Human Rights

in

World Politics

Seyom Brown

Brandeis University

 LONGMAN

An Imprint of Addison Wesley Longman, Inc.

New York • Reading, Massachusetts • Menlo Park, California • Harlow, England
Don Mills, Ontario • Sydney • Mexico City • Madrid • Amsterdam

Editor-in-Chief: Priscilla McGeehon
Associate Editor: Jennie Errickson
Marketing Manager: Megan Galvin-Fak
Full Service Production Manager: Denise Phillip
Project Coordination, Text Design, and
   Electronic Page Makeup: Thompson Steele, Inc.
Cover Design Manager: Nancy Danahy
Cover Designer: Keithley & Associates
Cover Illustration/Photo: Jeff Widener/© AP Wide World Photos
Senior Print Buyer: Hugh Crawford
Printer and Binder: The Maple-Vail Book Manufacturing Group
Cover Printer: Coral Graphics Services, Inc.

Cover photo caption: A Chinese man blocks a line of tanks heading east on Beijing's Cangan Avenue on Monday, June 5, 1989.

Library of Congress Cataloging-in-Publication Data

Brown, Seyom.
Human rights in world politics / Seyom Brown.
   p.   cm.
   Includes index.
   ISBN 0-321-02547-4 (alk. paper)
   1. Human rights.   2. World politics—1989–   I. Title.
JC571.B698   2000   99-37780
323—dc21   CIP

Please visit our website at http://www.awlonline.com

ISBN 0-321-02547-4

12345678910—MA—02010099

Contents

*To that prisoner who waits
for the next surge of pain,
wondering if anyone
in the world out there
knows or cares*

Preface

World politics is increasingly about human rights.

Any program of international studies that neglects the subject of human rights would be as seriously deficient as one that neglects the subjects of war and peace, political economy, or the global environment.

Why? Why are so many human rights struggles—usually initiated by domestic groups that feel mistreated by those in control of their countries—now "going international"? To what extent is the globalization of human rights transforming the nation-state system? And what is the impact of this globalization on the ability of people in various communities to promote and to achieve the rights they believe are theirs?

My decision to write such a book is itself a symptom of the rise of human rights issues to the top of the agendas of statespersons and foreign policy analysts. The content and style reflect my professional locus as an international relations generalist who periodically participates in the policy making process. It thus differs somewhat from more specialized texts on human rights that have been published in recent years—which, from my perspective, do not adequately explain or convey how or why human rights struggles are now the very stuff of world politics.

This book is only an introduction to these questions and to their unavoidably complex answers. It is written for laypersons and students in introductory courses in foreign policy and international relations, not for legal theorists, professional philosophers, or international lawyers. I do, of course, cite works of such experts and even quarrel with some of them. I include a chapter on the competing philosophical traditions underlying contemporary human rights debates and another chapter on the key international covenants. But I do not engage here in the kind of advanced critical interpretation of these texts that might be appropriate in a scholarly treatise.

Nor do I attempt to arbitrate among the competing definitions of human rights and ideologies that accord priority to certain types of rights. To some champions of particular definitions and ideologies, my neutral stance (for example, my unwillingness to endorse the proposition that human rights are rights claimed or possessed by individuals but not rights claimed by groups) may itself appear to be an ideological position, and they may have a point. But my present intention is not to expound a philosophy of human rights. My aim is to introduce readers to the ways in which these competing views have become the very stuff of world politics.

As such, this book presents an introductory survey of deeply held, popular and intellectual convictions about human rights for which people around the world have been willing to fight, often violently. I focus on those ideas and struggles that have found their way into contemporary *international* arenas, either in the form of international laws and institutions or as interventions (proposed and actual) on behalf of people who are allegedly denied justice in their own countries. And I offer some of my own speculations on how this internationalization of human rights issues is likely to affect the future of world politics.

ORGANIZATION

I have attempted to draw a fresh road map of the still roughly-charted domain of human rights in world politics—working as much as possible from primary sources and raw reports. The surveying and cartography has been informed, however, by a number of road maps already in existence. Closest to my own perspective is that of R. J. Vincent, *Human Rights and International Relations* (1986). I have also benefited from the knowledge and analysis in David P. Forsythe's *Human Rights and World Politics* (1989), and Jack Donnelly's *International Human Rights* (1993). Detailed analyses of the way human rights issues are handled in the United Nations are provided in the volume edited by Philip Alston, *The United Nations and Human Rights: A Critical Appraisal* (1992). A thick collection of essays and documents on international human rights law is amassed by Henry J. Steiner and Philip Alston in their *International Human Rights in Context: Law, Politics, Morals* (1996).

Chapter 1 introduces the issues that are elaborated on in the subsequent chapters.

Chapter 2 provides a sampling of some of the most intense contemporary human rights conflicts, still largely unresolved, that have been injected into the arenas of international diplomacy.

Readers who seek to probe for the philosophical logic of the contending arguments in the human rights struggles should find Chapter 3 of particular interest. But don't expect *too* much. The excerpts and analyses of the philosophical literature are themselves inevitably controversial (whole bookshelves are devoted the views of each of the philosophers I have selectively quoted); my purpose is to whet appetites for more comprehensive and thorough study.

Chapter 4 introduces the reader to key provisions in the covenants, declarations, and commission and court decisions in the rapidly growing corpus of international human rights law. The analysis shows that an understanding of why and how these often highly ambiguous provisions were adopted is crucial for a realistic assessment of the usefulness and limitations of international legal action in the human rights field.

Chapter 5 assesses the variety of international pressures and instruments available to people attempting to improve their human rights situation. The analysis surveys the full spectrum of methods than can be utilized, depending on the circumstances—from governmental action, ranging from condemnatory resolutions through military intervention, by the United Nations or regional institutions to commercial boycotts organized by nongovernmental organizations to coercive direct action, even terrorism.

Five case studies, each one illuminating in detail various of the philosophical and practical issues assayed in the previous chapters, are presented in Chapter 6. One is the dramatic success story of the abolition of the South African apartheid regime. Another analyzes the inability of the concerned international community to mobilize effective pressures on the Government of China to induce it to reform its problematical human rights practices. The third case study deals with the culturally sensitive controversy over the ritual cutting of the genitalia of young females in many of the predominantly Muslim countries in Africa. The fourth case reviews the international intervention against "ethnic cleansing" in Bosnia and Kosovo. The fifth analyzes the efforts to establish international tribunals with the power to try the perpetrators of at least the most heinous human rights crimes, such as genocide.

The way the United States in particular has been handling the growing prominence of human rights in world politics is analyzed in Chapter 7. The United States is singled out for analysis, since I can provide insights from my own participation in the policy process in this country and because what the United States chooses to push or oppose in the human rights field, like it or not, will profoundly affect the outcome of human rights struggles around the world in the years ahead.

Chapter 8 speculates on how the human rights developments discussed in the previous chapters are likely to affect the future of world politics: the structure and functioning of the state-sovereignty system itself and the prospects for the evolution of a significantly different system of world order and justice.

A guide to the proliferating source material in this field is provided in the Appendix. Prepared by Leslie Stebbins, Coordinator of Library Instruction at Brandeis University, the Appendix identifies the most useful hardcopy and electronic information on human rights available from governments, intergovernmental institutions, nongovernmental organizations, and independent experts.

Some of the most persistent and profound human rights dilemmas are illustrated in Controversy Boxes. These are specially designed to challenge students to debate and to make up their own minds on the central issues in this field; namely, which rights and duties should be prescribed for all people, which rights should be left to particular communities to adopt or reject for themselves, and which (and whose) rights should be accorded priority when they come into conflict?

ACKNOWLEDGMENTS

Human rights are everyone's business. Over the past three years while writing this book, I have bothered many of my colleagues at Brandeis University—often in corridor conversations—for insights and information, a good deal of which may be reflected (and transformed) in these pages but not sufficiently acknowledged in the footnotes. Let me partially remedy this lack of specific attribution by giving special thanks here to Jeffrey Abramson and Mark Hulliung (for instructing me in some issues in political philosophy), to Steven Burg (for helping me to sort out the self-determination issues in the former Yugoslavia), to Ruth Morgenthau and Wellington Nyangoni (for their perspectives of human rights problems in various African countries), to John Schrecker (for interpretation of Chinese classical thought) and to Dessima Williams (for analysis of what transpired at the 1995 World Conference on Women in Beijing).

Opportunities to "test-drive" some of the analysis offered here were provided by the Carnegie Council on Ethics and Boston University's Center for International Affairs, sponsors of a Conference on Great Power Responsibility in World Affairs, at which I presented a paper titled "My Brother's Keeper: International Rights and Responsibilities in Failed States" and by the Seminar on Ethnics and International Affairs at the Center for International Affairs, Harvard University, where I made a similar presentation.

During the revision process, I was fortunate to be able to have dialogues with Nancy Kokaz, whose doctoral studies in political philosophy at Harvard University are focused on many of the issues raised in these pages and who was a teaching assistant in my Harvard summer course on international relations at Harvard.

I would like to give very special thanks to Vanda Felbabova, one of my research assistants and a generously available interlocutor for me on political and philosophical ideas I've been grappling with. If the ideas can survive Vanda's keen scrutiny, I have less trepidation in their publication.

Early drafts of the complete manuscript were critically read by Michael Tomz, Harvard University; Piper Hodson, University of Illinois at Urbana-Champaign; Renee Marlin-Bennett, American University; Michael E. Salla, American University; Charles Taber, SUNY at Stony Brook; Leslie Vaughan, Santa Monica College; Kenneth L. Wise, Creighton University; and Deborah Cohen, Brandeis University, who also served as a research assistant on this project. Their constructive comments provided me a basis for rethinking and reformulating some of the key ideas for the final book. Mary Call also assisted by briefing me on current news of human rights issues.

A final note of appreciation to my two youngest sons, Matthew and Jeremiah, whose sparring with me about *their* rights helped me keep my feet on the ground instead of floating into clouds of pontifical discourse—which is the great temptation in this field.

It was never the people who complained of the universality of human rights, nor did the people consider human rights as a Western or Northern imposition; it was often their leaders who did so.

— Kofi Annan

If we can establish and spread the values of liberty, the rule of law, human rights and an open society, then that is in our national interests too.

— Tony Blair

Chapter

1

Introduction

Much of world politics is about human rights—about the priority to be given to the rights claimed by persons, peoples, and governments. On a typical day the news media are likely to feature stories such as these:

- Citing his encouragement of the brutal "ethnic cleansing" campaign conducted by Serbian forces against the Albanian population of Kosovo, the International Criminal Tribunal for the Former Yugoslavia has indicted Slobodan Milosevik for crimes against humanity and violations of the laws of war.

- Sinn Fein, the militant Catholic political organization in Protestant-controlled Northern Ireland, demands that members of the Irish Republican Army who have been arrested on suspicion of plotting terrorist attacks be released from British jails where they are incarcerated, allegedly in violation of their right to a fair trial.

- The Chechnyans continue to assert their right to full self-determination, meaning independent statehood, while the Russian government claims its sovereign right to put down Chechnya's secession.

- The Palestinian Liberation Organization demands that Israel cease building residential units in East Jerusalem prior to the conclusion of an international agreement on the future of the city.

- Lawyers for Salvadorians living in the United States in violation of U.S. immigration laws sue to prevent their deportation.

- Various labor and human rights organizations organize a boycott against athletic equipment manufactured in Bangladesh in conditions that violate international covenants on child labor.

- Asserting a right to individual land ownership, a Brazilian farm-labor organization stages an occupation of a forest area purchased by a multinational lumbering corporation.

• Claiming its "right to development," China opposes new global treaty provisions limiting the use of coal and oil in regional industrialization projects.

Human rights issues analogous to these, even if sometimes under a different label. have been around for thousands of years. They were involved in the imperial conflicts among ancient societies and in many of the conflicts within them. Medieval Europe was wracked by disputes among lords, vassals, kings, and bishops over their rights and duties vis-à-vis one another. Human rights were also deeply at issue since the fifteenth century in the consolidation and disintegration of the globe-spanning maritime empires. Finally, profound disagreements over the respective rights of persons, peoples, and governments have been at the core of many of the defining episodes in modern world history, including the American, French, and Russian revolutions, the Cold War, and the collapse of the Soviet Union.

Despite this historic lineage, today's human rights struggles are posing an unprecedented challenge to the world's political order.

In the past, the battles among countries and peoples had mostly to do with the location of borders, that is, they were battles about which state, or empire, had the right and power to exercise control over what population and territory. Conflicts within countries over the rights and privileges of various classes and groups were normally treated as domestic matters into which outsiders had no business interfering. From the middle of the seventeenth century until just the last few decades, such struggles over the rights of persons, peoples, and governments were handled *by* the world's state-sovereignty system and did not fundamentally challenge the norms and institutions of that system.

By contrast, many of today's human rights conflicts are shaking up the state-sovereignty system. Countries cannot avoid having to answer to one another, and to the world community at large, in response to serious charges that they are violating internationally accepted human rights principles—including the principle that governments are legitimate only to the extent that they are based on the uncoerced consent of the governed. How governments treat the people within their jurisdictions is no longer an issue to be worked out simply between governments and their domestic constituents.

Official commissions and courts of the United Nations and those of regional systems are acquiring the capacity to investigate, and in some cases adjudicate, complaints from nongovernmental groups and individuals that particular governments are violating the international human rights covenants. In other words, a "standing to sue" (meaning legal permission to bring one's case before a judicial body) is increasingly accorded in the international system to peoples and persons and no longer only to governments.

How significant are these developments for the structure and work-ings of the international system? Do they portend a fundamental erosion of its state-sovereignty norms? Are they the precursors of a significantly different kind of world political system, perhaps even of some kind of world government? Most importantly, from the standpoint of those who feel their human rights grievances are not being adequately tended to by their own governments, do these developments amount to a substantial opening up of opportunities to obtain redress in the wider international community?

The answers to these questions are currently in contention and will be shaped out of the intense debates and power contests now being waged in numerous international forums. Virtually all of the interna-tional dialogues and confrontations on human rights are explicitly, or implicitly, aspects of the increasingly explosive global issue of which rights are universally valid and which are the product of particular cul-tures or stages of societal development and appropriately left to local option.

In order to understand and participate effectively (for those who want to) in this progressively weighty aspect of world politics, one needs to keep abreast of

- what rights are being advocated by whom in the relevant interna-tional arenas

- philosophical sources and moral implications of the contending human rights positions

- the legal status of the various human rights that are being claimed

- the means (governmental and nongovernmental) available to human rights claimants for obtaining and protecting the rights they value

These topics will be introduced here and then elaborated on in subse-quent chapters. But, first, we must define the concept of human rights somewhat more precisely—yet with sufficient breadth to encompass the wide spectrum of definitions that are now contending for acceptance.

WHAT ARE HUMAN RIGHTS?

When people claim something as a human right, they usually mean that it is wrong for anyone to deprive them of it. Do they also mean to imply that *everyone* ought to have the particular protections, privileges, or opportunities being claimed? Frequently, the answer is yes; the insis-tence by people that something is a human right more often than not means that they have a right to it simply by virtue of the fact they are human beings, which implies that all other humans also should be able to enjoy that right. But, as is discussed below, not all participants in human rights debates accept such a universalistic definition.

Also, the insistence that something should be regarded as an essential aspect of human existence accords it a more profound status than that accorded ordinary demands, claims, or interests—such as, "I have a right to park my car in that space!"—which in everyday speech are often called rights.

Consistent with these common understandings, I use the term *human rights* to designate *philosophically justifiable claims by people to certain conditions of existence and privileges and amenities.* Such claims are not mere preferences or desires but are components of a system of beliefs, explicit or implied, about the way human society should be organized.

Various rights of this quality may already exist in a society's basic laws and thus can be claimed as legally guaranteed, or they may be advocated as rights that the society's laws should, but do not yet, incorporate. The claimed conditions, privileges, and amenities can range from elemental rights (security against physical violence, minimal subsistence needs, and the ownership of property and control over what happens to it) to special civic and procedural rights (for example, free speech, voting, and trial by jury).

Such rights are claimed not only for individuals but also for families, tribes, communities of different sizes and makeup, nations, states, transnational religions and cultures, producers of goods and services, economic classes, professions, and the organizations representing any of these entities. Indeed, some of the most fundamental disagreements in world politics today are over which of these entities should have their rights accorded priority and the overarching issue of how much global commonality and how much variation among the world's many communities with respect to human rights issues ought to be the basis of the emerging world order.

THE HUMAN RIGHTS DEBATE IN CONTEMPORARY WORLD POLITICS

In international forums today, the alignment of countries in human rights debates often finds the United States, Canada, and the countries of Western Europe on one side and China and most Third World countries on the other side. Japan, Russia, and the countries of Eastern Europe tend to associate themselves with one camp or the other depending on the issue at hand. (The alignment of the governments of countries, however, is only part of the story; for within most countries, there are deep disagreements among political parties and movements over which human rights are to be accorded priority.)

The groupings of countries in international forums correspond largely with their official positions on whether priority should be accorded to so-called *negative* rights (the rights of persons and groups against the power of governments, which are featured in the International Covenant on Civil and Political Rights) or to so-called *positive* rights (the rights of citizens to certain levels of economic well-being, health, education, and cultural amenities, which are featured in the international Covenant on Economic, Social and Cultural Rights). During the Cold War, the lineup of countries with respect to these two orientations rather closely matched the overall East-West polarization of the world into the Soviet-led and the U.S.-led coalitions—the East condemning the lack of economic equality in the capitalist countries and the West condemning the lack of political freedom in the communist countries. In the post–Cold War era, with very few countries professing marxist ideologies, the lineup is more congruent with the so-called North-South polarization between the industrialized countries and the developing countries. Within the Western/Northern grouping, however, there was, and continues to be, a wide spectrum of views, ranging from democratic socialism to laissez-faire capitalism, over the *degree* to which the state should be involved in running the economy and assisting those who are unable to compete effectively in the market.

Reflecting the history of political struggles against monarchical and autocratic power in North America and Western Europe, the United States and its allies in the so-called North Atlantic Community have by and large emphasized protections of individuals and private groups against governments, including the underlying principle that governments are legitimate only to the extent that they are based on the uncoerced consent of the governed. The ideology of limited government and free enterprise has been embraced most insistently by business interests confident of success in a minimally regulated market economy.

By contrast, the countries in both the Moscow-led and Beijing-led camps during the Cold War promoted the Marxist-Leninist philosophy that the equalization and improvement of the economic well-being of all citizens is the most important human right and that in a socialist "peoples democracy," it is the government's responsibility to bring it about. Moreover, those who stood in the way of this goal were enemies of the people and therefore could be treated harshly by the state. In the post–Cold War era, with the collapse of the Soviet Union, these views no longer hold sway in most of the countries formerly in the Soviet sphere (except in a few unreconstructed marxist countries such Cuba and Tadzhikistan), but they are still espoused by the Peoples Republic of China, Vietnam, and North Korea.

Many Third World countries, having waged their struggles for independence under the banners of "liberty" *and* "equality," are run by elites influenced by both the Western liberal and marxist traditions. But preoccupied with the difficult tasks of nation-building and economic development, and also frequently having to deal with militant self-determination movements by aggrieved ethnic or religious communities within their borders, most of the governments in the Third World today (some of them military dictatorships, such as Algeria and Burma) are unapologetically statist when balancing the rights claimed by persons and peoples against the presumed imperatives of public security. Even professed market democracies, such as Malaysia or Brazil, maintain they cannot afford the "luxury" of the kind of rights-based legal system championed by the United States. Increasingly, Third World statespersons and intellectuals argue that many of the human rights norms that the United States and its allies have been emphasizing are adverse to the precolonial, so-called non-Western cultural traditions of their societies in which the prerogatives of the community take precedence over the claims of individuals.

These international debates reflect and at the same time reinforce the conflicts of interest and of philosophical positions of rights claimants *within* countries. In virtually every country today, whatever the dominant cultural tradition, struggles over the priority to be accorded the rights of persons, peoples, and governments are, more than ever, the very stuff of domestic politics. Not all of these have become issues in *world* politics, which is the subject of this book. Yet most are potentially that, not only because of the worldwide monitoring by human rights organizations such as Amnesty International and Human Rights Watch, but also because of the globalization of commerce, which provides opportunities for human rights activists to mobilize international pressures against governments and businesses they believe to be in violation of human rights principles.

THE BASIC PHILOSOPHICAL ARGUMENTS

Many of the claims of the governmental and nongovernmental participants in these human rights struggles have a distinguished lineage, traceable to arguments formulated by the ancient Greek and Roman philosophers and developed further by the great political thinkers of medieval and modern times. Various of the most influential political philosophers, as well as the participants in rights struggles around the world, disagree on fundamentals. This realization can be disconcerting to those who have been operating under the assumption that their views are derived from self-evident truths and that only those who are ignorant or venal could disagree with them. On the other hand, the recognition that one's opponents may also be highly intelligent and ethically motivated can be the starting point for mutually respectful and constructive dialogue.

Ideas of particular philosophers that are pertinent to the contemporary human rights debates are analyzed in Chapter 3. The discussion here is a prelude to that analysis.

The philosophical controversies over human rights encompass five interrelated issues:

- The relationship between individuals and the communities to which they belong

- The question of which human characteristics and moral obligations are universal and which vary with time and place

- The relationship between rights and obligations

- The importance of particular rights and obligations

- The absolute or conditional quality of the rights that are most highly valued

Individuals and Communities   One of the major traditions of political thought, extending back to the Ancient Greeks and reflected in the views of contemporary communitarian philosophers, holds that human life has no meaning for individuals apart from the communities to which they belong; that is, communities are, in this sense, "prior" to persons. The rights of individuals and groups, from this standpoint, are created and sustained by particular political communities and accordingly are subordinate to needs of the communities. Extreme expressions of this kind of thinking are found in the state-glorifying ideologies of fascism and totalitarian socialism.

Non-western philosophies—notably Buddhism, Hinduism, and Confucianism—reject the dichotomy of individual versus state and conceive of persons and communities as inseparable parts of an integrated mosaic of mutual obligation. These religious-philosophical conceptions, however, when implemented in rigidly stratified societies, have often resulted in the oppression of the lower classes and occupational groups by the well-born elite, the latter exercising rights and privileges and the former mainly duties.

An alternative tradition, providing the philosophical sources of the human rights positions typically championed by the U.S. government in international forums, accords priority to certain presumably sacrosanct liberties of persons. As a minimum, governments are enjoined not to violate these liberty rights. Maximally, governments are also supposed to secure such rights for their citizenry. Drawing heavily on the British liberal thinkers of previous centuries and reflected in numerous rights-oriented opinions of twentieth-century U.S. Supreme Court justices, this philosophical tradition characteristically conceives of the rights of private citizens as being in tension with the preoccupations of officialdom with public order and regulation. Within this orientation, however, there is considerable variation: At one extreme are radical libertarians who regard virtually any governmental intrusion into their private lives as illegitimate. Then there are the neoconservatives who oppose state regulation of private enterprise but support laws upholding the moral standards of the community and tough law enforcement. Finally, there are the social-democracy liberals who tend to emphasize not only civil liberties and humane law enforcement but also interventions in the market for reasons of social justice to help the economically disadvantaged.

Universalism versus Relativism   Overlapping the opposition between the individualistically oriented and communitarian political philosophies, but not entirely congruent with it, is the opposition between

- the view that *all* people have certain rights simply by virtue of the fact that they are human beings

- the view that the distribution in any society of the rights and obligations of persons, peoples, and government is always (and rightly so) the product of that particular society's culture and unique historical experience

The universalism expressed in the first of these propositions has a lineage extending back to the Greek and Roman Stoic philosophers and is given religious sanction in the classics of Christian theology. Additional supports for universalism are provided by natural law, natural rights, and cosmopolitan thinkers whose treatises gave philosophical depth to the European Enlightenment of the seventeenth, eighteenth, and nineteenth centuries.

The strand of universalism closely associated with Christian theology seeks through a process of moral reasoning, called "right reason," to obtain knowledge of the moral principles that should govern how we highly imperfect human beings should treat one another here on Earth. This so-called natural law is supposed to put ultimate limits on what secular authorities, even legally sovereign nation-states, may do. As such, it provided the philosophical basis for the first major works on international law that date from the seventeenth century. Most of philosophizing in the early classics on international law dealt with relations among the states themselves (fishing rights, rules of navigation, the treatment of ambassadors, and noninterference in another's internal affairs). But part of the international legal discourse, and the treaties it spawned, was also directed toward establishing agreed-upon standards of civilized governance, particularly with respect to the toleration to be accorded religious minorities.

The reformist thinkers of the Enlightenment tended to emphasize natural *rights* as much as, or even more than, natural *law.* They characteristically grounded their prescriptions for the good and durable polity in premises about human nature (sometimes in the form of imaginings about human relationships in a precivilized state of nature). To the extent that humans possess characteristics that are given to all, by the gods or by nature, then, presumably, what is good for humans, what is their birthright, does not vary essentially by place or time. In the words of the American Declaration of Independence, "*All* men are created equal and they are endowed by their creator with certain unalienable rights. . . ." These rights are thus prior to laws and governments, which are established in order to secure such rights.

Another major strand of Western philosophy—idealism—derives universal principles of human rights from the assumptions about the essential quality of being human and the consequent imperative of mutual respect among persons. As formulated by the eighteenth-century exemplar of such thinking, Immanuel Kant, no person, anywhere in the world, should be treated simply as a means, but also as an end. There may be cultural variants in how this respect is accorded, but no nation, no state, has warrant to violate anyone's basic dignity.

Overlapping in time with the emergence of the nation-state system in Europe, many of the tenets of the rights-oriented philosophies spawned by the Enlightenment were widely embraced by the rising commercial and middle classes to justify the democratization of government (at least to the extent of giving *them* a say in how states were run). Most prominently in France, England, and North America, this took the form of political ideologies that gave highest priority to rights having to do with the acquiring and use of private property.

Whereas many Christian natural-law theologians and most Enlightenment philosophers regarded their prescriptions for good government as having global validity, other seminal thinkers (including some within these two traditions) have given greater weight to the cultural particularities of peoples and nations and, accordingly, have tended to reject universal prescriptions for the way societies should balance rights and duties. As with the universalists, there are also different schools of thought among the cultural relativists.

Relativist philosophers of a traditional or conservative bent regard the store of wisdom accumulated by each society, and embodying its historical experience, as the proper source of judgments about the legitimacy of the policies and laws of that society. These traditionalists and conservatives believe that ordinary citizens should defer to such accumulated wisdom and to those who, through study and accreditation by the institutions that are guardians of the society's traditions, are the society's designated authorities on such issues; outsiders especially, even those who have visited and studied a particular nation or cultural community, should not presume to tell it how to run its affairs.

Arguments on behalf of a relativist approach to human rights are also espoused by liberal proponents of cultural pluralism or multiculturalism.

Devotees of this position like to cite the Statement on Human Rights that the American Anthropological Association issued in 1947 in reaction to the effort to formulate the Universal Declaration of Human Rights. Observing that what was regarded as a human right in one society may be regarded as antisocial by another people, or by the same people in a different period in their history, and combining this with "the scientific fact that no technique of qualitatively evaluating cultures has been discovered," the Anthropological Association insisted that the Universal Declaration of the United Nations should affirm "respect for differences between cultures" and should not assume moral postulates that grow out of the beliefs of one culture are applicable to humankind as a whole.[1]

Relationships between Rights and Obligations If someone has a right, does someone else have a corresponding duty? The answer is usually yes—in either a strong or weak version. In the strong version, if I have a right, someone or some institution would be obligated to provide me with the wherewithal to enjoy that right. (Thus, if I have a right to enough food to keep me alive but am unable to earn enough money to buy the food, others who are capable of saving me from starvation have an obligation to do so.) In the weak version, the fact that I have a particular right would mean that others are obligated to respect my efforts to enjoy that right; that is, at least they should not try to prevent me from enjoying it. (Thus, if I have a right to freely express my political views, governmental officials should not attempt to suppress my speech or writing, no matter how critical I am of the government.)

Thinking about the relationships between rights and obligations points to the closely related question of moral responsibility for acts of omission as well as for acts of commission. If I know that through no fault of mine, your rights are being denied but I also know that I could substantially correct this through some initiative, do I have an obligation to act? And how direct must the connection be between my behavior or inaction and your rights-deprived situation for there to be a duty on my part to take appropriate action? (See Controversy Box 1 on page 11.)

The relationships between rights and duties are particularly difficult to work out in the international realm, where people who are remote from each other geographically and culturally can rather easily claim no responsibility for the well-being of one another. By contrast, *within* more organized communities—including most nation-states—many of the obligations corresponding to particular rights are lodged in public institutions responsible for implementing the law-and-order, regulatory, and social-welfare policies of the communities. The existence of these policies and implementing agencies in a community reflects the fact that the

---

1. American Anthropological Association, "Statement on Human Rights," *American Anthropologist* 49, 4 (1947), p. 539.

CONTROVERSY BOX
1

Rights, Obligations, and Crimes of Omission

Situation A   Near midnight, while Bertrand is hurrying to catch the last subway train home (he fears he is about to miss it), he passes an alley in which a man and woman are struggling. The woman yells, "Help! Rape! Rape!" There is a phone booth just inside the subway station entrance.

What, if any, are Bertrand's obligations (legal and/or moral)?

Situation B   A division of China's People's Liberation Army (PLA) enters Lhasa, Tibet—where they ransacked the Buddhist temples, beat the monks, and raped the nuns—on orders from Beijing, says the PLA commander, to punish the Buddhists for their role in fomenting a Tibetan secessionist movement.

What if any, are the obligations of other countries as the news of this event gets out?

In what respects is Situation B analogous to Situation A?

community as a whole already has decided (often as the outcome of intense political struggles) to take on the obligation to guarantee certain rights to its members. Some of these community obligations may be in the form of prohibitions against agents and agencies of the community acting to interfere with various specified rights of individuals or minorities. Other community obligations may be in the form of the provision of services, schooling, jobs, and other amenities to assure a specified minimum standard of living and quality of life to members of the community.

Which Rights Are Most Important?   The debates in international forums, like the national debates, over what rights are important enough to be made part of world law are expressions of a wide array of political philosophies; yet, as with the national debates, the contending philosophies cluster around a few central issues.

Political philosophies that give the highest value to guarantees of free speech, assembly, and protections of citizens against a repressive state usually also emphasize representative pluralistic (competitive) democracy in which government officeholders are selected by and are answerable to the electorate. By contrast, philosophies that focus on physical needs and economic interests typically assess the value of political and civil rights by their effectiveness in achieving the material values, not as unalienable ends in and of themselves; this subordination of political liberty to economics is characteristic of schools of thought across a wide spectrum, ranging from marxism to utilitarianism to free-market liberalism. A willingness to downplay the importance of the standard civil and political rights of individuals, often on grounds of the need to secure the country against its enemies, external and internal, can be found as well in philosophies that give primacy to national unity and/or cultural (sometimes religious) conformity.

Absolutism versus Consequentialism   Finally, philosophical positions on human rights can be distinguished by the extent to which they grant the need to compromise on the protected status of the encompassed rights in specific circumstances. No respectable political philosophy condones such extreme acts as genocide or rape, and rights to uncompromised protections against these crimes are universally affirmed. But short of the rights against such gross brutalities, different philosophies will place different sets of rights in an absolute (never-to-be-violated) category, as distinguished from the category of rights that might have to be limited on the basis of assessments of the consequences of their exercise in particular situations.

Thus, there is considerable variation among ethical and political philosophers when it comes to analyzing conflicts involving individuals or groups whose rights, if given a privileged status, could seriously interfere with the rights of others or with ways of life highly valued by society. Examples of hard cases of this sort include the right of a disaffected religious or ethnic minority to secede from a country in which the majority usually outvotes it on cultural issues; whether to waive a prisoner's rights against coercive interrogation when the prisoner is a member of a terrorist group and is suspected of knowing where and when the next terrorist bomb is going to be exploded; whether the right of family privacy overrides the right of a child to be protected against abuse by an alcoholic parent; the limitations to be put on speech that might be an incitement to riot; or, at a more mundane level, the respective rights of neighbors to hold loud parties or run their lawn mowers at different times of day or night.

THE INTERNATIONALIZATION OF HUMAN RIGHTS

The main arenas of international diplomacy are taken up, more than ever before, with issues involving charges that certain national governments are depriving, deliberately or by negligence, people within their jurisdictions of their legitimate rights. The disputes are not only over the truth or falsity of the particular allegations but also over the basic general question of the extent to which countries ought to be accountable to one another for how, in their own political systems, they balance the often-competing demands of liberty, public safety, cultural conformity, and economic well-being.

These issues were not always as central to international relations as they are now. What explains the change?

Traditional Statecraft: The Westphalian System

Traditional statecraft discouraged the admission into the diplomatic arena of claims against governments by individuals and nongovernmental groups. How governments treat their own people was supposed to be a matter to be worked out by the government and people of each country. The traditional view—reflected in the Peace of Westphalia (1648) that terminated the devastating Thirty Years War in which Protestants and Catholics crossed state lines to fight on behalf of their coreligionists—accorded primacy to the ruling dynasty of each state over what happens within its territorial boundaries; intervention by any state or group of states (or nonstate agency such as the Church) into the domestic affairs of any other state was prohibited.

The Westphalian sovereignty and noninterventionist principles were, of course, often systematically violated by imperialistic states in the three centuries following Westphalia. Indeed, under the banner of "the Rights of Man," Napoleon Bonaparte sent the French armies into other countries to "liberate" them from monarchical absolutism. Yet after the defeat of Napoleon, the rhetoric of statecraft and treatises on international law again embraced state-sovereignty as the basis for civilized world order.

The Challenge to State-Sovereignty Norms

In the twentieth century, the morality and legality of the traditional state-sovereignty principles have encountered increasing challenge. When President Jimmy Carter contended in his 1977 address to the UN General Assembly that "No member of the United Nations can claim that mistreatment of its citizens is solely its own business,"[2] he was affirming the U.S. government's recommitment to a worldview already codified in numerous post–World War II international covenants and UN resolutions. Carter's human rights emphasis put the United States once again prominently in the ranks of the countries pushing for international

---

2. *Public Papers of the Presidents of the United States: Jimmy Carter, 1977* (Washington, DC: GPO, 1977), pp. 444–450.

accountability in the field of human rights (the United States had temporarily erased human rights concerns from its diplomacy in the early 1970s as Richard Nixon and Henry Kissinger tried to revive a statist realpolitik reminiscent of nineteenth-century European diplomacy).

The assertion of individual and group rights against governments is, of course, nothing new. The history of virtually every country is a history of the struggles, sometimes bloody, to work this out within the national community. Indeed, many countries (the United States being an early exemplar) owe their origin to the popular embrace of the idea that all people have certain natural rights (see page 53–55) and that governments which attempt to take away these rights deserve to be overthrown. Under the principles of traditional international law and statecraft, however, it was presumed to be illegitimate for states to intervene in one another's jurisdictions on behalf of the opponents of the government in power; even in cases of revolutions or secessionist wars, outsiders were supposed to forbear from supporting the antigovernment forces.

What *is* new is the agreement by most countries since World War II that there is an *international* community interest in—and possibly even jurisdiction over—at least those situations where basic human rights are being systematically violated by particular national governments.

The War-Crimes Prosecutions

In the post–World War II war-crimes trials conducted by the victor powers, a threshold was crossed into a world legal order in which the heretofore-sacrosanct sovereignty of nation-states would be subject to a higher law of humankind. Legal scholars and political philosophers continue to debate whether this step should have been taken, but there is little doubt that the trials marked the start of a new era in international relations.

Nazi officials responsible for inflicting acts of genocide upon the civilian populations under their control, particularly the Holocaust against 6 million Jews, were charged with crimes against humanity. In the words of the charter of the Nuremberg Tribunal,

> CRIMES AGAINST HUMANITY . . . [include] murder, extermination, enslavement, deportation, and other inhuman acts committed against any civilian population, before or during the war, or persecutions on political, racial of religious grounds in execution of or in connection with any crime within the jurisdiction of the Tribunal, *whether or not in violation of the domestic law of the country where perpetrated.*[3] [emphasis added]

---

3. The text of the Nuremberg crimes-against-humanity count is from Victor H. Bernstein, *Final Judgment: The Story of Nuremberg* (New York: Boni & Gaer, 1947).

The Genocide Convention

The Nuremberg breakthrough was subsequently codified and universalized in the *Convention on the Prevention and Punishment of the Crime of Genocide*, adopted by the United Nations General Assembly in 1948 and entered into force in 1951. Called the "Genocide Convention," it outlaws "acts committed with the intent to destroy, in whole or in part, a national, ethnic, racial or religious group," including not only killing members of the group, but also causing "serious bodily or mental harm" or deliberately "inflicting on the group conditions likely to bring about its physical destruction."[4]

It is under the Genocide Convention that the United Nations set up international tribunals in the mid-1990s to try governmental officials and military commanders responsible for "ethnic cleansing" and other alleged war crimes committed by rival forces in the Balkan conflict and by the Hutus and Tutsis in Rwanda and Burundi. And the acts outlawed by the Genocide Convention are the primary crimes to be brought under the jurisdiction of the new International Criminal Court (ICC) that was approved by the representatives of more than 180 countries in 1998 (at the present time, the ICC statute still requires a number of formal national ratifications to become international law).

The Evolving United Nations Regime

Even before the full extent of Nazi atrocities were exposed at Nuremberg, it was a foregone conclusion that the post–World War II order would give unprecedented emphasis to the rights of people against governments. The democracies in the anti-Axis coalition, in order to sustain public enthusiasm for the war effort, claimed to be fighting Germany and Japan not only with the geopolitical motive of preventing these aggressor states from dominating the international system but equally to allow all peoples to enjoy the freedoms proclaimed in the Atlantic Charter by U.S. president Franklin Roosevelt and British prime minister Winston Churchill.

Accordingly, the United Nations Charter (adopted in 1945), in addition to making it clear that the world organization's overriding purpose is to preserve international peace and security, emphasizes in its preamble the signatories' determination "to reaffirm faith in fundamental human rights, in the dignity and worth of the human person, [and] in the equal rights of men and women." Moreover, Article 1 states that one of the basic purposes of the United Nations is "to achieve international cooperation in . . . promoting and encouraging respect for human rights

---

4. Convention on the Prevention and Punishment of the Crime of Genocide, 78 *United Nations Treaty Series* 277 (adopted December 9, 1948; entered into force January 12, 1951).

and for fundamental freedoms for all without distinction as to race, sex, language, or religion." And Article 55 enjoins members to promote "universal respect for, and observance of, human rights and fundamental freedoms for all."[5]

The embrace by the UN Charter of the rights of individuals and peoples vis-à-vis governments should not be exaggerated. In its main thrust the Charter remains a compact among national governments to respect one another's sovereignty. Article 2, Section 7, assures that "Nothing contained in the present Charter shall authorize the United Nations to intervene in matters which are essentially within the domestic jurisdiction of any state or shall require Members to submit such matters to settlement under the present Charter."

But the UN Charter's protectiveness of the state-sovereignty system lagged behind the growing popular support in the aftermath of World War II for rights-based democracy. The liberal democratic ethos was given a preliminary "charter" in the form of the *Universal Declaration of Human Rights* adopted by the General Assembly in 1948. The Universal Declaration was an omnibus enumeration, without clear prioritization, of virtually all the human rights demands—from demands that governments not interfere with civil liberties to demands that governments guarantee everyone basic amenities like a job, education, and health care—that were being directed against governments around the world.

Because the Universal Declaration of Human Rights was not a treaty requiring formal ratification by UN member governments but was only a resolution of the General Assembly, it was not legally binding on member governments; were it legally binding, it is doubtful that many governments would have voted for the Universal Declaration in 1948. Still, its adoption by the General Assembly was a concession by member governments to the strength of human rights ideas on the part of their constituents, who, in turn, over the coming decades invoked the declaration to give enhanced legitimacy political campaigns against governments deemed to be sluggish in responding to their human rights demands.

This strengthening of the human rights ethos resulted in the mid-1960s in the General Assembly's adoption of a set of covenants to be signed and ratified by the member governments. By acceding to these covenants, a national government would be indicating that the human rights provisions were potentially enforceable by citizens against the government in the country's domestic courts and perhaps even through intervention by international agencies. The core covenants (six in all), which together with the Universal Declaration are often referred to as

---

5. Charter of the United Nations (signed at San Francisco, June 26, 1945; entered into force October 24, 1945).

the "International Bill of Rights," include the International Covenant on Civil and Political Rights; the International Covenant on Economic, Social and Cultural Rights; the International Convention on the Elimination of All Forms of Racial Discrimination; the Convention on the Elimination of All Forms of Discrimination Against Women; the Convention on the Rights of the Child; and the Convention Against Torture and Other Cruel, Inhuman or Degrading Treatment or Punishment.

The persisting philosophical, legal, and operational issues raised by each of the components of this International Bill of Rights, plus various associated human rights instruments, are analyzed in subsequent chapters. The point emphasized here is that having been signed by a sufficient number of countries to qualify as international law (at least for the countries that have ratified them), the core human rights covenants have profoundly shifted the burden of justification in international discourse and diplomacy to those governments still insisting on sovereign immunity from international accountability for their human rights behavior.

Some governments—China, Singapore, Saudi Arabia, Turkey, and Cuba, for example—are holdouts for the traditional view that the burden of justification falls on those who would undermine the norm of noninterference by states in one another's domestic affairs. But the statist hard-liners are finding that a poor human rights record, despite their efforts to suppress the information, is likely to translate into considerable diplomatic friction, let alone embarrassing exposures by influential nongovernmental organizations, with countries who have embraced the human rights ethos. Countries with poor human rights records may be denied the benefits of full membership in regional and specialized international organizations with stringent human rights criteria. Such countries may also find themselves the targets of economic boycotts organized by transnational nongovernmental organizations.

To avoid the negative consequences of frontally opposing the new international norm of human rights accountability, the statist hard-liners have been lobbying in international forums for definitions of human rights that will make allowance for the traditions of diverse cultures.

How the attempt to reconcile cultural diversity and universalism will affect the respective roles of domestic and international agencies is still largely an open question, and highly controversial. But, consistent with the basic shift toward international accountability on human rights, the United Nations system—its assemblies, conferences, and commissions—is itself heavily involved in the process of determining what should be left to the national governments and what should be taken on by the international community. (The current responsibilities and procedures of the various UN agencies operating in the human rights field are described in Chapter 5.)

Regional Human Rights Regimes

One adaptation to the increasingly adamant Third World campaign against universalizing the implementation of the International Bill of Rights is to regionalize implementation regimes among sets of countries with basically similar cultural traditions and political values. From the standpoint of truly improving the condition of people around the world, rather than merely debating about human rights issues, this approach may turn out to have considerable merit.

CONTROVERSY BOX
2

Dealing with Burma

President Clinton (White House Press Release, April 22, 1997)
Today I am announcing my decision to impose a ban on new U.S. investment in Burma. I have taken this step in response to a constant and continuing pattern of severe repression by the State Law and Order Restoration Council (SLORC) in Burma. During the past seven months, the SLORC has arrested and detained large numbers of students and opposition supporters, sentenced dozens to long-term imprisonment, and prevented the expression of political views by the democratic opposition, including Aung San Suu Kyi and the National League for Democracy (NLD). I have therefore imposed sanctions under the terms of . . . the Consolidated Appropriations Act for Fiscal Year 1997 [which] . . . calls for investment sanctions if the Government of Burma has physically harmed, rearrested for political acts, or exiled Aung San Suu Kyi, or has committed large-scale repression of or violence against the democratic opposition. It is my judgment that recent actions by the regime in Rangoon constitute such repression.

New York Times (June 1, 1997) JAKARTA, Indonesia—Defying the wishes of the United States and brushing aside concerns over human rights abuses, the Southeast Asian political and economic bloc known as ASEAN announced Saturday that it would embrace Myanmar [Burma] as a member this year. . . . Political analysts say that the reason for Saturday's action was an assertion of regional autonomy, and they suggested that public pressure from the United States might have backfired with such independent-minded leaders as Prime Minister Mohamad of Malaysia, Lee Kuan Yew of Singapore and President Suharto of Indonesia. "To save face, ASEAN will have to admit Burma," Foreign Minister Surapong Jayanama of Thailand had said in May.

Are you supportive or critical of President Clinton's move? Could he have handled the situation differently?

It has the advantage of allowing those nations who are ready to experiment with supranational procedures for dealing constructively with actual human rights cases to do so without being accused of cultural imperialism; it also has the advantage of avoiding the frustrations and international acrimony encountered in efforts to get the universal-membership agencies of the United Nations to act on specific cases.

The furthest evolved regime for holding national governments accountable to, and developing practical means of implementing, international standards of human rights exists among the countries who belong to the Council of Europe. As signatories of the European Convention for the Protection of Human Rights and Fundamental Freedoms, these countries—who include the members of the European Union (EU) plus aspirants to EU membership such as Poland and Turkey—are constituent members of the European Human Rights Commission and the European Human Rights Court.

The most innovative feature of the Council of Europe regime is that most members have accepted the compulsory jurisdiction of the Commission and Court in cases of complaints against them "from any person, nongovernmental organization or group of individuals claiming to be the victim of a violation . . . of the rights set forth in . . . [the] Convention."[6] The Commission can receive and investigate petitions from private parties; the Commission can also represent individual petitioners or nongovernmental groups before the Court. And the Court has the authority to find member governments to be in violation of their obligations under the Convention and to order members to provide redress to the victims of abuse or neglect. (Additional details on the structure and workings of the European regime are provided in Chapter 5.)

The second most elaborated regional human rights regime has been constructed by the Latin American countries under the auspices of the Organization of American States. With a commission and court ostensibly modeled on the European regime, the countries of the hemisphere have been more active than any regional grouping outside Europe in taking official international cognizance of human rights allegations against member governments. But consistent with the nonintervention ideology and sovereignty-protecting traditions of the Latin American states, the Inter-American regime, unlike the European system, makes it easy for members to veto anything that smacks of supranational monitoring, let alone supranational enforcement.[7] (The Inter-American institutions are also analyzed in Chapter 5).

---

6. European Convention for the Protection of Human Rights and Fundamental Freedoms (entered into force 1953, plus protocols of 1964, 1967, 1968, 1983, 1985, 1986, 1990, and 1992.

7. American Convention on Human Rights (entered into force 1978).

The Organization of African Unity, in what is called the "Banju Charter," provides the most explicit statement of a regional approach to human rights quite different in philosophy from that given the dominant emphasis in the universal documents. A separate chapter on the duties of individuals toward the state and other legally recognized communities is given equal weight with the chapter that enumerates the usual catalog of rights. The enumerated duties of the individual include, for example, "to serve the national community by placing his physical and intellectual abilities at its service" and "not to compromise the security of the State whose national or resident he is." Like the Inter-American Charter, the Banju Charter establishes a regional Commission on Human and Peoples' Rights, structured to function essentially as an interstate consultative body and to protect the countries from any significant supranational monitoring.[8]

Asia and the Middle East have lagged behind other areas in developing region-centered institutions and norms for handling human rights issues. Insofar as they have fashioned common approaches, these have been directed more toward forging a common front against "culturally imperialist" intrusions from the industrialized West than on institutionalizing procedures for serious intraregional consultations on the human rights conditions in their countries. (See Controversy Box 2 on page 18.)

---

8. African Charter on Human and Peoples' Rights (entered into force 1986).

2

Human Rights in Contemporary World Politics: Claims and Counterclaims

Human rights issues enter the arenas of world politics when people outside of countries experiencing major human rights violations attempt to bring international pressures to bear on those alleged to be responsible for the violations. The results of these efforts to mobilize international pressures are affected significantly by how constituencies attentive to human rights issues around the world view the credibility and moral content of the claims and counterclaims of the parties to the human rights disputes. In the world politics of human rights, perhaps more than with other issues, "Right makes might," at least in part, as much as the reverse.

Thus, to understand how human rights issues are transforming world politics, we need to look at the substance, but also at the underlying moral logic, of the claims and counterclaims being made in today's prominent human rights disputes. This chapter maps the range of conflicting human rights claims that have become prominent in contemporary world politics. Chapter 3 provides guidance for understanding the underlying moral logic of these claims through a probe of the world's dominant philosophical traditions in search of the ideas that have been providing the dominant concepts and vocabularies for today's human rights debates. Chapters 4 through 8 analyze the practical effects of this ferment on international law and institutions, on the ability of people to enjoy what they believe are their human rights, on the foreign policy of the United States, and on the evolving shape of the world's political system.

The human rights claims that have become central issues in world politics are of basically four, partially overlapping, types: (1) those concerning charges that individuals are being mistreated by governments; (2) those concerning the demands of ethnic and religious communities for self-determination; (3) those in the private sphere (such as the respective rights and obligations of husbands and wives, of landlords and tenants, and of workers and employers and the claims of people with particular characteristics or lifestyles to equal or special treatment in society); and (4) those revolving around demands by governments for rights and benefits for the nation as a whole, such as the right to protect the country's resources against foreign exploitation and even the right to development.

THE RIGHTS OF INDIVIDUALS AGAINST GOVERNMENTS

Human rights disputes more often than not center on allegations that particular governments are depriving individuals within their jurisdictions of their legitimate rights. Typically, in such cases, the individuals who claim they are being wronged will cite provisions in the constitutions of their countries or in international covenants that state (or strongly imply) that all persons are entitled to certain kinds of treatment and that the government in control of the jurisdiction in which they are residing has the duty to assure or provide such treatment.

Allegations that a government is violating someone's human rights usually contain two essential components: (1) factual claims about the government's behavior and (2) claims that the government's action or negligence is legally or morally wrong; that is, its action (or inaction) falls within a category of behavior this is, or ought to be, legally prohibited (or required). It is not enough, however, for human rights advocates to establish that behavior falling within one of the categories which could make it a human rights violation has occurred; for in both moral and legal philosophy and in the relevant international treaties (see Chapter 4), a person's enjoyment of particular rights is often conditioned on such enjoyment not infringing on the rights of others as well as on certain important community values. Indeed, it is not unusual in such cases for the government that is the target of such allegations to defend its actions on the ground that they were required in order to maximize the enjoyment of human rights within its jurisdiction.

Regarding Torture and Other Extreme Measures

There is a special category of governmental mistreatment of individuals—either engaging in such actions or condoning them—to which virtually no government will admit. This category encompasses violations of

CONTROVERSY BOX
3

Torture and the "Ticking Bomb"

United Nations Press Release (May 9, 1997)   The Committee against Torture . . . [has been conducting] a spirited debate with Israel over Government-approved use during interrogation of what it termed "moderate physical pressure" in efforts to elicit information that could foil pending terrorist attacks.

Such interrogation methods apparently included restraining in very painful conditions; holding under special conditions; sounding of loud music for prolonged periods; threats, including death threats; violent shaking; and the use of cold air to chill. In the Committee's view, such methods constituted torture as defined by Article 1 of the Convention Against Torture.

It called among other things for Israel to "cease immediately" the use of those and any other interrogation procedures that violated the Convention, and emphasized that no circumstances—even "the terrible dilemma of terrorism" . . . faced by Israel—could justify torture.

Members of [the Israeli] Government delegation appearing before the Committee contended that such methods had helped to prevent some 90 planned terrorist attacks over the last two years and had saved many civilian lives, in one recent case enabling members of the country's General Security Service to locate a bomb. The delegation repeatedly denied that the procedures amounted to torture.

Do you agree with the Committee Against Torture or the Government of Israel? Why?

the individual rights that are protected against "derogation" by Article 4 of the International Covenant of Civil and Political Rights, especially[1]

- not to be arbitrarily put to death

- not to be subjected to torture or other cruel or inhuman punishment

- not to be held in slavery

- recognition as a person before the law

---

1. See Chapter 4, pp. 77–78 for further elaboration and analysis of the "no-derogation" principle.

The unalienable status that is supposed to be accorded these most fundamental individual rights is reaffirmed in numerous UN and regional documents and in the vast majority of national constitutions around the world. The strongest, absolute protection of this sort appears in the UN convention against torture, which states that

> No exceptional circumstances whatsoever, whether a state of war or a threat of war, internal political instability or any other public emergency, may be invoked as a justification of torture.[2]

Because of worldwide revulsion, governments that have been accused of torture, arbitrary executions, and other extreme practices either flatly deny the factual basis of any such allegations brought against them or attempt to redefine the acts they admit to so as to remove these acts from the category of absolutely prohibited practices. (See Controversy Box 3 on page 23.)

Regarding the Repression of Civil Liberties and Political Activity

The vast array of civil and political rights claimed by individuals around the world, however, are not unconditionally protected against legal suspension in national constitutions or in international covenants. Although governments normally are obligated to provide compelling justifications of the necessity for any such suspensions, the fact that the state-sovereignty regime in international diplomacy, with its deference to national decisions on domestic issues, is still powerful means that individuals who seek international remedies for any but the most brutal government actions face an uphill battle.

If an international spotlight is indeed turned upon an alleged infraction of civil or political rights, the targeted government may attempt to deny the factual basis of the charges against it, for example, saying, "We have not denied the arrested person the opportunity to contact his attorney." In some cases the government may attempt to turn the tables on its foreign critics, arguing, for example, that "This is the customary method of dealing with such situations here, and outsiders who are telling us what to do are insulting our community's way of life" (the *cultural-relativism* argument) and, moreover, that "It would be a violation of our national sovereignty if outsiders tried to impose their views on us" (the traditional *international-law* argument).[3]

---

2. Convention Against Torture and Other Cruel, Inhuman or Degrading Treatment or Punishment, Article 2 (1897).
3. See Stanley Cohen, "Government Responses to Human Rights Reports: Claims, Denials, and Counterclaims," *Human Rights Quarterly* 18, 3 (August 1996), pp. 517–543.

Cultural-relativism arguments and legalistic defenses of national sovereignty have become standard parts of what is called the "Asian" counter to complaints by the United States and Western European governments that some of the newly industrializing countries in giving priority to economic development have been trampling on civil and political liberties. A leading champion of the cultural relativist position, Lee Kuan Yew, the former prime minister of Singapore and now that country's most influential elder statesman, argues that

> [In the West] The expansion of the right of the individual to behave or misbehave as he pleases has come at the expense of orderly society. . . .
>
>   . . .
>
> In the East the main object is to have a well-ordered society so that everybody can have maximum enjoyment of his freedoms. This freedom can only exist in an ordered state and not in a natural state of contention and anarchy.[4]

In their culturalist arguments the Singaporians are revisiting a deeper controversy over the requisites of liberty and order that has divided liberals and conservatives (and their philosophical gurus) in many countries. The basic philosophical issues, as are shown in Chapter 3, antedate and transcend the contemporary North-South and East-West alignments that have surfaced in international forums.

An even more frequently voiced counter by governments to allegations that they are systematically violating the rights of individuals under their jurisdictions is that clear and present dangers to the security and safety of their nations require that some limitations be placed on the exercise of the standard liberty rights (the *state-of-emergency* argument).

The human rights lawyers who drafted the Covenant on Civil and Political Rights attempted to preempt an irresponsible use of excuses of internal security and public order by explicitly allowing (in Article 4) governments in time of public emergency to curtail many of rights underwritten by the covenant but by restricting this allowance only to an officially proclaimed "public emergency which threatens the life of the nation." As adopted, this allowance is further restricted by the stipulation that any such curtailments must be limited to measures "strictly required by the exigencies of the situation."[5] The UN Human Rights Committee, set up to monitor compliance with the covenant, has taken these restrictions seriously and issued in the 1980s a number of findings; for example, it found that the authoritarian government of Chile had

---

4. Fareed Zakara, "Culture is Destiny: A Conversation with Lee Kuan Yew, *Foreign Affairs* 73, no. 2 (March/April 1944), pp. 109–126, quotation from p. 111.
5. Covenant on Civil and Political Rights (1976).

proclaimed and was continuing to impose a state of emergency "without any objective justification" for the measures it was applying.[6]

Some countries—China being the most prominent case in point— have been more aggressive internationally in their responses to charges that they are unjustly curtailing political and civil liberties.

Stung by widespread criticisms for holding thousands of political dissenters in brutally administered prisons, usually without formal indictment or trial, Beijing has issued a series of what it calls "White Papers" that attempt to convince the world it has a laudable human rights record. In the most comprehensive of these White Papers, issued in November 1991, the regime cites provisions in its constitution that provide Chinese citizens with "freedoms of speech, the press, assembly, association, procession and demonstration." The White Paper also claims that under the constitution citizens have a right to criticize the government and to make charges against state organs or functionaries for violation of the law or dereliction of duty.[7]

But in exercising their freedoms and rights, says the White Paper, "citizens may not infringe upon the interests of the state, of society or the collective, or upon the lawful freedoms and rights of other citizens."[8] Such provisos, of course, are either implicit or explicit in the basic laws of most countries. The crucial question is *who* makes these determinations? And in China it is clear that the only officials who have such authority, whether they be administrators or members of the judiciary, are appointed by and expected to be loyal to the Communist Party hierarchy. So if there ever are conflicts between citizens' rights and the interests of the state (which according to communist ideology should never really happen in a communist-run state), those beholden to the regime's conceptions of its own interests will invariably be judges on their own behalf.

Beijing's persistent claims that it does not repress legitimate political dissent (for example, its official line that the 1989 student demonstration in Tiananmen Square, which it brutally suppressed, was designed to subvert public order) are not given much credence by international human rights groups or most other governments. China's ability to fend off formal UN-agency criticism for its dismal human rights record and to avoid punitive diplomatic and economic sanctions by the United States and other public champions of civil and political rights is analyzed in one of the case studies in Chapter 6.

---

6. Jaime Oraa, *Human Rights in States of Emergency in International Law* (Oxford: Clarendon Press, 1992), pp. 21–22.
7. "'White Paper' on Human Rights in China," Foreign Broadcast Information Service CHI-91-212 (November 1, 1991), pp. 27–37.
8. Ibid.

PRIVATE RIGHTS

In traditional interstate relations, which are reflected in orthodox treatises on international law, foreigners are not supposed to interfere with the norms of everyday human relationships that particular national cultures have adopted for themselves. But with the growing international mobility of people and information, the principle of noninterference in the domestic affairs of states, even with respect to norms of interpersonal behavior, has come under increasing challenge.

The Women's Rights Movement

The most prominent realm of interpersonal behavior, previously considered to be a purely domestic issue, that has come to center stage in world politics in recent years is that of relations between men and women. Women's rights groups, often organized on a transnational basis, have been demanding universal reforms in how the relationships between the sexes are regarded to bring about what in their view would be a full equalization of privileges, amenities, and power of women vis-à-vis men.

The targets of the women's rights groups are not just governments and other organizations of society that they perceive to be discriminating against women in personnel hiring, promotion, and wage policies but include also, even more basically, the social/cultural patterns prevailing within certain communities. Some feminists and various human rights advocates argue that governments around the world, in addition to being obligated to refrain from official policies and actions that hurt or discriminate against women, are obligated to *prevent* private groups and individuals from actions thought to be injurious or unjust to women. A wide range of practices, not all of which are universally prohibited or even condemned, are targeted and include wife battering, *sati* (widow burning), ritual genital cutting, rape, prostitution, nonviolent sexual harassment, veiling, exclusion from certain professions and kinds of education, and allocations of household privileges and responsibilities that are demeaning to women.

Not surprisingly, governments responsive to traditional communities that condone the practices offensive to Western feminists have been active in various international forums (especially those dealing with population policy and women's rights) in opposing efforts to promulgate international standards, let alone enforceable rules, on male-female relationships. Thus when Hillary Rodham Clinton built her speech to the 1995 Beijing Conference around the slogan "Women's rights are human rights!" she was not simply reiterating a self-evident proposition, but was taking sides on what for many delegates was a politically and culturally explosive issue.

This ideological divide—that is, the divide between those who maintain that each cultural community ought to retain autonomy over its own sexual customs and those who claim that universal human rights are involved—also extends to other matters of interpersonal behavior and private morals, including particularly controversies over the care and education of children and the respective roles of parents, community authorities, and the state.

THE RIGHTS OF ECONOMIC WELL-BEING

Often those governments that are frequently charged with human rights abuses by the mainline human rights organizations counterattack with the argument that, on the contrary, they are doing a better job overall in advancing the human rights of their citizens than are the countries of which their accusers are citizens. We just have our priorities right, they say, emphasizing that even the right to life means nothing if the person is starving; that the right to buy and sell and advertise one's goods freely in the open market is not worth much if the market is open to multinational corporate monopolists which can squeeze out local family entrepreneurs; and that even the right of citizens to vote and run for office means little if elections can only be won by those who can afford the enormous costs of publicizing themselves and their views on the electronic media.

Leading participants in this debate are in China, the government of which is on the defensive when it comes to liberty rights and loses no opportunity to favorably compare its emphasis on the equal social and economic rights of its citizens with what it implies is an unjust indifference by Western capitalist regimes to the plight of the lower classes.

Although in 1998, under pressure from the United States, China agreed to sign the Covenant on Political and Civil Rights (it had already signed the Covenant on Economic, Social and Cultural Rights), its priorities clearly continue to lie in the economic-development side of the human rights equation. The key document for understanding Beijing's position is still its 1991 White Paper on human rights.

The White Paper proudly claimed that in contrast to the situation in most of the Western industrial countries, only 2.5 percent of its urban work force was unemployed. Admitting that monetary wages in China were relatively low, the White Paper proudly claimed that the "government guarantees the basic necessities to every worker and his family . . . including financial subsidies for housing, . . . social insurance such as medical treatment, industrial injury and retirement pension and many other welfare items, which are not counted in the wages." Moreover, averred the White Paper, "Chinese workers are the masters of their enterprises, directly participating in the management and supervision of the enterprises through workers congresses."[9]

The Chinese position that various political freedoms may have to take a back seat to economic imperatives has been a standard argument not only of Marxist-Leninist regimes but also of many of the excolonial states in debates in the World Bank and other United Nations agencies active in the development field.

This emphasis by Third World governments on the economic well-being of peoples as a basic, if not the most basic, human right has become an increasingly prominent part of the international human rights dialogue. There is a virtual consensus among these governments, despite their differences on many other issues, on the following set of arguments: Just as national self-determination was the precondition for the realization of their peoples' civil and political rights and the politically sovereign nation-state remains the most appropriate instrument for advancing and protecting human rights, so too, the economic well-being of their people needs to be assured through the national collectivity. As a prerequisite to each person in each nation being able to enjoy a minimum standard of economic well-being, a certain level of economic development needs to be obtained by the country as a whole. This requires that the capacity of the nation-states to manage their economic development, as a minimum, should not be undermined by other states or powerful international corporations or banks and, optimally, in the case of poor countries, that the affluent countries should provide their governments with assistance to help them attain self-sustaining economic growth without undermining their political and cultural autonomy in the process.

In addition to insisting that the most important of the human rights treaties is the Covenant on Economic, Social and Cultural Rights (see Chapter 4 for its detailed provisions), the Third World coalition has successfully sponsored numerous supporting declarations by United Nations bodies in which the Third World countries command a substantial majority of the votes. One of the most controversial of these was the Charter of Economic Rights and Duties of States, passed by the General Assembly in 1975 by a vote of 120 to 6 with 10 abstentions (countries voting against were Belgium, Denmark, the Federal Republic of Germany, Luxembourg, the United Kingdom, and the United States).[10] In the spirit of the North-South polarization of the 1970s, the emphasis in the Charter on Economic Rights and Duties is as much on protecting the developing countries against neocolonial, rich-country and corporate

---

9. "'White Paper' of November 1, 1991," FBIS-CHI-91-212, p. 32.
10. Charter of Economic Rights and Duties of States (adopted by the United Nations General Assembly, 1974).

violations of their sovereignty as it is on assuring that the affluent would help in their development. The charter affirms that

> Every State has the sovereign and inalienable right to choose its economic system as well as its political, social and cultural systems in accordance with the will of its people, without outside interference, coercion or threat in any form whatsoever.

And it proceeds to catalog the national prerogatives that flow from the basic-sovereignty principle, giving special prominence to "the right" of each *state*

> To regulate and exercise authority over foreign investment within its national jurisdiction. . . .
>
> . . .
>
> To regulate and supervise the activities of transnational corporations within its national jurisdiction. . . .
>
> . . .
>
> To nationalize, expropriate or transfer ownership of foreign property. . . . [and] where the question of compensation gives rise to a controversy, it shall be settled under the domestic law of the nationalizing State. . . . .

The next major step in this effort of the Third World countries to enlarge the definition of human rights to include (and give priority to) their perceived needs was the United Nations Declaration of the Right to Development adopted by the General Assembly in 1986.[11] The argument of the Declaration is that since the economic well-being of every human being is an essential human right, every human being has a right to live in a country in which the conditions are present that will permit this right to be enjoyed by all. This means, in turn, that it is the *obligation of the affluent countries to provide the relatively poor countries with the means and facilities the poor countries need* to realize these conditions. But the document is very clear in its reiteration of the strictures of the Charter of Economic Rights and Duties of States that in fulfilling this obligation, the affluent countries are not in any way to infringe upon the sovereignty of the developing countries. In the words of the declaration,

> The right to development is an inalienable human right by virtue of which every human person and all peoples are entitled to participate in, contribute to, and enjoy economic, social, cultural and political development, in which all human rights and fundamental freedoms can be fully realized.

---

11. Declaration on the Right to Development (adopted by the United Nations General Assembly, 1986).

But, inadvertently perhaps, the emphasis in these and other development documents sponsored by Third World governments have provided
disadvantaged and disaffected peoples in their jurisdictions with moral
ammunition to assert their own claims of unjust treatment against these
governments.

THE RIGHTS OF PEOPLES

Assertion by communities of their collective or peoples' rights frequently emerge out of situations in which individuals are denied their
basic rights, not simply as individuals, but because they belong to a
group that the government or the dominant cultural group wants to suppress or weaken. This need not always take the form of the kind of direct
deprivation of individual rights that the mainline human rights groups
pay most attention to. Thus, even though an individual member of a
aggrieved group does not feel personally deprived of his or her individual
rights—such as equal protection of the laws, freedom of expression and
association, the opportunity to vote and run for office, and the guarantee
of due process in the courts—he or she may belong to a group whose
minority status in a given society does not allow the group to exercise
sufficient weight in shaping the rules and policies of that society. Such
feelings of relative powerlessness are widespread among members of a
religious or ethnic community that exists as a minority in a state where
the majority belongs to a rival religious or ethnic community; the resulting envy at the majority community (especially where its members
occupy the lion's share of a country's elite roles) is raw material for
mobilization into a self-determination or secessionist movement for the
establishment of an independent jurisdiction in which the formerly
aggrieved minority will now constitute the ruling majority.

Political leaders attempting to mobilize such autonomy or secessionist movements can invoke either of the two most important international covenants on human rights—the *International Covenant on Civil
and Political Rights* and the *International Covenant on Economic,
Cultural, and Social Rights*—in support of their demands. Even before
stipulating the rights of individuals, Article 1 in both of these documents
states the following:

> All peoples have the right of self-determination. By virtue of that
> right they freely determine their political status and freely pursue
> their economic, social, and cultural development.[12]

But this universally asserted right of self-determination has become a
problem for many of the very countries that, having recently achieved

---

12. *United Nations Treaty Series* 993 and 999.

independence from their colonial overlords, lobbied hard to give self-determination pride of place in the international human rights documents. The new states must now deal with culturally diverse peoples within *their* jurisdictions, some of whom consider themselves distinct nations meriting independent statehood.

Western liberals who previously championed the self-determination of peoples are also having second thoughts; for if the idea that any nation has a right to a state of its own is taken seriously by aggrieved ethnic communities around the world, the entire nation-state system as we know it could become dangerously unraveled. Only one in ten of the world's countries is ethnically homogeneous; three-quarters of the countries have ethnic minorities that make up over 5 percent of the population; and in one-tenth of the countries at least 40 percent of the population is distinct from the dominant ethnic group.[13] A global survey of ethno-nationality conflicts in the early 1990s found that as many as 200 disaffected ethnic communities (some spanning the borders of existing nation-states) were attempting to assert their rights against national governments, and as many as 20 of these were engaged in overt agitation for political autonomy.[14]

Self-determination Movements in the Wake of Retreating Empires

In many of the countries that have achieved independence from their European overlords since World War II, with the necessity of maintaining solidarity in the struggle against the colonial power now removed, communal groups with languages or religions different from those of the dominant group often are not content to allow the dominant group, even if it represents a majority of the population, to determine the way of life for the whole country.[15] Each is insisting that the "self" that should possess self-determination rights is its own cultural community and not necessarily the whole population that was arbitrarily included within the borders established by the former colonial power.

In some of the postcolonial states, the moral claims to self-determination are especially difficult to sort out because of the complicated history, and legacy, of the colonial regimes in their regions. This is

---

13. See Gunnar P. Mielson, "States and 'Nation-Groups': A Global Taxonomy," in Edward A. Tiryakian and Ronald Rogowski, *New Nationalisms of the Developed West* (Boston: Allen & Unwin, 1985), pp. 27–56.

14. Ted Robert Gurr, *Minorities at Risk: A Global View of Ethnopolitical Conflict* (Washington, DC: United States Institute of Peace Press, 1993). See also Ted Robert Gurr and Barbara Harff, *Ethnic Conflict in World Politics* (Boulder, CO: Westview Press, 1994).

15. See Donald L. Horowitz, *Ethnic Groups in Conflict* (Berkeley, CA: University of California Press, 1985).

particularly the case in segments of the colonies (for example, Southern Sudan) where imperial powers encouraged their religious missionaries to operate. When the colonial powers departed, the newly independent nations, even if relatively homogeneous racially, were comprised of some areas where the people considered themselves culturally distinct (on religious grounds) from the dominant group, but the dominant group could well claim that the people in this area were perpetuating the alien culture of the former colonial overlord. (See Controversy Box 4 on page 34.)

In some regions, such as South Asia, the cultural and religious legacies of successive imperial occupiers over the course of centuries have even further complicated the issue of what communities have legitimate claims to national self-determination. The Indian subcontinent's bloody intercommunal strife following the end of the British raj is a notorious case in point.

The genocidal conflicts in the former Yugoslavia are another tragic expression of the phenomenon whereby the legacy of religions superimposed on an ethnically homogeneous population by former imperial overlords become grist for communal demagogues to stir up incompatible demands for national self-determination (in this case by the Roman Catholic Croats, the Eastern Orthodox Serbs, and the Muslims of Bosnia).

Postimperial self-determination movements in the region formerly under Soviet domination have also become a predicament. With the end of the Cold War, the long-festering resentment of the diverse peoples that had been absorbed into the Soviet empire broke out in an epidemic of national independence and secession movements between 1989 and 1992. No longer motivated by the transnational communist ideology and no longer able to devote the economic and military resources required to sustain such a huge imperium, the Kremlin—much to the surprise of the international community—allowed many of the peoples it had formerly held in subjugation across the vast Eurasian landmass to defect nonviolently. But this set in motion a process of imperial unraveling that has yet to run its full course.

In what was the USSR itself, national self-determination, proclaimed as a right (but never really honored) in the Soviet constitution and in other basic laws of the USSR, was the concept embraced by the 15 member republics as they all successfully asserted their political independence during the 1989–1991 period of democratization initiated by Mikhail Gorbachev. The problem is that these newly sovereign states are themselves multinational societies.

In the former Soviet states outside of Russia proper, ethnic Russians comprise significant portions of the populations. Thus, more than 30 percent of the people of Estonia and Latvia are Russians, whom Moscow alleges are now being discriminated against.

In Ukraine, the ethnic Russians are 20 percent and are concentrated in the strategically important and resource-rich Crimean peninsula. The Ukrainian government, proud of its newly obtained independence from

CONTROVERSY BOX
4

Self-Determination for East Timor?

Responding to UN resolutions and decades of protest by international human rights groups supporting self-determination for the mostly Catholic people of East Timor (the former Portuguese colony that Indonesia forcibly annexed in 1976), Indonesian President Habibie offered the East Timorese the opportunity to vote for "wide ranging autonomy" under Indonesian soveriegnty in August 1999. President Habibie also announced, as an alternative to the autonomy option, that the Indonesian government would permit the East Timorese to vote for complete secession. But most East Timorese and international observers regard this second "full independence" option as a ruse that has virtually no credibilty but is designed to confuse and split the self-determination movement. In the months preceding the August vote, militiamen armed by the Indonesian military were formenting violence in the countryside in what appeared to be an effort to discredit the validity of the forthcoming plebiscite.

What role, if any, can and should the United Nations play in this type of situation to ensure free and fair elections?

the USSR but fearing the spread of the self-determination fever to the ethnic Russians within its jurisdiction, has imposed uncompromising culturo-linguistic conformity on the people of Crimea, which in turn has further stimulated the separatist tendencies the government was trying to repress.

Many of the most intense intercommunal conflicts are on Russia's southern periphery, where ethnic groups with a Muslim orientation are fighting groups who identify with the Orthodox Christian church. These situations are especially combustible in that they carry the danger of intervention from one or a combination of Islamic Middle Eastern nations, which Russia might perceive to threaten her national security and economic interests. The conflict in Azerbaijan over Nagorno-Karabakh is of this type: A mostly Christian Armenian enclave within largely Muslim Azerbaijan, Nagorno-Karabakh voted in 1991 to secede from Azerbaijan and merge with neighboring Armenia—a vote that provoked violence between the Muslims and Christians in Nogorno-Karabakh and then military intervention by the Azerbaijani government to coercively reverse the secession.

Finally, in the Russia federation many of the member republics, especially in the south and the east, have non-Russian Islamic and/or Asian majorities that are discontented with their subordinate status in the Russian-dominated federation. Chechnya and Tatarstan have refused to sign Russia's federal constitutive treaty, and further separatist rumblings have reverberated throughout this historically unstable fault line flanking the Russian empire. Moscow's military suppression of the Chechnyan secession was designed in part to deter the other republics from emulating Chechnya and Tatarstan, but instead Chechnya has become a human rights cause celebre, undermining both the international and domestic legitimacy of the Yeltsin regime.

Autonomy Movements in Muticultural Democracies

The right to substantial political/legal autonomy, if not full independence, has been asserted even against governments of the democracies in Western Europe and North America by minorities who feel that the one-person–one-vote basis of the democratic polity can result in their being kept in a condition of second-class citizenship by the prevailing majority. Particularly when a minority community that considers itself deprived is differentiated by a number of cultural factors—say, language, religion, concentration in certain occupations, or physical traits and geographic clustering—the situation is ripe for that group to be politicized and to demand autonomy.

Such is the situation in Canada, where 6 million Canadians of French ancestry are concentrated in Quebec and constitute 85 percent of that province's population. Although the French Quebecois are hardly of one mind with respect to how far to take their sense of being a distinct nation within the Canadian federation, they have approved legislation making French the first language of the province of Quebec and are governed by a political leadership that propagates the goal of full political autonomy.

In 1996 the Canadian government branded a pending Quebec declaration of independence unconstitutional, even if it were supported by a provincial referendum. The Canadian constitution requires that any such fundamental change in the makeup of the Canadian union must receive approval by all nine of the country's provinces, but the separatists argue that it is the Canadian constitution itself that is being rejected—deliberately!—and that in so doing, Quebecers are simply exercising their more basic human right to determine their own future. Although a full-blown civil war appears highly unlikely, violent tests of will over which community will have the final right of self-determination cannot be ruled out—even on Canada's traditionally peaceful streets.

An even more complicated debate over who is the "self" that has the overriding right to determine its way of life has been going on in Ireland for most of the century, frequently exploding into violence between the Irish Catholics and the Irish Protestants. Despite the historic Peace

Accord signed on April 10, 1998, between the United Kingdom of Great Britain and Northern Ireland on the one side and the government of Ireland the other, Ireland remains divided in two: the independent and sovereign Irish Free State, which is predominantly Catholic, and Northern Ireland, which is a province of the United Kingdom (Britain) and is predominantly Protestant.

Until the April 1998 Peace Accord, most Catholics in both parts of Ireland insisted that all the people on the island constitute the Irish nation and that the right of self-determination implies that this nation as a whole, through a single democratic referendum, should be permitted to determine whether or not it would be one country or remain divided. Were there to be a referendum of all the voters on the Irish Isle, the Catholics would constitute over 75 percent of the electorate and would undoubtedly support a unification of the island under a one-person–one-vote system. But that is precisely why the electorate in Northern Ireland, 60 percent of whom are Protestant, would never agree to such a single islandwide referendum, for the Protestants fear the outcome would be their permanent subordination as a minority in the larger Catholic country.

The historic breakthrough in April 1998, the product of a 22-month negotiation chaired by former U.S. Senator George Mitchell, featured a modification of the Irish Catholic demand for the single islandwide referendum in exchange for a start toward eventual confederation (though it wasn't called that) of the north and the south.

The new institutional start toward eventual confederation included a North/South Ministerial Council (to decide upon and coordinate policies requiring cross-border and all-island cooperation or joint action); a British-Irish Council representing the government of Ireland (Dublin) and the United Kingdom (to decide upon and coordinate policies requiring inter-island cooperation or joint action); a variety of implementation bodies for these two Councils; and a newly constituted, democratically elected Assembly for Northern Ireland (that would guarantee decision-making weight to the minority Catholic community and would provide for a multiparty coalition government).[16]

The concessions by the Catholics on the issue of a referendum to determine the island's future are contained in Article 1 of the Peace Accord, in which the Irish and British governments stated that they

> (i) recognize the legitimacy of whatever choice is freely exercised by a majority of the people of Northern Ireland with regard to its status, whether they prefer to continue to support the Union with Great Britain or a sovereign united Ireland;

---

16. Agreement between the Government of the United Kingdom of Great Britain and Northern Ireland and the Government of Ireland (signed at Belfast on April, 10 1998).

(ii) recognize that is for the people of the island of Ireland alone, to exercise their right of self-determination on the basis of consent, freely and concurrently given, North and South, to bring about a united Ireland, if that is their wish, accepting that this right must be achieved and exercised with and subject to the agreement and consent of a majority of the people of Northern Ireland;

(iii) acknowledge that while a substantial section of the people in Northern Ireland share the legitimate wish of a majority of the people of the island of Ireland for a united Ireland, the present wish of a majority of the people of Northern Ireland, freely exercised and legitimate, is to maintain the Union and accordingly, that Northern Ireland status as part of the United Kingdom reflects and relies on that wish; and that it would be wrong to make any change in the status of Northern Ireland save with the consent of a majority of its people.[17]

Although the basic agreement has been approved by the electorate in both the north and the south, there is still a long road to traverse to concrete institution building to implement its provisions. Obstructionist militants in both religious communities, each claiming the need to deter the other side, have not completely foresworn violence or disarmed their paramilitary units, and moderate factions in each community hold that unless the other side's militants decommission their weapons, there will not be an adequate context for the needed cooperation.

Some of the other festering multicultural conflicts in democratic states, involving essentially incompatible assertions of the right of self-determination, include the Flemish-Waloon rivalry in Belgium, pitting the 5.5 million Dutch-speaking Flemings in the traditionally agricultural north against the 4 million (but politically dominant) French-speaking Walloon of the more industrialized south, and outbreaks of anti-Spanish violence in the ethno-linguistic communities along the border between France and Spain, especially among some of the 1 million Basques who are dissatisfied with the considerable autonomy Spain has already allowed them and are demanding full independence.

Finally, there are the proliferating assertions of autonomy rights around the globe by so-called indigenous peoples, that is, ethnically distinct communities who usually reside in remote hinterlands and who have resisted, or been denied, assimilation into the dominant modernizing culture. A prominent example is the agitation by North American aboriginal tribes for extensive rights to the resources of the land they occupy and the waters they live near. Instead of insisting on equal treatment as Americans and as Canadians and full integration (if not assimilation) into the majority cultures, the dominant thrust of the contemporary rights movements of Native Americans (on the U.S. mainland) and of the

---

17. Ibid.

Inuits (in Canada and Alaska) is toward restoring the authentic dignity, including the political autonomy, of their own cultures. To many of the new leaders, self-determination means immunity from, rather than equal protection of, the laws of the dominant Euro-American political systems into which their communities have been subordinated (often forcibly) during the past 300 years.[18]

THE PERVASIVE DEBATE: UNIVERSALISM VERSUS CULTURAL PLURALISM

In light of the conflicts and controversies recounted in this chapter, how do we explain the declaration adopted in Vienna at the 1993 World Conference on Human Rights meeting in Vienna? In this declaration, official representatives of most of the world's national governments reaffirmed

> the solemn commitment of all States to fulfill their obligations to promote universal respect for, and observance of, all human rights and fundamental freedoms for all in accordance with the Charter of the United Nations, other instruments relating to human rights, and international law. The universal nature of these rights and freedoms is beyond question.[19]

Although there was considerable debate among the Vienna conferees over the last sentence of this paragraph in particular, the final reaffirmation of the "universal character of these rights" was consistent with the phraseology in virtually all of the human rights declarations and covenants adopted by the United Nations since 1948. But because of the contradictory or ambiguous provisions in most of these documents (analyzed in detail in Chapter 5), the 1993 reendorsement of their universal character would still leave their implementation up to the varying interpretations the different parties would give them.

Indeed, to make sure the pluralism of implementation and interpretation would also continue to be accorded legitimacy, the Asian states at their Regional Preparatory Meeting for the Vienna Conference in Bangkok issued their own declaration, stating that

> while human rights are universal in nature, they must be considered in the context of a dynamic and evolving process of international norm-setting, bearing in mind the significance of the

---

18. Paradoxically, an independent Quebec itself would become a major target of the indigenous peoples' self-determination movement (the Inuit and Cree peoples claim territory amounting to two-thirds of Quebec's 594,860 square miles).
19. United Nations, Doc. A/CONF. 157/22 (1993).

national and regional peculiarities and various historical, cultural, and religious backgrounds.[20]

And when a new UN High Commissioner of Human Rights was appointed, the cultural relativism of the Bangkok Declaration was included in his mandate.

If anything, the evolution of the international human rights consensus since 1948 along the universalism-pluralism spectrum has been in the direction of greater pluralism. This reflects both the increased influence of the non-Western nations in international forums and, paradoxically, the increased empowerment worldwide of nongovernmental groups committed to the universal expansion of basic human rights. As constituencies mobilize transnationally to compel national governments to take human rights seriously and as national governments, responding to these pressures, fashion international instruments to hold one another accountable to human rights norms that have widespread support, the substantive content of these norms can no longer be regarded as lacking in political force. As this happens, culturally distinct communities around the world are becoming all the more determined to protect their special ways of life from erosion by the new universalist currents. Governments, subjected to these contrary pressures, are therefore *simultaneously* taking international human rights diplomacy more seriously than ever, while trying to preserve their traditional sovereign prerogatives and to protect their more culturally sensitive constituents.

In summary, human rights considerations, no longer the subject merely of international rhetoric, have moved to the center of very real, high-stakes world politics.

---

20. United Nations, Doc. A/CONF. 157/PC/59; quoted by Philip Alston, "The UN's Human Rights Record: From San Francisco to Vienna and Beyond," *Human Rights Quarterly* 16 (1944), p. 382.

Chapter 3

Philosophical Issues and Insights

Those who claim their human rights are being denied and those who dispute these claims sometimes argue over the facts (for example, Did such and such events actually take place? Did the acts in question happen exactly the way some parties allege?). Sometimes the main arguments are over the law (such as, Are the acts or policies in question in violation of or protected by certain international covenants, treaties, or findings of international judicial bodies?). Often, however, the human rights disputes that find their way into international arenas are over the more basic issue of whether certain kinds of actions or policies *should* be internationally prohibited or protected. Indeed, some of the most prominent alignments and antagonisms in contemporary world politics are traceable to differing positions on this philosophical core of the human rights question.

Moral and political philosophers (classical, theological, modern, Western, and non-Western) have had a good deal to say that is pertinent to the current ferment over human rights. Their thinking is probed here for insights that bear especially on the international controversies over the priority that should be given to the rights of persons, peoples, and governments and the related controversies over which rights should be universally guaranteed and which should be left to various communities to decide in accordance with their own cultural traditions.

Much of today's human rights debate, now conducted in the international arena among diplomats and international lawyers relies—sometimes explicitly, often unknowingly—on arguments systematically developed by the world's great philosophers concerning the profound and interrelated questions of the relationships between individuals and their communities, the universality or cultural uniqueness of human characteristics and social norms, and the relationship among and priority to be accorded various rights and duties when they come into conflict.

The analysis here draws selectively on works that are intellectually powerful statements of the main contending points of view. It is not meant to be a comprehensive survey of the range of views but rather to highlight the fact that the principal human rights issues now at the center of world politics are neither new nor easily disposed of and that they are matters on which great minds have fundamentally disagreed—within countries, across continents, and for thousands of years.

Table 3.1 on page 42 anticipates in highly summary form the discussion of the major philosophical schools of thought in this chapter. The table should be used only as a simplified map of the analysis ahead and not as an adequate exposition of the contending views.

CLASSICAL GREEK AND ROMAN VIEWS

Aristotle on the Priority of the State

Consistent with the political ideas prevailing in the Greek city-states in the fourth century B. C., Aristotle (good student of Plato that he was) held that "the state is by nature clearly prior to the family and to the individual, since the whole is of necessity prior to the part."[1] The words *prior to* in this context mean an *essential condition for* rather than *earlier in the sequence of societal development.* Aristotle elaborates as follows:

> The proof that the state is a creation of nature and prior to the individual is that the individual, when isolated, is not self-sufficing; and therefore he is like a part in relation to the whole. But he who is unable to live in society, or has no need because he is sufficient for himself, must either be a beast or a god; he is no part of a state. A social instinct is implanted in all men by nature, and yet he who first founded the state was the greatest of benefactors. For man, when perfected, is the best of animals, but when separated from law and justice, he is the worst of all."[2]

Aristotle's project in his *Politics* was to discover, both through logic and through a comparative historical analysis of constitutions, the essential characteristics of the good and just state. In the end, his preferences for the alternative forms of true governments (and their perversions)—monarchy (tyranny), aristocracy (oligarchy), and constitutional government (democracy)—remained somewhat ambiguous. But he did make it clear that in his view the good *of* the state—its survival and ability to

---

1. Aristotle, *Politics,* translated by Benjamin Jowett (New York: Random House, New American Library, 1943), Book I, Chapter 2, p. 55.
2. Ibid.

Table 3.1   Preview of Philosophical Views

	Aristotle	Cicero	Premodern Non-West	Aquinas	Grotius	Hobbes	Locke	Rousseau	Burke	Kant	Hegel	Bentham	J. S. Mill	Walzer	Current Non-West	Shue	United States (Gov.)	China (Gov.)
Human nature is the same everywhere	Y	Y	Y	Y	Y	Y	Y	Y	N	Y	Σ	Y	Y	Σ	Y	Y	Y	Σ
All humans should have the same basic rights and duties	N	Y	Σ		Y	Y	Y	Y	Σ	Y	Σ	N	Σ	Σ	Y	Y	Y	N
The international community should intervene in countries to secure human rights					Y									N	N	Y	N	N
Priority should be given to individual rights	N		N			N	Y	N	N	Y	N	N	Y	N	N	Y	Σ	N
Highest priority should be given to civil liberties	N		N			N	Y	N	N	Σ	N	N	Y	N	N	Σ	Σ	N
Government should be based on democratic consent	Σ		N			N	Y	Y	N	Y	Σ	Y	Y	Σ	N	Y	Y	N
Government should be limited by higher moral law	Y	Y	Y	Y	Y	N	Y	N	Σ	Y	Σ	N	Σ	Σ	Σ	Σ	Σ	N
Self-determination should be allowed for ethno-national communities						N	Y		Σ	Σ			Σ	Σ	Σ	Σ	Σ	N
Human traits are deeply shaped by each community	Y	N							Y		Y			Y	Y		N	Σ
Foreign intervention into domestic affairs should be prohibited						Y	Σ	Σ	Y	Σ			Σ	Σ	Y	N	Σ	Y
Priority should be given to the needs of the whole country	Y					Y		Y	Y		Y	Y			Y	Σ	Σ	Y
Highest value should be accorded to basic physical and economic needs												Y		Σ	Y	Y		Y

Note: Y = Largely supports idea
          N = Largely opposes idea
          Σ = Has complex views (neither supports nor opposes)
          Blank = Does not emphasize idea

*Table designed by Vanda Felbabova

minister to the common needs of its citizenry—overrides the claims upon the state by any individuals within it.

Moreover, Aristotle maintained that states could not perform what they were designed to do well unless they were small, legally autonomous, and culturally homogeneous, on the model of the Greek city-state.[3] But not all the prominent philosophers of the time agreed. The Stoics, with a universalistic view of the scope of the human community, had a very different conception of the relationships between particular states and the individuals within them; and it was the Stoic view that, understandably, became the official public philosophy of the Roman Empire.

The Cosmopolitan Natural-Law Philosophy of Cicero

The most prominent political theorist of the Roman Empire, the lawyer-statesman Cicero (106–45 B.C.), wrote in his *De Re Publica* that

> True law is right reason in agreement with Nature; it is of universal application, unchanging and everlasting. . . . We cannot be freed from its obligations by senate or people; and we need not look outside ourselves for an expounder or interpreter of it. And there will not be different laws at Rome and at Athens, or different laws now and in the future, but one eternal and unchangeable law will be valid for all nations and all times. . . .
>
> [T]he most foolish notion of all is the belief that everything is just which is found in the customs or laws of nations.[4]

Of major significance for subsequent assertions of the rights of individuals and peoples against the prerogatives of governments, Cicero's formulation holds that *both* the state and the citizenry, anywhere in the world, are bound by the authority of the higher law of nature. "This whole universe," he said, is "one commonwealth of which both gods and men are members." If taken seriously, this would make it legitimate for individuals or groups to disobey the laws of the state claiming jurisdiction over them, and even to revolt against existing governments, on grounds of the incompatibility of the local or national laws with natural law.

But revolutionary implications, outrunning what Cicero himself would have wanted, might also be read into Cicero's contention that "we

---

3. Ibid., Book VII, pp. 278–319.
4. Cicero, *De Re Publica*, translated by Clinton Walker Keyes (Cambridge: Harvard University Press, 1943), p. 385–387.

need not look outside ourselves for an expounder or interpreter" of natural law. If each individual could be an interpreter of when the higher law justified disobedience of local or national law, would this not be a license for anarchy that could tear apart even the presumably just cosmopolitan commonwealth? Cicero's answer was that the just commonwealth would be sustained by "right reason"—the capacity of all humans to discern what regime of laws for the commonwealth would best fulfill nature's design for humans to live virtuous lives of service to others, generosity, and mutual love.

Cicero's optimism was, of course, not borne out as the real-world cosmopolis in which he placed his faith—an empire overstretched economically and militarily to sustain its vast frontiers, and weakened from within by self-serving as well as enlightened subverters of imperial law—ultimately gave way to centuries of anarchy across the length and breadth of the European continent.

PREMODERN NON-WESTERN POLITICAL THOUGHT

In parallel with the flourishing of political philosophy in ancient Greece and Rome, various of the intellectually rich civilizations of the Orient were also developing bodies of thought about the relations between the ruler and the people within the ruler's sphere of control. Why some of these are today called "non-Western"—as in the case of Islam but not of Judaism or Christianity—has much to do with their not being assimilated into European culture. Although in its religious origins Islam was a direct offshoot of Judaism and Christianity, in its political evolution Islam (largely insulated from the European renaissance of Greco-Roman thought and then the European Enlightenment) resembled more closely the Asian cultures, some of which it strongly infiltrated, in resisting the secularization of philosophy.

As with ancient Greek and Roman philosophy, the early non-Western thought clearly is deeply divided on many of the basic issues relevant to human rights questions. Accordingly it would be inappropriate to invoke *the* non-Western—or even *the* Asian—tradition as if it constituted a coherent counterstatement to *the* Western tradition. Each of the schools of thought (and their subschools) has grappled in their own way with the pertinent philosophical questions, and each can be mined for unique insights. This introductory look at various non-Western approaches highlights the fact that fundamental philosophical debates on these issues have taken place as much within "civilizations" as between them. The same holds true for other traditions not sampled here, such as that of Africa, of the pre-Columbian Western Hemisphere, and of the indigenous peoples in the South Pacific and the Arctic regions.

The Great Asian Traditions

Much of what presents itself today as the non-Western reaction to an imposed Euro-American philosophy of human rights is claimed to be derived from the great philosophical traditions of the East—Hinduism, Buddhism, and Confucianism. The Asian/non-Western views, while reflecting a wide array of cultures and religions, do converge around the primary emphasis they gives to beliefs about the inseparability of individuals and community.

Common to the various schools of Hinduism, explains Sarvepalli Radhakrishnan, is the view that

> Human society is an organic whole, the parts of which are naturally dependent in such a way that . . . the whole is present in each part, while each part is indispensable to the whole.
>
> . . .
>
> The political and the economic life of the community is expected to derive its inspiration from the spiritual. This principle saves the State from becoming a mere military despotism. The sovereign power is not identified with the interests of the governing classes but with those of the people at large.[5]

Buddhist philosophies in the main (whether of the Hinayana, Mahayana, or Zen types) are not directly concerned with politics since they are preoccupied primarily with the inner spiritual development of the person. Yet even in its focus on the inner being, Buddhism is profoundly political in the sense of its absolute respect for the inherent worth and potential spiritual excellence of each individual (a view that anticipates Immanuel Kant's[6] imperative always to treat persons as ends, never simply as means). This puts Buddhism at odds with statist and totalitarian ideologies. Moreover, in its views of the essential characteristics of the human creature and of human potentialities and paths to excellence, Buddhism is also unapologetically universalistic—even while recognizing pragmatically that there are different cultural environments to which its insights and ethical precepts may have to be adapted.

The richest source of ancient non-Western ideas pertinent to contemporary human rights debates is the Chinese humanist tradition that emanated from the thinking of Confucius (who lived in the fifth century B.C. and more than a century before Aristotle). But the idea that in a virtuous state there could be legitimate rights claims of individuals against the governing authorities was foreign to Confucius' own thinking; for in

---

5. S. Radhakrishnan, *The Hindu View of Life* (London: Allen & Unwin, 1954), pp. 107–109.
6. See pages 58–59 for a discussion of Kant's views.

his view a virtuous state exhibits "no distinction, no separation, no confrontation between the individual and society, but an essential unity and harmony," with justice regarded as what contributes to that harmony.[7] All people in society have a duty to contribute to that essential harmony, and officials of the state up and down the hierarchy are especially responsible for demonstrating and cultivating in themselves and others the traits of mutual respect and civility that are at the core of the just society. Thus, according to the *Analects* (the collection of sayings by Confucius and his pupils),

> Confucius said, "Lead the people with governmental measures and regulate them by law and punishment, and they will avoid wrongdoing but will have no sense of honor and shame. Lead them with virtue and regulate them by the rules of propriety (*li*), and they will have a sense of shame, and moreover, set themselves right." (2:3)
>
> . . .
>
> Chi K'ang asked Confucius about government, saying, "What do you think of killing the wicked and associating with the good?" Confucius replied, "In your government what is the need of killing? If you desire what is good, the people will be good. The character of a ruler is like wind and that of the people is like grass. In whatever direction the wind blows, the grass always bends."[8] (12:19)

In the elaborations of some of Confucius' prominent successors, however, the picture of a virtuous officialdom presiding over a willingly compliant society was substantially modified. The reality was that tensions between the people and their governments might require more than refresher courses in the *Analects* for imperial bureaucrats.

One school of thought, led by Mencius, the most influential disciple of Confucius, located the basis for the virtuous and just state in the natural ability of ordinary humans to understand and do good. The occurrence of evil is a result of "external" influences that interfere with this natural capacity—one such influence being badly run government.

Remarkably, for the times—this was still three centuries B.C.— Mencius put the people's innate sense of justice ahead of their obligation to obey the governing elites. He advised his king that

> When all your immediate ministers say that a man is worthy, it is not sufficient. When all your great officers say so, it is not suffi-

---

7. Louis Henkin, "The Human Rights Idea in China: A Comparative Perspective," in R. Randle Edwards, Louis Henkin, and Andrew J. Nathan, *Human Rights in Contemporary China* (New York: Columbia University Press, 1986), p. 21.
8. Excerpts from the *Analects of Confucius,* 2:3 and 12:19, in Wing-Tsit Chan, *A Source Book in Chinese Philosophy* (Princeton, NJ: Princeton University Press, 1993), pp. 22, 40.

cient. . . . When all your people say [that a man is *not* worthy],
look into the case, and if you find him to be no good, then dismiss
him. . . . Only in this way can a ruler become the parent of the
people.[9]

Mencius even strongly implied the right of revolution and popularly supported assassination of unjust rulers, not excluding the king. Asked by
the King of Ch'i, "Is it right for a minister to murder his king?" Mencius
replied, "He who injures humanity is a bandit. He who injures righteous-
ness is a destructive person. Such a person is a mere fellow. I have heard
of killing a mere fellow. . . ." Having lost the "Mandate of Heaven," a
king may be deposed, by violence if necessary.[10]

Another prominent student of Confucius, Hsun Tzu, went in a different direction and focused rather on what he regarded as the evil in
human nature that needed to be effectively countered by strong and
incorruptible rulers. In Hsun Tzu's words,

Mencius said, "The nature of man is good." I say this is not true. . . .
Man's nature is evil. Therefore the sages of antiquity, knowing that
man's nature is evil, that it is unbalanced and incorrect, and that it
is violent, disorderly, and undisciplined, established the authority
of rulers to govern the people, set forth clearly propriety and right-
eousness to transform them, instituted laws and governmental
measures to rule them, and made punishments severe to restrain
them, so that all will result in good order and be in accord with
goodness.[11]

Premodern Islam

The political ideas in premodern Islam—actually, the political *implications* of its theology—have proven remarkably durable. The views of the
religion's founder, the Prophet Muhammad (570–632 A.D.), are invoked
today as justifications for actions by governments and political movements representing as much as 15 percent of the world's population.

The meaning of the Prophet's words, which are transcribed in the
Koran (or Quran) and other reports of what he said and did, have been fer-
vently disputed by his disciples. Accordingly, the legally enforceable
meanings, which are supposed to be derived by juridical and theological
scholars from the Prophet's basic teachings and which make up the basic
Law of Islam, or *shari'a*, have varied with time and place. Indeed, the

---

9. *The Book of Mencius, Meng Tzu*, excerpts in Chan, ibid., pp. 51–83; quotation from
   pp. 61–62.
10. Ibid., p. 62.
11. From *The Hsun Tzu*, excerpts in Chan, *A Sourcebook of Chinese Philosophy*, ibid.,
    p. 131.

shari'a's rules governing the property rights of husbands and wives, for example, may well be quite different in Baghdad, Teheran, and Istanbul. Yet most Muslims subscribe to at least the following politically significant tenets:

1. Allah (God) is the only one true sovereign. He is omniscient and omnipotent. As stated in the Koran,

   > All that is heaven and earth gives glory to Allah. His is the sovereignty, and His the glory. He has power over all things.[12]
   > . . .
   > His is the kingdom of the heavens and the earth. He ordains life and has power over all things.
   > He is the first and the last, the visible and the unseen. He has knowledge of all things.[13]

2. In all of Islam, everyone—the rulers and the ruled, high- and low-born—is equal in the most important law of life: duty to the will of Allah.
3. It is the will of Allah, and the aim of Islamic law on Earth, that ruler and ruled alike are obligated to serve the well-being of the Islamic *Ummah* (community) as a whole.[14] The *Ummah* takes precedence over the wants and needs of any individual or family, local community, or official, no matter of how high in rank.

These foundational principles of Islamic theology translate into a basic political philosophy in which, according to Professor Bernard Lewis,

> The ruler owes a collective duty to the Islamic community as a whole, to defend its interests, to protect it against enemies, and advance its cause; he also owes a duty to the individual believer, to enable him to live the good Muslim life in this world, and thus prepare himself for the next. In return for these services he is entitled to command the obedience of his subjects in everything except sin. The duty of the subject is to render this obedience. . . . His expectation is that the ruler will fulfill his obligations and conduct himself in accordance with what is usually called justice.[15]

---

12. *The Koran,* translation by N. J. Dawood (London: Penguin Classica, 1956), p. 87.
13. Ibid., pp. 104–105.
14. Ann Elizabeth Mayer, *Islam and Human Rights: Tradition and Politics* (Boulder, CO: Westview, 1999), pp. 43–49.
15. Bernard Lewis, *The Political Language of Islam* (Chicago: University of Chicago Press, 1988), pp. 69–70.

The view that both the ruler and subject are subordinated to a higher will, the will of Allah, leaves open the question of *who* determines what that will is when ruler and subject come into conflict and each believes (or claims to believe) he is acting as Allah prescribes. This issue has been hotly disputed among Islamic philosophers and jurists throughout the ages and, as might be expected, has been at the center of some of the most violent conflicts for power within Islamic states. At one pole are those who have transposed the religious concept of *tawid* (oneness, or the sovereignty of a singular god over the entire universe) into absolute power for the ruler who, as Allah's designated authority over the community, must be obeyed.[16] At the other pole are those who insist (quoting the Prophet's instruction, "Do not obey a creature in transgression against the Creator") that there are limits to any ruler's power on Earth and that it is a right, even a duty, of the pious Muslim to disobey a ruler who violates the higher law.[17]

The dominant traditional theology, emphasizing the oneness of members of the religious community all submitting to the will of God, tended to discourage open dissidence by subjects of an Islamic state against the current governing authorities. If the ruler was indeed acting contrary to the will of Allah, he would be punished in the afterlife. Characteristically, the pious Muslim was one who respectfully submitted to the prevailing theocracy's interpretation of the holy law and who would be rewarded by Allah for his piety. Such passive respectfulness toward regimes in power is, of course, no longer the norm in the contemporary world of Islam.

THE NATURAL-LAW DOCTRINES OF THE UNIVERSAL CHURCH

Another tradition of thinking about relations between rulers and their subjects can be found in the great classics of Christian theology that deal with the moral laws to which secular rulers should be held accountable. This philosophical tradition evolved between the collapse of the Roman Empire at the end of the fifth century A.D. and the emergence of the nation-state system. It grew out of the efforts by the Christian Church to superimpose some standards of order and justice on the otherwise brutish feudalism that pervaded most of Europe during the Middle Ages.

The Church assumed its role of active guardian of the moral order on Earth as a duty to God, who, as preached by Christ and his contemporaneous disciples, considers all humans to be his children. (The universe of

---

16. See Nazith Ayubi, *Political Islam: Religion and Politics in the Arab World* (New York: Routledge, 1991), pp. 14–17.
17. Lewis, p. 70.

God's children was soon reduced by Christian theologians to encompass only those who accepted the validity of the Gospels; but as a result of the Church's missionary zeal, the bulk of the peoples that had previously been under the control of Rome came to be included.) Throughout Europe, legions of Church officials fanned out cross the lands of the former empire to provide good offices, counsel, and mediational and adjudicatory services and sometimes to handpick and install local and regional rulers. In performing its secular work, the Church claimed to be guided by the natural laws of the universe which in turn were governed by divine law. Actually, the natural-law doctrines it articulated to explain its policies were mainly a synthesis of the Platonic, Aristotelian, and Stoic philosophies that pre-Christian Rome had used to legitimize its imperial domain.

Most fully developed in the treatises of the thirteenth-century theologian St. Thomas Aquinas, the Church's doctrines on the sources and principles of natural law bear a striking resemblance to Cicero's formulations. Thus, in his *Summa Theologica*, St. Thomas opined,

> That which is not just seems to be no law at all. Hence the force of a law depends on the extent of its justice. Now in human affairs a thing is said to be just from being right, according to the rule of reason. But the first rule of reason is the law of nature. . . . Consequently, every human law has just so much of the nature of law as it is derived from the law of nature. But if in any point it departs from the law of nature, it is no longer a law but a perversion of law.[18]

As with Cicero, human beings would appear to have the right to refuse to obey an unjust (meaning unnatural) law. But in the Catholic version of such a conditional obligation to obey the laws of states, the right to disobey in particular cases usually must be authorized by the Church. Even so, the Thomistic philosophy provided a theological foundation for later individualistic or populist human rights challenges to governmental policies, particularly those in countries where a Catholic population perceived itself to be badly treated by those in control of the state. Also, the philosophy has provided radical Catholics around the world (quite numerous in some countries) with a philosophical justification to support certain revolutionary secular movements.

---

18. St. Thomas Aquinas, *Summa Theologica*, I–II, Question 95, Article 2, quoted in Melvin Rader, *Ethics and the Human Community* (New York: Holt, Rinehart and Winston, 1964), p. 24.

THE GROTIAN TRADITION
OF INTERNATIONAL LAW

The next major contributions to philosophical discourse on the subjugation of state power to moral and legal norms were, ironically, part and parcel of the historical expansion of state power vis-à-vis the Catholic Church in the late Middle Ages. The post-fourteenth-century consolidation of states into larger and more powerful units (a consequence of technology-driven developments in warfare and commerce) put many of the modernizing rulers on a collision course with the Church. In their desire to control their own affairs, some of these statespersons found support among dissident Christian religious groups— called "Protestants"—who were also struggling against the heavy hand of the Roman ecclesiastical authorities. The result was the century of bloody religious wars from the mid-1500s to the mid-1600s that pitted Protestant monarchies (in alliance with the followers of Martin Luther or John Calvin) against the kingdoms still loyal to or controlled by the Catholic Church.

The Peace of Westphalia (1648), ending the wars of religion, was in substantial part a codification of the arguments for state autonomy that had been developed by legal theoreticians in the Protestant states—most prominently the Dutch lawyer Hugo Grotius. Although Grotius died three years before the peace accords were signed in 1648, the terms "Westphalian" and "Grotian" are often used interchangeably to refer to the tradition of international law emanating from that defining historical moment.

Melding the postmedieval state-centric theories of Jean Bodin and Alberico Gentili with the classical natural-law legacy of Cicero and Aquinas, Grotius regarded the governments of countries as both the subjects and objects of international law. The governments simultaneously created, and were bound by, "customary law"— the practical interstate arrangements they negotiated and the recurring patterns of their interaction. But to avoid having such customary law merely reflect prevailing power relationships (in which "Might makes right"), Grotius insisted that the interactions of states must also be constrained by the higher natural law of humankind, the content of which could be ascertained by right reason from the essentials of human nature.

Like Aristotle, Grotius held that the human being is essentially a political, or "sociable," animal

> This sociability . . . or this care of maintaining society in a manner conformable to the light of human understanding, is the fountain of right, properly so called; to which belongs the abstaining from that which is another's, and the restitution of what we have of another's, . . . the obligation of fulfilling promises, the reparation

of damage done through our own default, and the merit of punishment among men.[19]

From his premise of human sociability, Grotius reasoned that the natural law of humankind has as its highest purpose the maintenance of stable communities of law and justice, which in turn require that the governments of the separate states must be sovereign within their own realms:

> All men have naturally a right to secure themselves from injuries by resistance. . . . But civil society being instituted for the preservation of peace, there immediately arises a superior right in the State over us and ours, so far as is necessary for that end. Therefore the State has a power to prohibit the unlimited use of the right toward every other person, for maintaining publick peace and good order, . . . for if that promiscuous right of resistance should be allowed, there would be no longer a State, but a multitude without union. . . .[20]

The world community of order and justice therefore is first and foremost a society of mutually respectful governments, that is, governments respectful of one another's territorial integrity and domestic jurisdiction. As reflected in the Westphalian accords, the rights of peoples and individuals within the borders of the officially recognized countries are distinctly secondary to the maintenance requirements of the state-sovereignty system.

The Grotian philosophy of a state-centric system of order and justice, which still provides the foundational assumptions of contemporary international law, does not *exclude* domestic-justice considerations (including what we now call human rights) from its purview. Grotius himself was concerned with such matters, particularly when domestic injustices and turmoil were so severe as to provoke cross-border violence. And many of his modern disciples, especially those who have also adopted Lockean liberal philosophies of domestic justice (see page 53), have tried to infuse the natural-law aspects of the international jurisprudence with human rights in addition to world-order imperatives.[21]

Indeed, the inclusion of human rights provisions in the United Nations Charter and the push for an International Bill of Rights have been largely the result of international lawyers identifying with the Grotian tradition. But a true Grotian normally would still accord pride of place *in international law and international arenas* to the sovereignty

---

19. Hugo Grotius in *The Rights of War and Peace* [1625] as quoted by Richard Tuck, *Natural Rights Theories: Their Origin and Development* (London: Cambridge University Press, 1979), p. 72 [text edited for conventional capitalization].
20. Grotius, in Tuck, pp. 78–79.
21. See the essays in Hedley Bull, Benedict Kingbury, and Adam Roberts, eds., *Hugo Grotius and International Relations* (Oxford: Clarendon Press, 1990).

prerogatives of national governments, especially where efforts to advance the rights of individuals and peoples threaten to seriously undermine stability of the larger state-sovereignty system.

SOCIAL CONTRACT THEORIES

Locke on Natural Rights, Natural Law, and the Obligations of Government

The idea that the rights of persons are prior—in a moral sense—to the rights of governments became an influential strand in political philosophy with John Locke's publication in 1690 of his *Second Treatise on Government*. The relations of humans uncontrolled by governments are natural claimed Locke. Governments are artificial creations and are designed to implement the more basic "social contract"—one that Locke imagined people in a "state of nature" would have fashioned to secure their liberties and well-being. Intelligent people can through rational inquiry discover the natural-law principles that should be embodied in the social contract and hold governments accountable to these principles.

The fiction of a social contract emerging from a pregovernmental state of nature had been developed by Locke's great predecessor, Thomas Hobbes. But unlike Locke, who used this philosophical construct to argue for limiting the powers of government, Hobbes used it to justify an all-powerful state, which he called the *Leviathan*.[22] (The differences between Locke's and Hobbes' views are reminiscent of the debate, described above, between Mencius, who believed that humans have a natural capacity for doing good, and Hsun Tzu, who believed that humans are basically motivated by evil desires.) Hobbes' natural men, fearing for their lives in the anarchic state of nature, forego the freedom that is making their existence nasty, brutish, and short.

By contrast, Locke's state of nature has many aspects he believed should be preserved. He imagined people in

> a state of perfect freedom to order their actions and dispose of their possessions and persons as they think fit, within the bounds of the law of nature, without asking leave or depending upon the will of any other man.
>
> A state also of equality, wherein all the power and jurisdiction is reciprocal, no one having more than another, . . . without subordination or subjection. . . .[23]

---

22. Thomas Hobbes, *Leviathan* [1651], edited by C. B. MacPherson (New York: Penguin Books, 1982).
23. John Locke, *The Second Treatise of Government* [1690], edited by Thomas P. Peardon (New York: Liberal Arts Press, 1956), p. 4.

Although this is a "state of liberty," cautioned Locke, "it is not a state of license." He reminded us that

> The state of nature has a law of nature to govern it, which . . .
> teaches all mankind who will but consult it that, being all equal
> and independent, no one ought to . . . take away or impair the life,
> or what tends to the preservation of the life, the liberty, health,
> limb, or goods of another.[24]

The only exceptions to these prohibitions are in the event of transgressions against the law of nature itself; in such cases it may be appropriate to punish the offender by depriving him of what otherwise would be his natural rights.[25] But it is precisely the prospect of such transgressions and having to deter and deal with them fairly that convinces humans in the state of nature of the need to enter into social contracts and to establish governments. Without forming themselves into such a political society, they would live in a condition of anxious insecurity, fearing that some of their fellow humans may disrupt the natural order and transform the benign state of nature into a state of war. "Thus mankind, notwithstanding all the privileges of the state of nature, but being in an ill condition when they remain in it, are driven into society."[26]

In contracting with one another to construct a stable political society and then to establish a government, the people do not surrender their natural rights; they simply entrust the government with the responsibility for securing them. Moreover, the people can take back the powers they have delegated to the government and indeed can "dissolve" it, if "the legislative or the prince act contrary to . . . the trust reposed in them"—that is, "when they endeavor to invade the property of the subject, and to make themselves . . . arbitrary disposers of the lives, liberties, or fortunes of the people."[27]

Locke's ideas were put to practical effect by the American colonists in the next century, as both stimulus to and justification for their war of secession from England. In an eloquent restatement of the logic of the *Second Treatise*, the American Declaration of Independence (the prose is largely Thomas Jefferson's) proclaimed,

> We hold these Truths to be self-evident, that all Men are created
> equal, that they are endowed by their Creator with certain unalienable

---

24. Ibid., pp. 5–6.
25. Ibid., pp. 6–10.
26. Ibid., pp. 70–71.
27. Ibid., p. 123.

Rights, that among these are Life, Liberty, and the Pursuit of Happiness—That to secure these rights, Governments are instituted among Men, deriving their just powers from the Consent of the Governed, that whenever any Form of Government becomes destructive of these Ends, it is the Right of the People to alter or abolish it, and to institute new Government. . . .[28]

In addition to providing the philosophical grounding for the American revolution, the Lockean social-contract arguments chalked out the space for debate over rights for generations to come and continue to be invoked even today.

Rousseau's Subordination of Individual Rights to the General Will

In popular political discourse, the ideology of the American Declaration of Independence (based largely on the social-contract arguments of John Locke) and the ideology of the French Revolution of 1789 (which borrowed in considerable part from the popular-sovereignty arguments of Jean-Jacques Rousseau) are often lumped together as constituting the core of the human rights tradition. But just as the regime that supplanted British rule in the United States was very different from the regime that supplanted the monarchy in France, so the political philosophies of Locke and Rousseau are substantially at variance in their basic assumptions and also in their logical implications.

Taking issue with the Lockean premise that certain rights possessed by individuals in the state of nature were unalienable, Rousseau envisioned a "moral and collective body" that results from the "total alienation to the whole community of each associate with all his rights. . . without reserve."[29] How is it that the revolutionary critic who complained that "Man was borne free, and everywhere he is in chains,"[30] ended up arguing for a "social pact" that "gives the body politic an absolute power over all its members"?[31]

The answer to the apparent paradox is found in Rousseau's argument, developed at length in his *Discourse on the Origin of Inequality*, that although humans are naturally good, they are corrupted and perverted by

28. A Declaration by the Representatives of the United States of America, U.S. Congress Assembled, (July 4, 1776).

29. Jean-Jacques Rousseau, *The Social Contract* [1762]; quotation from the Lester G. Crocker edition of *The Social Contract and Discourse on the Origin of Inequality* (New York: Pocket Books, 1967), pp. 18–19.

30. Ibid., Book I, Chapter 1, p. 7.

31. Ibid., Book II, Chapter 4, p. 32.

so-called civilized society into selfish, property-acquiring, power-seeking beings. Maintaining in *The Social Contract* that there is no possibility of returning to the state of nature, Rousseau reasoned that the only way humans can avoid the worst consequences of civilization and try to retrieve some of their authentic goodness is through their total and therefore equal subordination to (and into) a state that will be directed by the general will of all the citizenry.

In striking contrast to Locke's social contract, in which there is a highly limited, conditional, and retrievable granting of powers to the state, Rousseau held that

> the essence of the social contract . . . is reducible to the following terms: "Each of us puts in common his person and his whole power under the supreme direction of the general will; and in turn we receive every member as an individual part of the whole."[32]

Moreover, once the body politic, or "sovereign," has been formed, that body in making laws is not itself bound by any fundamental law of nature or whatever. Reflecting the "general will," its acts are supreme. Rousseau reasoned that

> the sovereign, being formed only of the individuals that compose it, neither has nor can have any interest contrary to theirs; consequently the sovereign power needs no guarantee towards its subjects, because it is impossible that the body should wish to injure all its members. . . and it can injure no one as an individual.[33]

A society in which the sovereign embodies the general will need not, should not, permit to arise any distinction between the rights of individuals as citizens and their duties as subjects of the body politic. To allow individuals to pose their particular wills against the general will "would bring about the ruin of the body politic." Unwittingly providing the rationale for the French revolutionary government's reign of terror and foreshadowing the presumption of modern totalitarian dictatorships that because they are peoples' republics, they always act for the good of the entire society, Rousseau prescribed that

> whosoever refuses to obey the general will shall be constrained to do so by the whole body; which means nothing else than that he shall be forced to be free. . . .[34]

---

32. Ibid.
33. Ibid., p. 21.
34. Ibid., p. 22.

If, as Rousseau would have it, "the general will is always right and always tends to the public advantage," the means of ascertaining the general will becomes crucial for preventing this whole scheme of governance from degenerating into blatant tyranny. Rejecting representative or republican forms of indirect democracy, Rousseau conceived of the general will taking shape out of direct, face-to-face, deliberate processes in which each citizen has a voice and through which majoritarian decisions are rendered. The implication is that for the general will to materialize in this way, the state must be small, like the city-state of Geneva in which Rousseau lived for a time, that is, one based on the model of the self-sufficient polis favored by Plato and Aristotle. The policies produced by such direct democracy are presumed to be supreme and absolute, binding on government officials, jurists, and citizens alike and not subject to appeal on grounds of either natural law, natural right, or any other concept of a universal or higher morality.

EDMUND BURKE'S CONSERVATIVE STATE

If Rousseau can be viewed as an intellectual godfather of the revolutionary state, claiming obedience to no principle other than its obligation to effectuate the general will of the people, Edmund Burke, reacting to what he considered the disastrous implications of this philosophy, can be viewed as the intellectual godfather of the conservative nation-state. Yet, the views of both Rousseau and Burke are remarkably similar in that they leave little room for individuals or minorities to claim rights against the state.

The true liberties of Englishmen, claimed Burke, are not derived from any abstract principles of the rights of man, but rather are an

> *entailed inheritance* derived to us from our forefathers, and to be transmitted to our posterity; an estate belonging to the people of this kingdom without any reference whatever to any other more general or prior right. . . .[35]

The alternative philosophy propounded by the French Jacobins of rights of men deduced from an intuited set of abstract natural rights or an imagined state of nature is a prescription for anarchy, argued Burke, allowing each generation of revolutionaries to arrogate unto itself the prerogative of drawing up a totally new constitution. By contrast, asserted Burke,

---

35. Edmund Burke, *Reflections on the Revolution in France* (New York: Holt, Rinehart and Winston, 1959), pp. 37–38.

> We have an inheritable crown; an inheritable peerage; and an house of commons and a people inheriting privileges, franchises, and liberties from a long line of ancestors.
>
> This policy appears to me to be . . . the happy effect of following nature, which is wisdom without reflection, and above it. . . . By a constitutional policy, working after the pattern of nature, we receive, we hold, we transmit our government and our privileges, in the same manner in which we enjoy and transmit our property and our lives.[36]

As passed down from generation to generation, these principles and institutions have come to constitute an organic national community, distinct and separate from the totally abstract universal community of humankind.

Burke's views, more than those of any other political philosopher, provide intellectual ammunition for today's neoconservative wing of the communitarian school in the United States and Britain (see page 64–67) in their arguments against the champions of individual rights.

KANT'S UNIVERSAL ETHIC

It has always been easier for the Burkean conservatives to attempt to rebut disciples of Locke or Rousseau than champions of universal human rights who rely on arguments developed by the late-eighteenth-century philosopher Immanuel Kant. This is because in Kant's ethical system—although it is also based on the presumed capacity of individuals anywhere in the world to formulate the good society on the basis of reason rather than tradition—the ordinary civil and political rights of humans are inextricably tied to *inviolable obligations* that all humans have toward themselves and one another. The most profound of these universal obligations is Kant's "categorical imperative" that each person

> Act in such a way that you always treat humanity, whether in your own person or in the person of any other, never simply as a means, but always at the same time as an end.[37]

Kant makes the universalistic implication of the categorical imperative explicit in his statement that

> I ought never to act except in such a way that I can also will that my maxim should become a universal law.[38]

---

36. Ibid., p. 38.
37. This formulation of the "categorical imperative" appears in Kant's *Groundwork of the Metaphysics of Morals,* quoted in Chris Brown, *International Relations Theory: New Normative Approaches* (New York: Columbia University Press, 1992), p. 30.
38. Ibid.

The imperative (as both a source of obligations and of rights) is binding equally on all persons, on the communities they belong to, and on the states in which they may happen to reside. In this sense most contemporary human rights advocates are Kantian, although the communitarians would leave to national communities a greater role in determining its application in particular circumstances than would the cosmopolitans, who would have it translated into quite detailed universally binding international laws.

Kant's insistence that every human being is to be treated as an "end," and "never simply as a means," is also widely embraced as a core human rights credo today by liberal universalists and communitarian relativists alike. The debates among those who accept the premise are over the intrinsic and essential characteristics of the human being that are never to be violated or severely compromised in the service of other ends and over the national and international policy implications of the differing conceptions of human nature.

G. W. F. HEGEL AS COMMUNITARIAN GURU

With Hegel we encounter a synthesis of earlier community and state-centered philosophies—a synthesis that is consistent with his theory of how ideas progress through history and that is supposed to embody a higher intellectual and spiritual awareness of the good than did the thought of his predecessors. As did Aristotle, Hegel viewed the human being as a socially formed animal, fragmented and alienated from the self and other humans beings unless fully integrated into the community. Similar to Rousseau, Hegel conceived of an ideal, complete harmony between the interests of individuals and the good of the community, a harmony that can be realized through informed deliberation among the members of the community and freedom that can only be achieved in such a community. Like Burke, however, he conceived of the spirit of the times (called *Zeitgeist*) that animates the community "Idea" at any particular time as an historically evolved *Geist*, as are the prevailing complex of ethical and practical relationships that embody the Idea. And Hegel would agree with Burke that Rousseau's ahistorical general will, constructed freshly by the people out of whole cloth, is shallow, if not dangerous. But neither is the past a sufficient guide to the higher good (and in this he differs from Burke), for the absolute freedom of the individual within the perfect state is a continually developing idea.

Hegel's idealized vision of the relationship between individuals and the state is conveyed in his *Philosophy of Right*, where he maintained that

> The state is the actuality of concrete freedom. But concrete freedom consists in this, that personal individuality and its particular interests not only achieve their complete development . . . but . . .

they also pass over of their own accord into the interests of the universal. . . .[39]

. . .

The state is [an] absolutely rational . . . end in itself, in which freedom comes into its supreme right . . . . [And]this final end has supreme right against the individual, whose supreme duty is to be a member of the state.[40]

Hegel's writings, although dense and often obscure, are experiencing a revival among contemporary communitarians (see page 67) who seek arguments against what they believe to be the excessive individualism and universalism pervading the Western industrialized democracies.

BRITISH NINETEENTH-CENTURY LIBERALISM

Bentham's Utilitarianism

The British version of the rational state popular among leading British liberals in the nineteenth century was in many ways just as dismissive of Lockean and Kantian notions of the inviolable natural rights of individuals as were organic statist views of Burke or the mystical theories of Hegel. But this was not the main task of the liberals' political philosophy. Rather, its purpose was to develop a scientific grounding for the enfranchisement of the rising middle classes and their demands that legislation deal with their needs in contrast to the traditional elitist philosophies which assumed that wisdom about the good society resides in the aristocracy and/or the minds of brilliant philosophers.

The leading philosopher for this rational, empirical, utilitarian, and essentially democratic school of thought was Jeremy Bentham. In his *Principals of Morals and Legislation* (first published in the 1780s), Bentham located the determination of what is good for individuals in their own perceptions of their own interests—or, more precisely, in that which they either want because it gives them pleasure or want to avoid because it gives them pain. This principle, which Bentham called "utility," he defined as that which "augments the happiness of the party whose interest is in question." Elaborating, Bentham wrote

By utility is meant that property in any object, whereby it tends to produce benefit, advantage, pleasure, good, or happiness (all of this in the present case comes to the same thing) or . . . to prevent the

---

39. G. W. F. Hegel, *Philosophy of Right*, Section 260, quoted in Paul Lakeland, *The Politics of Salvation: The Hegelian Idea of the State* (Albany, NY: State University of New York Press, 1984), p. 40.
40. Hegel, *Philosophy of Right*, Section 258, quoted in ibid., p. 55.

> happening of mischief, pain, evil, or unhappiness *to the party whose interest is considered.*[41] [emphasis added]

The state ought to be organized, then, to maximize the opportunity for individuals to realize their self-interests, which, by definition, would be conceived of (subjectively) by each person. Having stated the principle, Bentham recognized the complications, and the rest of his book is devoted to attempting to resolve them.

The subjective utilities of individuals will unavoidably clash at times, and in such cases it will be necessary to determine whose happiness should prevail. Bentham attempted to solve this problem though postulating measures for assessing the value to each individual of the competing pleasures and pains; namely, to take into consideration their "intensity," "duration," "certainty or uncertainty," and "propinquity or remoteness." But these criteria of value are themselves in need of further measurement criteria.

Presumably, much of the valuation of utilities can take place in the free market, on the basis of decisions by individuals to buy or sell or to invest with the resources at their disposal (and indeed, many of the utilitarians became devotees of a laissez-faire economy as being the best overall arbiter of utility). Still, there are "goods" and "bads" in society that require some form of public allocation—the building of public roads and seaports, the provision of day-to-day safety on the streets, the provisioning of armies to defend the realm, and the collection of money for these tasks and its disbursement. What was Bentham's solution?

> Take an account of the *number* of persons whose interest appear to be concerned. . . . Take the *balance;* which, if on the side of *pleasure,* will give the general *good tendency* of the act, with respect to the total number or community of individuals concerned; if on the side of pain, the general *evil* tendency, with respect to the same community.[42]

Bentham had no illusion that he had devised a perfect calculus of choice for social policy. "It is not to be expected," he cautioned, "that this process should be strictly pursued previously to every moral judgment, or to every judicial operation." He did insist, however, that "as near as the process actually pursued . . . approaches to it, so near will such process approach to the character of an exact one."[43]

---

41. Jeremy Bentham, *An Introduction to the Principles of Morals and Legislation* [1789] (New York: Hafner Publishing Co., 1948), p. 2.
42. Ibid., p. 31.
43. Ibid.

It is from this complicated process of balancing interests that rights come. "Right is the child of law; from real laws real rights come," not from "imaginary" concepts like "natural law." Bentham was scathing in his criticism of the Lockean and Rousseauistic traditions. "Natural rights," he wrote in *Anarchical Fallacies*, "is simply nonsense, . . . nonsense upon stilts."[44] In the utilitarian calculus, no *one* person's happiness, by virtue of some natural qualitative superiority of his or her interests, is by definition unalienable. And, ultimately, individuals or minorities must forego their interests if the sum of all the interests of the people (the greatest happiness of the greatest number) requires it. There can, in other words, be no sacrosanct bill of rights against the public interest.

John Stuart Mill's Libertarianism

It took someone from within the utilitarian school, a son of one of the most prominent utilitarian writers (James Mill), to powerfully expose a major, and potentially disastrous, pitfall in the Benthamite approach—disastrous, that is, to the idea of the limited state so central to British and U.S. traditions. John Stuart Mill anticipated a problem that would preoccupy political theorists and jurists in twentieth-century Britain and America: the concern that the representatives of the people, in the name of majority rule and catering to the happiness of the greatest number, would attempt to legislate controls on the speech, art, private morality, and even the thinking of nonconformist minorities.

In his famous tract, *On Liberty*, Mill insisted that there is, as he put it, "one very simply principle" that is "entitled to govern absolutely" the attempts of society to control individuals:

> That principle is that the sole end for which mankind are warranted, individually or collectively, in interfering with the liberty of action of any of their number is self-protection. That the only purpose for which power can be rightfully exercised over any member of a civilized community, against his will, is to prevent harm to others.[45]

The burden is always on the state to demonstrate that without the socially imposed restrictions individuals will indeed harm one another. Moreover, self-inflicted harm is not the business of the state.

---

44. Jeremy Bentham, *Anarchical Fallacies*, quoted by Maurice Cranston, "Human Rights Real and Supposed," in D. D. Raphael, ed., *Political Theory and the Rights of Man* (Bloomington, IN: Indiana University Press, 1967), pp. 43–53, quote on p. 44.
45. John Stuart Mill, *On Liberty* [1859] (New York: Liberal Arts Press, 1956), p. 13.

> . . . The only part of the conduct of anyone for which he is amenable to society is that which concerns others. In the part which merely concerns himself, his independence is, of right, absolute. Over himself, over his own body and mind, the individual is sovereign.[46]

Prefiguring the efforts of twentieth-century civil libertarians to protect free speech and political activity against nationalistic repression, Mill argued that such repression is even "more noxious when exerted in accordance with public opinion than when in opposition to it." If only one person in the whole world were the dissenter, "mankind would be no more justified in silencing that one person than he, if he had the power, would be justified in silencing mankind."[47]

Still claiming to be a utilitarian, Mill justified the preservation of free speech on the grounds that without it, society will have a reduced opportunity for the self-correction induced by the exposure of error. This is "utility in the largest sense," said Mill, utility "grounded on the permanent interests of man as a progressive being." Along with his foundational and firmly stated principle that no limitation of speech and other civil liberties is justifiable unless clearly required to prevent harm to others, this broadened conception of Mill comes close to embracing a "natural" basis for these rights that the Benthamites and other British empiricists were hoping to discredit.

THE POST-GROTIAN PHILOSOPHY OF INTERNATIONAL LAW

Both in the practice and theory of international statecraft in the 250 years following the Peace of Westphalia, as the struggle *within* states increasingly concerned the rights of citizens via-à-vis governments, the external sovereignty of national governments via-à-vis one another was being solidified. During this era of the maturing of the nation-state system, the realpolitik diplomacy and power politics of European states was legitimized by post-Grotian legal theorists who embraced the Dutch jurist's "positivistic" analysis of the practice of states as a source of international law but who effectively discarded his insistence that state practice needs to be limited by the moral principles of natural law.

Writers like S. Pufendorf, Emeriich von Vattel, and Christian Wolff, adopting and embellishing the doctrines of Jean Bodin, held that, to the extent that there is any natural law at all, it is a law for the protection of

---

46. Ibid.
47. Ibid., p. 21.

the sovereignty of states. In the words of Christian Wolf, "A perfect right belongs to every nation not to allow any other nation to interfere in any way in its government. For if any nation interferes with the government of another, it does this in contravention of the other's right."[48] The international rules with any real effect on the actions of states, therefore, are those that the official representatives of states agree in treaties to be bound by; and since princes and ministers would never agree to be accountable to outsiders for how they deal with their own citizenry, there could not, and should not, be any international law on what we now call human rights.

More than did Grotius, these state-sovereignty positivists provided the philosophical foundations for the dominant doctrines of modern international law in the nineteenth century and well into the twentieth century. The orthodox doctrines are currently under major challenge, however—particularly as a result of the growth of the contemporary international law of human rights analyzed in Chapter 5.

THE CONTEMPORARY DEBATE

The New Communitarianism

A major division among contemporary political philosophers engaged in the debate over human rights is between those in the lineage that includes Cicero, Locke, and Kant (the liberals or cosmopolitans) and those in the lineage of that includes Aristotle, Rousseau, Burke, and Hegel (many of whom like to call themselves communitarians). The new communitarians, like their predecessors, hold that the life of humans has no real meaning independent of the particular communities in which they live and of the moral ideas they absorb from the culture of these communities and that therefore no human being has any rights beyond those that are derived from and encompassed by the way of life of his or her community.

The list of prominent contemporary communitarians includes the ethical philosopher Michael Walzer, the legal theorist Cass Sunstein, political theorists Alasdair MacIntyre and Michael Sandel, and the popular social theorist Ematai Etzioni.

The new communitarians tend to be critical of human rights philosophies that derive a large, and presumably universally valid, set of human rights from characteristics that all humans are supposed to have

---

48. Christian Wolf, *The Law of Nations* [1749], translation by T. J. Hemelt; quote from selection in Evan Luard, *Basic Texts in International Relations* (New York: St. Martin's Press, 1992), pp. 152–155.

in common. As put by MacIntyre, an exemplar of the politically conservative wing of the communitarian school,

> I am never able to seek for the good or exercise the virtues only *qua* individual . . . because what it is to live the good life varies from circumstance to circumstance. . . . [W]e all approach our own circumstances as bearers of a particular social identity. I am someone's son or daughter, someone else's cousin or uncle; I am a citizen of this or that city, a member of this or that guild or profession; I belong to this clan, that tribe, this nation. Hence what is good for me has to be good for one who inhabits these roles. As such, I inherit . . . a variety of debts, inheritances, rightful expectations and obligations. These constitute the given of my life, my moral starting point. This is in part what gives my life its own moral particularity.[49]

Such moral-community particularity, especially one's national identity, argues MacIntyre, can never be left behind, nor can it be absorbed or obliterated into the idea of the community of humankind.

> The notion of escaping . . . into a realm of entirely universal maxims which belong to man as such, whether in its eighteenth-century Kantian form or in the presentation of some modern analytical moral philosophies, is an illusion and an illusion with painful consequences.[50]

Michael Walzer, an exemplar of the reformist-humanist wing of the communitarian school and also less categorical in his rejection of Kantian ethics, recognizes that there are some values and conditions of life that may be universally sought and that may even need to be secured by some international rules and institutions; but the universal values, says Walzer, are very "thin," as compared with the "thick" commonalities of values and mutual interest that are located within coherent societies. "Societies are necessarily particular because they have members and memories, members *with* memories not only of their own, but also of their common life." By contrast,

> Humanity . . . has members but no memory, and so it has no history and no culture, no customary practices, no familiar life-ways, no festivals, no shared understanding of social goods. It is human

---

49. Alasdair MacIntyre, *After Virtue* (Notre Dame: University of Notre Dame Press, 1981), pp. 204–205.
50. Ibid., pp. 205–206.

to have such things, but there is no singular human way of having them.[51]

Even John Rawls, perhaps the most influential neo-Kantian philosopher of social-welfare liberalism, backs away from Kantian universalism when it comes to prescribing his principles of "justice as fairness" for humankind as a whole.[52] His outline of what he recommends for a "law of peoples," in addition to reiterating the standard sovereignty rights of traditional international law, does require that "peoples are to honor human rights." But he defines these rights so thinly (to use Walzer's concept) as not to offend what he calls "well-ordered hierarchical societies." These societies are "illiberal" in the Western sense, but each is governed by a system of law that "impose[s] moral duties and obligations on all persons" within its jurisdiction, a system of law "guided by a common good conception of justice."[53]

Rawls cautions against insisting upon universal human rights laws based on "a quite deep philosophical theory that many if not most hierarchical societies might reject as liberal or democratic, or in some way distinctive of the Western political tradition and prejudicial to their cultures." He does not consider it too much to ask of all societies, including hierarchical ones, that they

> at least uphold such basic rights as the right to life and security, to personal property, and the elements of the rule of law, as well as the right to a certain liberty of conscience and freedom of association, and the right to emigration.[54]

But he emphasizes that

> For these things to hold does not require that persons are first citizens and as such free and equal members of society who hold these basic rights as the rights of citizens. It requires only that persons be responsible and cooperating members of society who can act in accordance with their moral duties and obligations.[55]

And to explain how human rights need not be based on the assumption of *individual* freedom, Rawls invokes Hegel's vision of a well-ordered state in *The Philosophy of Right* in which he states, "persons belong first

51. Michael Walzer, *Thick and Thin: Moral Argument at Home and Abroad* (Notre Dame: University of Notre Dame Press, 1994), p. 8.
52. John Rawls, *A Theory of Justice* (Cambridge: Harvard University Press, 1971).
53. John Rawls, "The Law of Peoples," in Stephen Shute and Susan Hurley, eds., *On Human Rights: The Oxford Amnesty Lectures 1993* (New York: Basic Books, 1993), pp. 41–82; quotes from p. 60.
54. Ibid., p. 68.
55. Ibid., p. 69.

to estates, corporations, and associations" that "represent the rational interests of their members" in a "just consultation hierarchy." Rawls is not overly bothered by the way the individual, functioning in such a group-based civil society, does not directly assert his rights against the state in the Hegelian scheme. Rather, that is the virtue of the "associational" (translate communitarian) approach, for "Human rights understood in the light of that condition cannot be rejected as peculiar to our Western tradition."[56]

The Non-Western Renaissance

In much of the post-Colonial Third World, new generations of leaders and political philosophers have emerged with interests and worldviews less in tune with Lockean-liberal ideas than were their predecessors, who had relied on the doctrine of unalienable and universally valid natural rights as a weapon in their struggles for independence. In many countries, the governing elites, now preoccupied with regime consolidation and nation-building, are embracing either authoritarian models of development or precolonial and non-Western religious and cultural traditions, or a combination of both, that give primacy to the community and/or state over the individual.

The fact that these approaches are often at odds with concepts championed by the leading transnational human rights groups and embodied in many of the international human rights treaties (see Chapter 4) and that they are opposed as reactionary by some of the liberal modernizers in their own countries has not discouraged their articulation. On the contrary, the realization by many Third World intellectuals that they are participants in a significant new East-West debate seems only to have encouraged the current new propagation and elaboration of the non-Western (sometimes *anti*-Western) philosophies.

One branch of this non-Western philosophical renaissance—traditionally authoritarian, yet modernist when it comes to economic development—has come to the defense of the kind of autocratic state-directed capitalism featured in countries like Peru, Singapore, Indonesia, and South Korea. These views are exhibited in a Singaporian philosopher-statesman's criticism of the American and European human rights approach, which he characterizes as foreign to the "historical experience" of his part of the world.

> [Our] experience sees order and stability as preconditions for economic growth, and growth as the necessary foundation of any political order that claims to advance human dignity. . . .

---

56. Ibid., p. 70.

> . . . East and Southeast Asians tend to look askance on the
> starkly individualistic ethos of the West in which . . . rights are an
> individual's "trump" over the state. Most people of the region pre-
> fer the situation in which the distinctions between the individual,
> society, and state are less clear-cut, or at least less adversarial.[57]

Another branch of the non-Western philosophical renaissance is
decidedly antimodernist. Its most prominent expressions are found in
the Islamic fundamentalist movements now flowering across the Middle
East and North Africa (where in some countries, like Iran and
Afghanistan, they have captured the government and in others, like
Algeria and Egypt, they are in militant opposition to the secular modernizers who are in control of the state). Representatives of a wide range of
these fundamentalists, meeting under the auspices of the nongovernmental international Islamic Council promulgated their own Universal
Islamic Declaration of Human Rights (UIDHR) in 1981. The UIDHR,
like the Constitution of the Islamic Republic of Iran on which it draws,
stipulates that it is a part of, and unequivocally subject to, the *shari'a*.
This proviso, in effect, leaves it up to juridical and theocratic authorities
in each Islamic state (or movement) to invoke the more basic Islamic law
as it implements, and curbs, if necessary, the rights enumerated in the
Islamic Declaration.[58]

Antimodernist reactions to the philosophical foundations of the
Western human rights movement are also evident in the new self-
determination movements blossoming among indigenous peoples from
Australasia to the Americas, from the equator to the Arctic. And it is
perhaps from these so-called Fourth World peoples that the deepest challenges will be coming. Increasingly, in international forums indigenous
peoples that have been previously silent are presenting *their* worldviews.
A sampling follows:

> The Earth is the foundation of Indigenous Peoples. It is the seat of
> spirituality, the fountain from which our cultures flourish. . . .
>
> . . .
>
> The oneness of the earth has been shattered by commercial and
> industrial practices that poison air, land and water and the crea-
> tures dependent on them. . . . We have seen this pattern of destruc-
> tion repeated around the world by societies that base their way of
> life on excessive industrialization. We who have tried to take from
> Mother Earth only what we need. . . have had our land base eroded
> and stolen by industrial societies whose . . . greed causes them to
> fight with each other over the spoils of a spoiled earth.
>
> . . .

---

57. Bilahari Kausikan, "Asia's Different Standard," *Foreign Policy* 92 (fall 1993), pp. 24–41;
quote from pp. 35–36.
58. Mayer, *Islam and Human Rights*, pp. 76–78.

> The natural law is that all life is equal in the great creation; and we the human beings are charged with the responsibility . . . to work for the continuation of life. . . . It now seems that the natural world people are the ones who have kept to this law.[59]

The Reassertion of Universalism

The rediscovery of the validity of their own philosophical traditions by non-Western peoples simultaneous with a revival of Hegelian/Burkean political philosophy among Western intellectuals has produced a counter-response on the part of liberal cosmopolitans who fear that the new communitarianism can become a rationalization for indifference to the methods that dictators, autocrats, and even intolerant popular majorities often use to repress those who dare to criticize them.

Today's cosmopolitans, like their intellectual predecessors, regard political institutions as instruments for basic security, well-being, dignity of peoples, not as ends in themselves. They also regard human well-being and dignity, although varying in they way they may be defined and realized in various cultures, as requiring certain conditions of existence that are absolutely essential to their realization, no matter where a person might live. It is from assumptions (often scientifically supported) about such necessary conditions for any individual's basic security, well-being, and dignity (rather than from natural-law postulates) that the contemporary cosmopolitans typically derive their catalogs of universal human rights. Among the prominent contemporary cosmopolitans are the ethical philosopher Henry Shue, legal theorists Ronald Dworkin and Amy Gutmann, and political theorists Charles Beitz and Brian Barry.

Such a grounding is well laid out in Henry Shue's disquisition on *Basic Rights*.[60] "Basic rights," says Shue, "are everyone's minimum reasonable demands on the rest of humanity. They are the rational basis for justified demands the denial of which no self-respecting person can reasonably be expected to accept." Why? Because "the enjoyment of them is essential to the enjoyment of all other rights." These rights include

> *physical security*—a right . . . not to be subjected to murder, torture, mayhem, rape, or assault.
>
> . . .

---

59. Public statements of indigenous-peoples spokespersons at international conferences; quoted in Franke Wilmer, *The Indigenous Voice in World Politics* (Newbury Park, CA: Sage Publications, 1993), pp. 117–118.

60. Henry Shue, *Basic Rights: Subsistence, Affluence, and U.S. Foreign Policy* (Princeton, NJ: Princeton University Press, 1996).

> No one can fully enjoy any right that is supposedly protected by society if someone can credibly threaten him or her with murder, rape, beating, etc., when he or she tried to enjoy the alleged right.
>
> . . .
>
> [and] *minimal economic security, or subsistence, . . .* to have available for consumption what is needed for a decent chance at a reasonably healthy and active life of more or less normal length, barring tragic interventions.
>
> . . .
>
> No one can fully, if at all, enjoy any right that is supposedly protected by society if he or she lacks the essentials for a reasonably healthy and active life. Deficiencies in the means of subsistence can be just as fatal, incapacitating, or painful as violations of physical security.[61]

And in a challenge to those who relegate subsistence rights to a subordinate position below the right to be secure from physical attack, Shue argues that people who lack protection against those who would violate their physical security can, "if they are free, fight back against their attackers or flee, but people who lack essentials, such as food, because of forces beyond their control, often can do nothing and are on their own utterly helpless."

Shue also claims that some liberty rights (as he calls them) should be regarded as so basic to human well-being that no one should be denied. Most of these, he argues, are encompassed by the concept of the opportunity for *effective participation* in the basic decisions of society necessary to the provision of security and subsistence. But on this score, Shue's essentially pragmatic criteria for what is a basic right are an invitation to exactly the kind of relativistic (culturally dependent) assessments that cosmopolitans find objectionable in communitarian political philosophy. If Shue does ground the case for certain liberty rights on the premise that they are necessary for human dignity, he must then engage the communitarians on their own turf.

Other contemporary cosmopolitan liberals continue to reassert the universal validity of liberty rights of the kind that have matured in Western democracies and indeed seek to engage the communitarians on their own ground over the wider implications of the communitarian valuation of societal particularity. The new cosmopolitan argument (well represented in Charles Beitz's *Political Philosophy and International Relations*[62]) is that in the increasingly interdependent world, multiple com-

---

61. Ibid.; quotes from pp. 20–25 [emphasis added].
62. Charles R. Beitz, *Political Theory and International Relations* (Princeton, NJ: Princeton University Press, 1979). See also Seyom Brown, *International Relations in a Changing Global System: Toward a Theory of the World Polity* (Boulder. CO: Westview, 1996).

munities exist on a international and global basis as they never have before and that many of these communities are transnational as well as trans-state. Those who share a commitment to individual rights-based democracy can be found throughout Asia, Africa, the Arab Middle East, and Latin America as well as in Scandinavia and the United States; the same can be said for the devotees of the more statist philosophies. Just as the world of material interdependence (with its high mobility of things, people, and information) produces crosscutting tangible interests in most countries, communities, and individuals, so most of us are also cross-pressured by our multiple cultural and ideological identities and commitments. As put by Ronald Dworkin in a debate with Michael Walzer,

> The idea that the world is divided into distinct moral cultures, and that it should be the goal of politics to foster the value of "community" . . . is once again fashionable in political theory, but its proponents have paid insufficient attention to their central concepts. Moral traditions are not clubs into which the peoples of the world are divided so that everyone carries a membership card in one but only one.[63]

Chapter 4 reveals the degree to which the often competing philosophical legacies described above are reflected in the evolving international law of human rights.

---

63. From an exchange between Ronald Dworkin and Michael Walzer in the *New York Review of Books*, April 14 and July 21, 1983; reprinted in Markate Daly, *Communitarianism: A New Public Ethics* (Belmont, CA: Wadsworth Publishing Co., 1994), pp.110–120; quote from p. 119.

Chapter 4

The International
Law of Human Rights

The philosophical issues discussed in Chapter 3 are reflected in the international law of human rights. This sector of international law encompasses the rapidly growing corpus of treaties, UN resolutions, opinions by judicial bodies and commissions, and state practices dealing with the internationally recognized rights that individuals and groups have been asserting, usually against the governments in whose jurisdictions they reside.

Although much of this evolving international human rights law thus has attributes of what international lawyers and legal scholars call *customary* international law, the present chapter focuses primarily on the legal obligations to which countries have explicitly bound themselves as parties to particular international treaties.[1] The analysis shows that even the international laws that have gone through a deliberative drafting process and that have been voluntarily signed and ratified by member countries remain highly controversial with respect to the substance of what these countries have indeed bound themselves to and its enforceability, let alone what obligations such new international laws establish for nonsignatory countries.[2]

---

1. Various so-called customary sources for determining countries' legal obligations (the precedents governments have established by prior patterns of behavior; the decisions of national courts; the findings of international and regional commissions; virtually universal moral prohibitions on extreme acts such as genocide and torture) are, to be sure, crucial aspects of the context and negotiating history of human rights treaties and have a great deal to do with how governments and international agencies attempt to apply or escape from their provisions. They inform the analysis in subsequent chapters; but this book refrains from entering into the complex and controversial debates that preoccupy international law scholars over the role of custom in international law, particularly in the unique field of human rights law.
2. For a sampling of these conceptual debates, see Henry J. Steiner and Philip Alston, *International Human Rights in Context: Law, Politics, Morals* (New York: Oxford University Press, 1996), pp. 27–30, 37–38, 40–42, 55–56, 60–71, 132–148, and 770–788.

The principal human rights treaties and covenants contain provisions that are often contradictory or vague. These contradictory and vague provisions are not the result of careless drafting, however. Just the opposite.

The negotiators of the international agreements on human rights are appointees of countries with widely differing constitutional systems and political traditions. To obtain sufficiently widespread support to achieve the status of international law, a human rights covenant must include a range of provisions reflecting these differing traditions (becoming a self-contradictory document) and/or provisions that obscure the differences in ambiguous phrases (allowing signatories to interpret them in a way that is consistent with their own traditions).

Some countries, most notably the United States and Britain, are largely Lockean and tend to champion international measures for protecting citizens against arbitrary state power. Others, particularly the countries of Eastern and Central Europe, have been strongly influenced by the ideas of Rousseau or Hegel and give greater emphasis than do the Anglo-Americans to the prerogatives of communities over individuals. Then there are countries whose political evolution has been influenced by socialist (utilitarian or marxist) philosophies and for whom human rights have as much, if not more, to do with the distribution of income and other economic amenities than with limiting the reach of government. Finally, on the part of many Third World countries, the experience of their struggle for self-determination has been transmuted into the felt need to oppose postcolonial intrusions by the West (often cloaked in the ideology of universal human rights) on their newly won national sovereignty. Countries where a traditional religious culture exists that is threatened by the secular implications of various human rights ideas will be all the more anxious to circumscribe the universal thrust of the pertinent international covenants and agencies in order to assure that their writs do not undermine indigenous ways of life.

Self-contradictory or not, ambiguous or not, the existence of such international human rights covenants and of intense negotiation and debate over their provisions is itself symptomatic of the ongoing transformation of world politics discussed in the Chapter 1—from a simple state-sovereignty system to a more complex polyarchy in which the national governments are becoming increasingly accountable to one another and to communities transcending their territorial jurisdictions. No longer can a government legally claim that the condition of the people within its jurisdiction is no one else's business.

The set of international instruments at the core of this evolving global accountability system has come to be called the International Bill of Rights. The discussion focuses on the principal provisions in these documents, commenting not only on their legal content but also on their underlying philosophical assumptions and their implications for the functioning of the international system. This is followed by a brief discussion of other important documents in the rapidly growing corpus of international human rights law.[3]

HUMAN RIGHTS IN THE UNITED NATIONS CHARTER

According to the Preamble of its Charter,[4] the United Nations was established not only "to save succeeding generations from the scourge of war" but also "to reaffirm faith in fundamental human rights, in the dignity and worth of the human person, in the equal rights of men and women and of nations large and small." One of the basic purposes of the organization enumerated in Article 1 is "to achieve international cooperation in . . . promoting and encouraging respect for human rights and for fundamental freedoms for all without distinction as to race, sex, language, or religion."

But the statespersons and international lawyers who constructed the United Nations had no intention of eroding the sovereignty of nation-states in the name of human rights. Accordingly, Article 2, Section 7 assures that "Nothing contained in the present Charter shall authorize the United Nations to intervene in matters which are essentially within the domestic jurisdiction of any state or shall require Members to submit such matters to settlement under the present Charter." Notably, the reiterated obligation in Article 55 to "promote . . . universal respect for, and observation of, human rights and fundamental freedoms for all" is presented as a *means* of ensuring the conditions of stability and well-being necessary for peace and security, not as an end equal in value to peace and security.

THE INTERNATIONAL BILL OF RIGHTS

The circumscribed human rights provisions of the UN Charter lagged behind the growing support in the aftermath of World War II for rights-based democracy. This liberal democratic ethos was given early expression in the Universal Declaration of Human Rights adopted by the General Assembly in 1948 and then accorded more solid legal status in the next few decades by the accession of most countries to the International

---

3. The legal documents cited in the chapter are available in numerous collections of documents. See the list of widely available sources in the Appendix to this book.
4. Charter of the United Nations (signed at San Francisco June 1945; entered into force October 1945).

Covenant on Civil and Political Rights (and its Optional Protocol) and the International Covenant on Economic, Social and Cultural Rights. Popularly called the International Bill of Rights, these documents—particularly the covenants—provide a basic legal grounding for claims by individuals and groups that particular countries are violating their internationally guaranteed human rights.

A country becomes a party to an international covenant, convention, or treaty—the terms are used interchangeably—after completing a two-stage formal process: The covenant is (1) *signed* by the highest official(s) of the country's government and (2) *ratified* by whatever official process is required in the laws of the country to certify that the body politic has approved its provisions.[5] In its statement of ratification, a country can attach reservations or conditions that indicate the provisions which it rejects or which it is redefining to make them acceptable to the country's polity. Countries typically tolerate each other's reservations (instead of demanding new negotiations) as long as the reservations do not blatantly contradict the main purposes and spirit of the treaty.

Having become a party to a covenant, a national government is then accountable to the other parties to the covenant and to whatever international agencies may have been designated in the covenant to exercise monitoring or adjudicatory authority over its implementation. The ratification process in most countries also makes the covenant part of domestic law, meaning that the officials of the government are accountable internally to the institutions (and, in democracies, the citizenry) of the country for adhering to its provisions.

Because the international agencies have few means at their disposal for assuring that countries will faithfully adhere to their treaty obligations, the implementation of the International Bill of Rights, like other international law, is highly dependent on self-enforcement by the parties within their own jurisdictions. Such decentralized enforcement can have substantial impact, however, especially where nongovernmental human rights groups act as watchdogs on their governments' adherence (or lack of it) to the international covenants and where they mobilize political and legal action to compel officials to implement the law.

Thus, if people around the world take the words in the International Bill of Rights seriously—as we do in this chapter—the governments *can* be held accountable for, and be compelled to implement, what they have signed.

---

5. Alternative steps, sometimes provided for in a particular treaty or recognized in the common law of treaty making, can satisfy the basic requirements; for example, declarations of accession by governments not present at the original signing and legislative or administrative acts of signatory states that are not called ratification but are functionally equivalent to it in the sense of solidly establishing the fact of approval by the responsible body politic.

The Universal Declaration of Human Rights

A nonprioritized collection of virtually all the human rights claims that up to 1948 had been directed against governments around the world, the Universal Declaration of Human Rights[6] is not, by itself, international *law*. Being only a resolution of the UN General Assembly, and not submitted for signature and ratification by member governments, the Universal Declaration is more of a mutual admonition to promote the enumerated human rights rather than a formal obligation to do so. Even so, as pointed out by the United Nations Secretary General in his 1971 Survey of International Law,

> During the years since its adoption the Declaration has come . . . to have a marked impact on the pattern and content of international law and to acquire a status extending beyond that originally intended for it. In general, two elements may be distinguished in this process: First, the use of the Declaration as a yardstick by which to measure the content and standard of observance of human rights; and, second, the reaffirmation of the Declaration and its provisions in a series of other instruments. These two elements . . . have caused the Declaration to gain a cumulative effect.[7]

The International Covenant on Civil and Political Rights

Ratified by more than one hundred countries, the Covenant on Civil and Political Rights[8]—emphasizing mainly (Lockean) rights of individuals against arbitrary governmental power, equal protection of the laws, and citizen rights of participation in the polity—builds on the first 21 articles in the Universal Declaration.

The Covenant recognizes *some* of these rights are so important, so basic, that they are never to be sacrificed—not even for reasons of national security. The remainder, less sacrosanct, can sometimes be put aside.

---

6. Universal Declaration of Human Rights, Resolution 217 A [III] of the UN General Assembly, (December 10, 1948). The vote was 48 to 0 with 8 abstentions: the USSR, Ukrainian SSR, Byelorussian SSR, Czechoslovakia, Poland, Yugoslavia, the Union of South Africa, and Saudi Arabia.

7. UN Secretary General U Thant, *1971 Survey of International Law*, Document A/CN.4/245 at 196, quoted in Louis Henkin, Richard Crawford Pugh, Oscar Schachter, and Hans Smit, *International Law: Cases and Materials* (St. Paul, MN: West Publishing Co, 1993), p. 607.

8. International Covenant on Civil and Political Rights, adopted in Resolution 2200 [XXI] of the UN General Assembly (1966; entered into force March 1976 upon receiving the required number of ratifications).

Rights Protected by the No-Derogation Clause Although the Covenant permits governments to "derogate from" (the legal term for "reduce") their human rights obligations in situations of public emergency, it fences off a number of rights even from such emergency exceptions. Thus Article 4, paragraph 2, stipulates that "No derogation from Articles 6, 7, 8 (paragraphs 1 and 2), 11, 15, 16, and 18 may be made." These specially protected parts of the Covenant contain the following provisions:

> *Article 6.* 1. Every human being has an inherent right to life. This right shall be protected by law. No one shall be arbitrarily deprived of his life.
>
> 2. In countries which have not abolished the death penalty,[9] sentence of death may be imposed only for the most serious crimes. . . . This penalty can only be carried out pursuant to a final judgment rendered by a competent court.
>
> . . .
>
> 3. . . . [I]t is understood that nothing in this article shall authorize any State Party to the present Covenant to derogate in any way from any obligation assumed under the provisions of the Convention on the Prevention and Punishment of the Crime of Genocide.
>
> 4. Anyone sentenced to death shall have the right to seek pardon or commutation of the sentence. . . .
>
> 5. Sentence of death shall not be imposed for crimes committed by persons below eighteen years of age and shall not be carried out on pregnant women.
>
> . . .
>
> *Article 7.* No one shall be subjected to torture or to cruel, inhuman or degrading treatment or punishment. In particular, no one shall be subjected without his free consent to medical or scientific experimentation.
>
> *Article 8.* 1. No one shall be held in slavery: slavery and the slave-trade in all their forms shall be prohibited.
>
> 2. No one shall be held in servitude.
>
> . . .
>
> *Article 11.* No one shall be imprisoned merely on the ground of inability to fulfill a contractual obligation.
>
> *Article 15.* No one shall be held guilty of any criminal offense on account of any act or omission which did not constitute a criminal

---

9. Only a few countries, the United States among them, still retain the death penalty.

offense, under national or international law, at the time when it was committed. Nor shall a heavier penalty be imposed than the one that was applicable at the time when the criminal offense was committed. . . .

Article 16. Everyone shall have the right to recognition everywhere as a person before the law.

. . .

Article 18. 1. Everyone shall have the right to freedom of thought, conscience, and religion. This right shall include freedom to have or adopt a religion or belief of his choice, and freedom, either individually or in community with others and in public or private, to manifest his religion or belief in worship, observance, practice and teaching.
2. No one shall be subject to coercion which would impair his freedom to have or to adopt a religion or belief of his choice.
3. Freedom to manifest one's religion or beliefs may be subject only to such limitations as are prescribed by law and are necessary to protect public safety, order, health or morals or the fundamental rights and freedoms of others.
4. The States Parties to the present Convention undertake to have respect for the liberty of parents and, when applicable, legal guardians to ensure the religious and moral education of their children in conformity with their own convictions.

Rights Subject to the Escape Clause   Most of the provisions of the Covenant on Civil and Political Rights are not protected by the no-derogation clause. Rather, the states party to the Covenant have preserved as much as possible of their traditional sovereign prerogative to subordinate any international obligations to their national security needs, which, of course, each state still could unilaterally define on its own behalf. Accordingly, Article 4 states that

In time of public emergency which threatens the life of the nation and the existence of which is officially proclaimed, the States parties to the present Covenant *may take measures derogating from their obligations under the present Covenant* to the extent strictly required by the exigencies of the situation, provided that such measures are not inconsistent with their other obligations under international law and do not involve discrimination solely on the ground of race, colour, sex, language, religion, or social origin. [emphasis added]

By this escape clause the national governments have allowed themselves, with respect to a wide range of rights, to take back legally with one hand what they have legally given to their constituents with the other.

These internationally guaranteed yet potentially recallable rights include:

- the right of "all peoples" to "self-determination," meaning to "freely determine their political status and freely pursue their economic, social, and cultural development" (Article 1)
- the right not to perform "forced or compulsory labor" (Article 8, Section 3)
- the standard "due process" rights, including protections against "arbitrary arrest or detention" and guarantees of a fair trial (Articles 9 and 14)
- "liberty of movement" and freedom to choose one's residence within the territory of a state and the freedom to leave any country and the right to return (Article 12)
- the right to "freedom of expression," including "freedom to seek, receive and impart information and ideas of all kinds, regardless of frontiers, either orally, in writing or in print, in the form of art, or through any other media" (except that "Any advocacy of national, racial or religious hatred that constitutes incitement to discrimination, hostility or violence shall be prohibited by law") (Article 19)
- the right of "peaceful assembly" (Article 21)
- the right to "freedom of association with others, including the right to form and join trade unions" (Article 22)
- the right of men and women to marry and to enjoy "equality of rights and responsibilities . . . during marriage and at its dissolution" (Article 23)
- the right to "take part in the conduct of public affairs, " including the right to vote and run for office "by secret ballot, guaranteeing the free expression of the will of the electors" (Article 25)
- the right of "ethnic, religious or linguistic minorities" to enjoy their own culture, to profess and practice their own religion, or to use their own language" (Article 27)

Although the Covenant allows that these rights may be limited in times of emergencies that threaten the life of the nation, the wording of the derogation provision (quoted on page 77) puts the burden of proof on the national governments to demonstrate that such limitations are indeed justified by the nature of the threats (see the Controversy Box 5 on page 81). Thus the existence and basic thrust of this Covenant, despite its escape clause, are both a symptom and an agent of the dramatic changes that have been occurring worldwide in the legal standing of individuals and nongovernmental groups vis-à-vis states.

The Covenant provides more than an enumeration of moral rights and duties. It also prescribes some rudimentary machinery for implementation in the form of a United Nations Human Rights Committee mandated to receive and consider communications from a state party to the Covenant to the effect that another state party to the Covenant is not fulfilling its obligations (Articles 28 and 41). The work of the Human Rights Committee and related human rights agencies is elaborated and evaluated in Chapter 5.

Despite efforts to give the United Nations a monitoring role, the legal authority to enforce the Covenant's provisions still resides almost exclusively in the world's decentralized, sovereignty-protecting system for implementing international law.

A potential wedge that could be used to open up of the state-sovereignty system is available in the Optional Protocol to the International Covenant on Civil and Political Rights, also adopted by the General Assembly.[10]

A state acceding to the Optional Protocol recognizes the competence of the UN Human Rights Committee to receive and consider communications from *individuals* claiming that the Protocol state is violating their human rights. As yet only some 15 of the more than 100 countries who are parties to the Covenant have become parties to the Optional Protocol.

International Covenant on Economic, Social and Cultural Rights

The drafters of the early UN human rights documents originally intended to parallel the Universal Declaration by writing one omnibus treaty. But the fact that such a treaty would be legally binding gave greater seriousness to the differences in human rights philosophy between the advocates of minimal government and the champions of socialism or state-sponsored cultural communitarianism. The result of this ideological division was to separate off into a distinct covenant—the Covenant on Economic, Social and Cultural Rights[11]—those provisions dealing with economic amenities and conditions of social well-being.[12]

The differences between the Covenant on Economic Social, and Cultural Rights and its companion covenant—the International Covenant on Civil and Political Rights—are evident in the call in Article 2 of the Covenant on Economic, Social and Cultural Rights for the countries to

---

10. Optional Protocol to the International Covenant on Civil and Political Rights (adopted in Resolution 2200A [XXI] of the UN General Assembly (1966; entered into force in March 1976).
11. International Covenant on Economic, Social and Cultural Rights, adopted in Resolution 2200A [XXI] of the UN General Assembly (1966; entered into force March 1976).
12. Although the Covenant on Economic, Social and Cultural Rights was signed by President Jimmy Carter in 1977, the U.S. Congress has still failed to ratify it.

CONTROVERSY BOX
5

The Emergency State in Algeria

The 1991 elections to the Algerian national parliament—which were free—would have resulted in the Islamic Salvation Front forming a government, had not the Algerian army staged a coup, outlawing the Islamic Salvation Front and jailing many of its leaders.

The leaders of Algerian army claimed the Islamic Salvation Front was preparing to impose an Islamic state and to dismantle the democratic/electoral system that they rode into power. The coup polarized the country into supporters of the Islamists and supporters of the military regime and precipitated a bloody conflict, which during its worst phases caused over 10,000 deaths a year.

The government has attempted to establish its legitimacy by holding and winning a series of national elections since 1992, but it still denies the outlawed Islamic Salvation Front, which it brands a terrorist organization, the right to compete in these elections.

What does international law say about this situation?

achieve "progressively" the full realization of the rights recognized in the Covenant by all "appropriate means" to the maximum of their "available resources." Unlike civil and political rights, most of which the citizens presumably already possess and which the Covenant on Civil and Political Rights admonishes governments not to violate, many of the rights in the Covenant can only be realized if countries can marshall new resources to provide the stipulated amenities.

The obligations taken on by countries in the Covenant on Economic, Social and Cultural Rights *are* linked to civil and political rights, however, through the basic nondiscrimination clause of Article 2, in which the parties to the Covenant

> undertake to guarantee that the rights enunciated in the present Covenant will be exercised without discrimination of any kind as to race, color, sex, language, religion, political or other opinion, national or social origin, property, birth or other status.

The positive rights enumerated in the Covenant include:

> *The Right to Work (Article 6)*—This right includes "the right of everyone to the opportunity to gain his living by

work which he freely chooses or accepts." The governments agree to take "steps . . . to achieve full realization of
this right" in the form of training programs for their citizens and also by tending to their country's economic,
social, and cultural development.

The wording of Article 6 is unclear on the extent of each
person's free choice of employment and how this might
legitimately be limited by one's talents, professional skills,
and other job-related qualifications. Nor is the wording
clear as to whether and to what extent labor unions can
limit access to jobs (but see the discussion trade unions and
Article 8 on page 83).

Also, societies wedded to free-market concepts—where a
certain amount of unemployment (say roughly 5 percent of
the potential workforce) is held to be a normal and acceptable consequence of the freedom of management and entrepreneurs to invest capital in different product lines and productive technologies and in general to move their facilities
from place to place in response to changes in supply and
demand—might object to the implied obligation that they
provide *full* employment.

Conditions of Work and Remuneration (Article 7)—The
states who are parties to the Covenant "recognize the right
of everyone to . . . just and favorable conditions of work"
and, in particular, to "fair wages and equal remuneration for
work of equal value" that as a minimum will provide workers with "a decent living for themselves and their families."
Employees are also to have "equal opportunity to be promoted to an appropriate higher level, subject to no consideration other than those of seniority and competence." Article 7 makes clear that the provisions on equal pay for equal
work and promotions refer in particular to women, who
should be "guaranteed conditions of work not inferior to
those enjoyed by men."

In addition, all employees have a right to "safe and
healthy working conditions" plus rest, leisure and reasonable limitation of working hours and periodic holidays with
pay, as well as remuneration for public holidays."

Much of the effort of translating these general provisions
into more specific guidelines has been undertaken by the
International Labor Organization (ILO), which has stipulated, for example, that a 40-hour week falls within the cri-
terion of "reasonable limitation of working hours." But in
deference to the concerns of many Third World countries
that they may be singled out for failing to deliver on their

legal obligations, the ILO has issued a covering guideline that indicates provisions in the Covenant "imply not a fixed standard of protection, but continuing action for the mobilization of available resources within balanced programmes of social and economic development."[13]

The Right of Everyone to Form Trade Unions and to Join Trade Unions (Article 8)—This right is not entirely consistent with the right of everyone right to a job of his or her choice. And indeed the potential contradictions are not resolved by the statement in Section 1(a) that

No restrictions may be placed on the exercise of this right other than those prescribed by law and which are necessary in a democratic society in the interests of national security or public order or for the protection of the rights and freedoms of others.

In fairness, however, human rights law should not be given the burden of resolving the social-reform paradox inherent in organized labor's need to control the supply of available workers in order to bargain effectively against management for fair wages and healthy working conditions.

The paradox is carried forward in the article's inclusion of the right to strike in the compass of organized labor's rights, subject only to the proviso that it be "exercised in conformity with the laws of the particular country."

The Right to Social Security (Article 9)—This article states only that the parties to the Covenant "recognize the right of everyone to social security, including social insurance." Its unelaborated formulation reflects the intense debate and ultimate lack of agreement among the countries involved in the drafting on what is to be comprehended by "social security" and "social insurance" and the respective roles of the government and private sources in providing the amenities. What the drafters finally did agree to (by implication), and the UN General Assembly endorsed, is that such policies are best left to each country to work out on its own. But even in its vague and open formulation with respect to the design of a social security *system*, Article 9 does appear to commit states to the principle that there is some minimum

---

13. *Second Report* by the Committee of Experts on the Application of Conventions and Recommendations of the International Labour Organization on Progress in Achieving Observance of the Provisions of Article 6 to 9 of the International Covenant on Economic, Social and Cultural Rights, UN Doc E/1979/33, at 7 (1979).

standard of health and welfare that society as a whole must guarantee to each individual throughout his or her life, and such a minimum standard is indeed the subject matter of Articles 11 and 12 (see pages 84–86).

Special Privileges for Child-Bearing Women (Article 10, Section 2)—The wording establishes a standard that most countries, including the United States, have not enforced on employers throughout their jurisdictions: "Special protections should be accorded to mothers during a reasonable period before and after childbirth. During such period working mothers should be accorded paid leave or leave with adequate social security benefits."

Prohibitions on the Exploitation of Children (Article 10, Section 3)—Although allowing for varying interpretations of some of its phrases, the intent of this provision is clear.

Children and young persons should be protected from economic and social exploitation. Their employment in work harmful to their morals or health or dangerous to life or likely to hamper their normal development should be punishable by law. States should also set age limits below which the paid employment of child labour should be prohibited and punishable by law.

The Right to an Adequate Standard of Living" (Article 11)—One of the most controversial parts of the Covenant, Article 11 recognizes

the right of everyone to an adequate standard of living, . . . including adequate food, clothing and housing, and to the continuous improvement of living conditions. The States Parties will take appropriate steps to ensure the realization of this right. . . .

Cognizant of the inability of many of the poor countries to implement this provision on their own, Article 11 emphasizes "the essential importance of international cooperation" but grants—in a realistic concession to the way the international system works—that the international help should be "based on free consent."

Particularly emphasized are the obligations of national governments *and* of the international community when it comes to the alleviation of starvation.

The States Parties to the present Covenant, recognizing the fundamental right of everyone to be free from hunger, shall take, individually and through international cooperation, the measures which are needed:

(a) To improve methods of production, conservation, and distribution of food . . . [including] reforming agrarian systems in such a way as to achieve the most efficient development and utilization of natural resources;

(b) Taking into account the problems of both food-importing and food-exporting countries, to *ensure an equitable distribution of world food supplies in relation to need.* [emphasis added]

This text makes is evident why the U.S. Congress has balked at approving the Covenant since the mid-1970s (when it was signed by the Carter administration and reported to the Congress with a recommendation for ratification). An incorporation of the provisions of Article 11 into U.S. law would obligate the government not only to intervene in the domestic market to deal with the problems of homelessness and borderline starvation but also, given the relative affluence of the United States, to contribute a nontrivial portion of its wealth and knowledge to the alleviation of poverty around the globe. With the exception of the Scandinavian countries and of the Netherlands, other affluent countries have also refrained from taking the international obligations in Article 11 seriously; most governments that have ratified the Covenant have simply interpreted these provisions as goals to be worked toward rather than as operative mandates.

Neither have many Third World countries been willing to institute the internal redistributive policies that are implied by the terms of Article 11. And they have taken umbrage at efforts by international agencies (such as the World Bank) to induce them to do so.

The Right to Health and Health Care (Article 12)—The stipulation of a "right of everyone to the enjoyment of the highest standard of physical and mental health" and the obligation of the governments to institute measures to assure its realization, like the obligation of governments to secure certain standards of living for everyone, stands at the center of controversy between the those who look toward an activist state to tend to the well-being of the citizenry and those who want as little interference as possible with the free market.

States acceding to the Covenant are obligated to take steps necessary for the "reduction of the stillbirth rate and of infant mortality;"[14] the "healthy development of the child;" the "improvement of all aspects of environmental and industrial hygiene;" the "prevention, treatment and control of epidemic, endemic, occupational and other diseases;" and the "creation of conditions which would assure to all medical service and medical attention in the event of sickness."

Unlike Article 10, Article 11 does not explicitly mandate international action to help the poorer countries provide their populations with the conditions of well-being. But the global disparities in capacities to provide adequate health care, plus the assignment in Article 18 to the Economic and Social Council and appropriate specialized agencies of the UN (particularly the World Health Organization and the United Nations Environmental Program) responsibilities for monitoring progress toward the various rights in the Covenant, have been read by the delegates and officials of these agencies as sufficient grounds for becoming active in designing implementation programs and specially funneling resources to the poor countries to help them (or induce them) to deal with their adverse health conditions.

The Right to Education (Articles 13 and 14)—Affirming that education is essential to human dignity and to the full exercise and enjoyment of many the other basic human rights, Article 13 lays out the public policy implications; namely,

(a) Primary education shall be compulsory and available free to all;

(b) Secondary education in all its different forms, including technical and vocational secondary education, shall be made generally available and accessible to all by every appropriate means, and in particular by the progressive introduction of free education;

(c) Higher education shall be made equally accessible to all, on the basis of capacity, by every appropriate means, and in particular by the progressive introduction of free education.

In implementing their universal, free education policies, however, the states are enjoined to allow leeway for private

---

14. "Stillbirth" here refers to the *involuntary* death of the fetus. The enormously controversial issue of voluntary abortion lacks sufficient international consensus for it to achieve status in such covenants.

education, especially for religious reasons; accordingly, the parties to the Covenant agree to

have respect for the liberty of parents . . . to choose for their children school, other than those established by the public authorities, which conform to such minimum educational standards as may be laid down or approved by the State and to ensure the religious and moral education of their children in conformity with their own convictions.

The importance the framers of the Covenant gave to education is driven home by Article 14, which commits any state that does not yet (at the time of ratifying the Covenant) have a system of universal free primary education to adopt "within two years . . . a detailed plan of action for the progressive implementation" and to commit itself to implement this plan within a reasonable period of time.

Rights Concerning Culture and Science (Article 15)—This article recognizes the "right of everyone" to "take part in cultural life" and to "enjoy the benefits of scientific progress and its applications." It also recognizes the rights of the author of any scientific, literary, or artistic production to special "moral and material interests" (what are referred to in other documents as "intellectual property rights") in such original work.

Article 15 recognizes that for these rights to be realized, states should "undertake to respect the freedom indispensable for scientific research and creative activity" and should encourage "international contacts and cooperation" in these fields. As with other provisions in the Covenant, the implication is logically inescapable (although often resisted in practice for political reasons) that in order for countries to make substantial progress in delivering economic, scientific, and cultural rights to their citizens, they must also adhere to most of the provisions in the Covenant on Civil and Political Rights.

OTHER INTERNATIONAL LEGAL INSTRUMENTS

There are other major international legal instruments on human rights that, because they are treaties (as are the two core covenants), imply commitments by the acceding governments to incorporate their provisions into their domestic legal systems. And they imply, even where they do not explicitly state it, that the parties to such treaties may hold one another accountable for major failures to live up to their treaty obligations.

These other treaties for the most part are elaborations in detail of provisions codified in more general terms in the two core covenants. Some are earlier conventions that were strengthened by the later instruments.

In addition to the 1951 Convention on the Prevention and Punishment of the Crime of Genocide[15] (discussed in the Chapter 1), the major human rights treaties dealing with particular subjects are as follows:

> *The Convention Against Torture and Other Cruel, Inhuman or Degrading Treatment or Punishment (1987)*—Next to the Genocide Convention, the most absolute of the human rights treaties, this Convention prohibits
>
> any act by which severe pain or suffering, whether physical or mental, is intentionally inflicted on a person for such purposes as obtaining from him or a third person information or a confession, punishing him for an act he or a third person has committed or is suspected of having committed . . . (Article 1)
>
> Moreover, in the words of Article 2,
>
> No exceptional circumstances whatever, whether a state of war or a threat of war, internal political instability or any other public emergency, may be invoked as a justification of torture.
>
> The Convention Against Torture established a Committee Against Torture of ten experts elected by the parties to monitor, investigate, and evaluate complaints of noncompliance. Two optional articles allow a government to declare in advance of any specific allegation that it recognizes the competence of the Committee Against Torture to receive and consider complaints against it; by Article 21, the Committee is permitted to consider such complaints from any other state party to the Convention; and by Article 22, the Committee can consider complaints from individuals under the jurisdiction of a government that has accepted the article. Some one hundred states have become parties to the antitorture Covenant, and of these about half have declared their acceptance of Articles 21 and 22.
>
> *Convention on the Elimination of All Forms of Racial Discrimination (1969)*—Another absolutist human rights docu-

---

15. The dates of these instruments indicate when they entered into force (that is, when the requisite number of ratifications to be binding on the parties were obtained).

ment, this Convention, to which most countries are party, outlaws

any distinction, exclusion, restriction or preference based on race, color, descent, or national or ethnic origin which has the purpose or effect of nullifying or impairing the recognition, enjoyment or exercise, on an equal footing, of human rights and fundamental freedoms in the political, economic, social or any other field of public life.(Article 1)

Not only does the Convention prohibit governments and their officials from engaging in such acts of racial discrimination, but it obligates the governments to outlaw and punish all such acts by private organizations and persons, including "propaganda activities, which promote and incite racial discrimination" (Article 4).[16]

The Convention on the Elimination of All Forms of Discrimination Against Women (1981)—Parties to this convention agree to prohibit within their jurisdictions

any distinction, exclusion or restriction made on the basis of sex which has the effect or purpose of impairing or nullifying the recognition, enjoyment or exercise by women, irrespective of their marital status, on a basis of equality of men and women, of human rights and fundamental freedoms in the political, economic, social, cultural, civil or any other field (Article 1).

The commitments of states adopting this convention extend to the taking of "all appropriate measures . . . to modify the social and cultural patterns of conduct . . . which are based on the idea of the inferiority or of either of the sexes or on stereotyped roles for men and women" (Article 5).[17]

---

16. The convention also includes an affirmative-action provision that allows, but does not mandate, "special measures for the sole purpose of securing adequate advancement of certain racial and ethnic groups" to achieve equal enjoyment of their human rights. These policies (according to Article 1, paragraph 4) "shall not be deemed racial discrimination, provided . . . that such measures do not . . . lead to the maintenance of separate rights for different racial groups and that they shall not be continued after the objectives for which they were taken have been achieved."
17. Similar to the Convention on the Elimination on All Forms of Racial Discrimination, this convention states that "temporary special measures aimed at accelerating de facto equality between men and women shall not be considered discrimination . . . but shall in no way entail, as a consequence, the maintenance of unequal or separate standards; these measures shall be discontinued when the objectives of equality of opportunity and treatment have been achieved" (Article 4).

The Convention on the Rights of the Child (1990)—This convention is designed primarily to commit countries to protect children within their jurisdictions "from all forms of physical or mental violence, injury or abuse, neglect or negligent treatment, maltreatment or exploitation including sexual abuse" (Article 19). In addition, "State Parties recognize the right of the child to the enjoyment of the highest attainable standard of healthy and to facilities for the treatment of illness and rehabilitation of health" (Article 24) plus the right to free primary education (Article 28).

Convention Concerning Indigenous and Tribal Peoples in Independent Countries (1991)—This convention applies to peoples whose local customs and traditions constitute ways of life distinguished from other segments of the nation-states in whose jurisdictions they reside and who wish to preserve their unique (usually premodern) ways of life. It attempts to deal with the dilemma of how to accord them the rights (and obligations) of full citizenship in the larger nation-states while respecting their desire for maximum autonomy to run their own affairs.

Thus, Article 3 states that "Indigenous and tribal peoples shall enjoy the full measure of human rights and fundamental freedoms without discrimination," while Article 4 provides that "Special measures shall be adopted as appropriate for safeguarding the persons, institutions, property, labor, cultures and environment of the peoples concerned." The Convention's attempts to reconcile these competing values in some 35 carefully worded articles have not been entirely successful, as the practical politics and litigation of conflicting claims of dominant majorities and indigenous minorities around the world are making this issue one of the most highly contentious areas in the human rights field.

Convention Relating to the Status of Refugees (1951) and the Protocol Relating to the Status of Refugees (1967)—Governments party to these treaties obligate themselves to provide most of the economic, social, and cultural rights to persons admitted as legal refugees that they provide to their own nationals. Refugees are also to be accorded most of the rights appearing in the Covenant on Civil and Political Rights, except the rights to vote in elections and run for public office. Each government retains the sovereign right to determine whom to admit as legal refugees. But once a government has granted someone refugee status, it may not expel or return (*refouler*) that person to any country "where his life or freedom would be threatened on account of his race, religion, nationality, membership of a particular social group or political opinion" (Article 33 of the 1951 Convention and incorporated into the 1967 Protocol).

The right to seek asylum from political persecution, and the implied moral obligation of states to admit such asylum seekers as refugees, although endorsed by the UN Declaration on Territorial Asylum (1968), does not have treaty status. In other words, under existing international law, an individual has the right to leave any country but not the right to enter another country.

International Convention on the Protection of the Rights of All Migrant Workers and Members of Their Families (opened for signature in May 1991)—This convention deals with the rights of the person (and of that person's family) who is living in a country "of which he or she is not a national" in order to "engage in remunerative activity." The Convention extends to migrant workers many, but by no means all, of the protections normally available to full citizens that are contained in the Covenant on Civil and Political Rights and the Covenant on Economic, Social and Cultural Rights. Even more so than with refugees, migrant workers are assumed to be residing in the host country temporarily, so there is no reason to extend them rights to participate in the political processes of making the laws and selecting the lawmakers. But in most other respects, the emerging transnational consensus, reflected in this document, holds that those who are temporarily and legally residing in a country for reasons of gainful employment ought to be treated with respect for their human dignity and provided with the rudimentary requirements of basic health and welfare that are provided to ordinary citizens.

In many countries the migrant workers, being from a different culture, ethnic group, or religion and speaking a different language, are sometimes thought to be competing for scarce jobs and are vulnerable to hostility from resentful elements of the majority community. The pervasiveness of such tensions is reflected in the provision that "Migrant workers and members of their families shall be entitled to effective protection by the State against violence, physical injury, threats and intimidation, whether by public officials, groups, or institutions" (Article 16).

Some of the provisions of the Convention are directed particularly to the complicated legal situation of temporary residents in a foreign country—such as making sure, if they get into trouble with law enforcement agencies, that they are informed of their rights and the charges against them "in a language they understand" and that they are provided with the opportunity of invoking the assistance of the consular or diplomatic authorities of the countries of which they are citizens.

The related, and growing, issue of the treatment of illegal immigrants—a subject of intense controversy within many countries—has not yet resulted in an international covenant.

In addition to the international human rights law designed to commit *all* countries to their provisions, there are a number of major human rights instruments reflecting agreements among sets of countries in particular regions on ways of implementing the global treaties in their area; some of these go beyond the global documents in substance and specify human rights that may not yet be acceptable on a universal basis.

The key regional human rights treaties are

The European Convention for the Protection of Human Rights and Fundamental Freedoms (1953) and its Protocols—No. 1 (1954); No. 2 (1970); No. 3 (1970); No. 4 (1968); No. 5 (1971); No. 6 (1985); No. 7 (1984); No. 8 (1985); Nos 9 and 10 (not yet in force)

The European Social Charter (1965)

The Final Act of the Conference on Security and Cooperation in Europe (1975)

The American Convention on Human Rights (1978); its Protocol to Abolish the Death Penalty (1991); and its additional Protocol on Economic, Social, and Cultural Rights (not yet in force)

The African Charter on Human and Peoples Rights (1986)

IMPLEMENTING THE LAW

How the countries who have acceded to the various conventions should implement them in their own legal systems—that is, what precisely are they legally and morally obligated to do—is the very stuff of continuing international dialogue and debate among the countries and, of course, domestic debate within each of their political systems.

Law libraries around the world have had to allocate large amounts of shelving space to accommodate the proliferating interpretive and theoretical treatises on human rights law.[18]

As indicated, on both the negotiation and implementation sides of international human rights law, the toleration of ambiguity has been functional: It has allowed countries with very different traditions to agree (or at least appear to agree) to a range of basic, universal principles of person-people-polity relationships without forcing them first to attempt to resolve their irreconcilable philosophical differences. The willingness to agree on such universal principles before clarifying the varying meanings these principles have to the countries that have agreed to them defers disputes over their meaning to the implementation stage; this means that often such disputes may *not* be resolved even in the implementation phase due to the political reality of decentralized, country-specific implementation.

Such accommodation to cultural relativism, which may well be the necessary price for having any international human rights law at all, does not always sit well the victims of human rights abuses who have been unable to get adequate attention to their claims within their countries. But this is exactly where the transnational human rights movements and organization come in, for once the international covenants are on the books, groups who have a common interpretation of their meaning can propagate their views across borders in an attempt to give aggrieved human rights claimants stronger grounds for holding their own governments accountable to the emergent universalistic human rights norms.

This open-ended character of much international human rights law has been reflected during the 1990s in various world conferences, which in large part have been the result of popular political pressures—often mobilized by nongovernmental organizations (NGOs)—upon the governments to resolve their differences, flesh out their obligations, and make new commitments to implement them. The major, official global conferences devoted largely or in substantial part to human rights issues have been the World Conference on Human Rights (Vienna, 1993), the International Conference on Population and Development (Cairo, 1994), the World Conference for Social Development (Copenhagen, 1995), and the World Conference on Women (Beijing, 1995).

The main purpose of the global conferences has been consensus-building and the clarification of the rights of people and of the obligations

---

18. There will be no attempt in the present volume to add to, or to analyze, this literature of exegesis. The emphasis here is on the practical reasons for and implications of ongoing human rights struggles under the often-ambiguous provisions in the legal documents.

of governments around the world. But at times, as in the Conference on Population and Development, they do just the opposite and expose deep divisions among peoples on the issues—divisions within countries and across national borders to which the governments have been falteringly and sometimes ineptly responding. In such cases, the declarations produced by these conferences, by papering over bitter fights among nongovernmental as well as official delegates, provide little in the way of clarification or guidance on the specifics of the human rights policies the governments should pursue in implementing the vaguely formulated international covenants. This experience supports the view that the way to keep the evolving international law of human rights robust is to maintain enough vagueness at the level of universal covenants to allow for flexible implementation in varying cultural contexts.

While for the time being much of the implementation must remain within the jurisdiction of the domestic legal systems of the participating countries, there has been a proliferation in the last few decades of intergovernmental monitoring and investigatory machinery in both global and regional institutions. This machinery is discussed in some detail in Chapter 5.

Obtaining Justice
in the World System

Human rights enter the arenas of international relations and world politics when individuals or communities believe they are not obtaining justice (meaning, fair treatment) within the nation-state that has jurisdiction over them and when some outsiders are willing to take up their cause. This has been happening more and more. Human rights issues have not only become internationalized but have moved to center stage in world politics. The basic international covenants analyzed in Chapter 4 have resulted from, and in turn further encouraged, this internationalization of human rights concerns.

But heightened concern, and even the creation of new international law, provides no guarantee that justice will be done. This chapter surveys the means available to people trying to improve their human rights situation.

In contrast to previous eras, today people who feel their human rights are not being adequately served in their own countries can attempt to invoke one or more of the numerous international human rights instruments in support of their claims. But not many of the provisions of these instruments have weighty legal standing in international or domestic courts around the world, and governments vary in the extent to which they are willing to modify their human rights behavior in response to international exposure or pressure.

To be sure, the state-sovereignty system remains heavily stacked against the ability of persons to obtain redress for human rights violations perpetrated or inadequately handled by their own national governments. Yet, globally, international assertions of human rights continue to grow—in number and intensity.

What methods, then, are individuals and communities (and the nongovernmental organizations that take up their causes) using to press their human rights claims in the arenas of international law and world politics? Such methods range from attempts to rely on standard procedures of existing international institutions, to efforts to embarrass particular governments for their moral failings, to support for political parties and organizations that can affect legislation and elections in the target countries, to the use of coercive methods (such as economic boycotts, work stoppages, nonviolent disruptions of government, terrorism, and international military intervention) to pressure or bring down regimes held to be responsible for the human rights violations.

The case studies in the next chapter examine how these various methods of mobilizing international pressure on behalf of victims of human rights abuses succeed or fail in particular situations.

THE ACTIVATION OF INSTITUTIONAL PROCEDURES

There are various official international procedures of limited effectiveness that can be activated against governments which have ratified the core human rights covenants (especially those governments that also are parties to optional protocols and accept complaints from private parties). The most advanced international procedures, in terms of giving individuals and minority communities standing to sue for their rights beyond their own national courts, are available to the people of most of the countries of Europe under the auspices of the Council of Europe. The human rights agencies of the Inter-American system provide some private-party access in theory but in practice lag far behind the access provided as a result of the innovations of the European system. I discuss these regional regimes later in the chapter after describing UN human rights procedures—which for most of the world's peoples provide the only hope beyond their national legal systems of obtaining a hearing for their human rights claims.

The United Nations

In the UN system, responsibility for overseeing adherence by countries to the key UN covenants is lodged primarily in the Human Rights Committee set up by the Covenant on Civil and Political Rights and, increasingly, in the Commission on Human Rights, which is responsible to the Economic and Social Council. Both of these agencies have evolved from being mere creatures of the sovereignty-protecting states that established them into more probing investigatory bodies, with staffs and special rapporteurs; they are often assisted by nongovernmental organizations that sometimes quite assiduously attempt to obtain information on problematic human rights situations.

The Human Rights Committee   Comprised of 18 juridical experts, who are elected by the states that are parties to the Covenant on Civil and Political Rights, the Human Rights Committee is mandated to over-see the parties' adherence to the Covenant's provisions. It is also man-dated to oversee adherence to the Convention Against Torture and Other Cruel, Inhuman or Degrading Forms of Punishment. It performs these roles by reviewing periodic *reports* from the parties (which all the treaty parties are obligated to submit) as well as *complaints* against them.

The regular reports, being self-evaluations by the national govern-ments, are unlikely to exhibit much candor on matters that could be embarrassing to their authors. But the complaints procedure, if skillfully utilized, has the potential for inducing a certain amount of governmental accountability. Formal complaints can be of two kinds:

- *Complaints from State Parties to the Covenant*—These are made against those governments who have declared their acceptance of the competence of the Committee to receive such complaints about them. About one-third of the parties have made such decla-rations, but reflecting the traditional reluctance of member gov-ernments to use UN machinery to undermine one another's sover-eignty, this procedure remains virtually unused.

- *Complaints by Individuals (and Nongovernmental Organiza-tions)*—These are made against those governments that have acceded to the Optional Protocol to the Covenant; about two-thirds of the nearly one hundred ratifying states have done so. And hundreds of individual complaints (from private persons or from nongovernmental organizations) have been received.[1] If a commu-nication meets the Committee's standards of admissibility (about 50 percent do qualify), the Committee examines its substance in detail; asks follow-up questions of the relevant parties, as appropri-ate; and upon completion of its review, forwards its findings (called "views") to the government concerned and the com-plainants.[2]

Although the impact of the individual-complaints procedure is lim-ited by the secrecy of actual deliberations during the review process, the Committee does publish the texts of its final views. And a negative find-ing on a country can be used by nongovernmental groups within that country and by other countries to legitimize domestic and international pressures on the offending government to change its ways.

---

1. Torkel Opsahl, "The Human Rights Committee," in Philip Alston, ed., *The United Nations and Human Rights: A Critical Appraisal* (Oxford: Clarendon Press, 1992), pp. 369–443.

2. The principal standards of admissibility are that the alleged violations must concern one of the rights recognized in the Covenant, the complaint cannot be anonymous, it must be well substantiated, the complainants must have exhausted all domestic reme-dies, and the matter must not be under examination by another international agency.

The Commission on Human Rights   The most visible UN organ for dealing with violations of human rights, the Commission on Human Rights was established as a special agency of the Economic and Social Council (ECOSOC) in conformity with Article 68 of the UN Charter. Its visibility is a function of the fact that its seats are governmental seats occupied by high-ranking official diplomats from most of the member countries of the UN. Its decisions, like the decisions of the ECOSOC, must be in the form of resolutions supported by most of the member governments. This visibility and formal (state-representing) structure limits the Commission's effectiveness in helping aggrieved peoples obtain redress for the human rights violations they are suffering. It can, however, serve to reinforce and give official legitimacy to widespread popular condemnation of notorious human rights infractions, since a government that is called prominently into account by other governments in the Commission is put on the defensive before the world and more than ever will be subject to pressures from its own citizenry to reform its ways. Especially in cases of systematic and persisting violations of basic human rights norms, the Commission's judgment can be a catalyst to the mobilization of diplomatic pressure, including the application of economic sanctions and other means of internationally ostracizing the offending government. (The abolition of the South African apartheid regime—analyzed in Chapter 6—is the most noted example of how such pressures can bring about reform.)

The Commission's role blossomed after 1967, when it took on the function of overseeing the implementation of the Convention on the Elimination of All Forms of Racial Discrimination; since then, it has also become the official international oversight agency for the conventions on the rights of women, children, refugees, migrant workers, and tribal and indigenous peoples.

Countries acceding to these various conventions—and their optional clauses allowing governments to be the object of complaints from private persons—are subject to procedures established under the authority of two ECOSOC resolutions (Resolutions 1235 and 1503, passed in the late 1960s) that give the Commission on Human Rights responsibility for receiving and investigating the complaints of individuals and nongovernmental groups.[3]

> *The 1235 Procedure*—Under this procedure the Commission holds an annual public debate on allegations of gross violations of human rights submitted to it by member governments, other international agencies, or nongovernmental organizations. The outcome of the debate on the policies

---

3. For a detailed account of the evolution of the work of the Commission under the 1235 and 1503 procedures, see Philip Alston, "The Commission on Human Rights, " in Alston, *The United Nations and Human Rights*, pp. 126–210.

of a country accused of infractions can be a resolution of condemnation or a request for reform or the initiation of additional investigations through the appointment of special rapporteurs, independent experts, and working groups. Their reports then inform the Commission's subsequent debates.

Countries that are singled out for special 1235 procedures cannot be forced to cooperate with the Commission's investigators, but the governments are under considerable moral pressure to cooperate, given the public knowledge that they are subject to allegations that the Commission considers serious enough to warrant deeper probes. When coming under such focused international scrutiny, offending governments may well attempt to reform the practices that brought on the allegations so that in the next round of the Commission's debates, they can be given a clean bill of human rights health.

The 1503 Procedure—This is the initial method, and usually the only one, by which the Commission screens out or takes action—confidentially—on the enormous number of the complaints it receives each year. (Complaints—a large proportion of them involving violations of the right to leave and return from one's country—peaked at about 300,000 annually during the flourishing of anticommunist uprisings against the Eastern European governments in the 1989–1991 period. A communications working group sorts through the huge number of complaints; categorizes them by country of origin; and weeds out all those that are either anonymous, fail to show serious efforts by the complainants to have exhausted all domestic remedies, or lack clear evidence of consistent patterns of gross violations. Typically, the actionable complaints come mainly from citizen groups in countries that are experiencing major domestic political turmoil.[4]

A working group "nominates" those countries for which it has complaints that it considers appropriate to be reviewed by the Commission at its annual meeting. These recommendations then are reviewed by a subcommission which decides whether and which files to send to the full Commission for consideration. Another working group is convened to gather addition information and draft recommendations for action by the Commission

---

4. The information of the workings of the 1503 procedure comes from Alston, ibid., pp. 145–155.

on the relevant cases. Complaints against about ten countries a year are reported to the Commission itself by this process.

At its annual meeting, the Commission devotes only a few days in secret session to the reports from the subcommission and working groups. At the conclusion of the secret deliberations, the chairman of the Commission announces publicly the names of the countries that have come under its review, but no details are revealed about the allegations or the actions taken by the Commission. The actions may involve the Commission simply asking the claimants and the governments to submit more information for the next annual round of reviews, appointing special emissaries or committees to conduct confidential investigations with the cooperation of the concerned governments, or seeking a friendly solution that the Commission could endorse at its next annual meeting. All of this is confidential.

Either at the time of its first annual review of allegations against a country or in its subsequent reviews, the Commission on Human Rights can decide to transfer the country's case to the public 1235 procedure. Conversely, a country whose human rights record is about to be exposed through public deliberations of the Commission under the 1235 can maneuver to have its case transferred to the 1503 procedure, thereby cutting off the public deliberations. Thus, through the device of the 1503 procedure, there are many opportunities along the way for a country to prevent the Commission from publicly exposing, or even taking note of, its human rights situation. This has frustrated the work of such nongovernmental organizations as Amnesty International and Human Rights Watch for which the 1503 procedure is the route to official UN review of the information on gross violations they have gathered. In its *Report 1995*, Amnesty International complained that

> Time and again governments with abysmal human rights records have won the support of enough other governments, acting in their perceived self-interests, to block action in the UN, particularly by the Commission on Human Rights. Through such concerted obstruction governments evade accountability, and the UN system for human rights protection in undermined.[5]

Under the Council of Europe

The most developed international mechanisms for holding governments accountable to one another and to their citizenry for their compliance with the covenants they have accepted operate under the auspices of the

---

5.   Amnesty International, *Report 1995* (London: Amnesty International, 1995), p. 40.

Council of Europe (to which members of the European Union plus most of the most of the other countries of Europe belong). Members of the Council are also parties to the European Convention for the Protection of Human Rights and Fundamental Freedoms that, in addition to reaffirming most of the human rights and governmental obligations in the core UN documents, gives jurisdiction over disputes arising out of the Convention to the European Commission on Human Rights and the European Court of Human Rights. These two investigatory/adjudicatory bodies have been accorded unprecedented authority as supranational institutions for making authoritative judgments on the policies of member states.

The European Commission on Human Rights   The European Convention confers on the Commission the authority to "receive petitions from any person, nongovernmental organization or group of individuals claiming to be the victim of a violation by one of the High Contracting Parties of the rights set forth in this convention, provided that the High Contracting Party against which the complaint has been lodged has declared that it recognizes the competence of the Commission to receive such petitions.[6] (Most of the members of the Council of Europe have signed such declarations). In such cases, the petitioner and the involved governments are obligated to cooperate with the Commission's investigation.

The Commission is composed of as many members as there are parties to the Convention; one individual from each country, typically a jurist or law professor, is elected by the Council of Europe to act in his or her individual capacity. Its work is facilitated by a permanent secretariat with a staff of over 50, some 30 of which are lawyers.

As in the rules for private complaints in the UN system, the petitioner must have exhausted domestic legal remedies, must not be anonymous, and so forth. In a typical year the Commission may formally register close to 1500 applications, out of which it will declare about 200 admissible.

The Convention stipulates that having admitted a petition, the Commission must then review the situation to ascertain the facts and, if necessary, to conduct its own investigation, "for the effective conduct of which the States concerned shall furnish all necessary facilities."[7]

The Commission is mandated to attempt to secure a friendly settlement; but if it is unable to do so, it must draw up a report that states "its opinion as to whether the facts found disclose a breach by the State concerned of its obligations under the Convention" and that proposes the

---

6. European Convention for the Protection of Human Rights and Fundamental Freedoms, 213 *United Nations Treaty Series* 221, Article 25.
7. Ibid., Article 28.

next steps to a Committee of Ministers of the Commission (actually comprised of the foreign ministers of the member states and thus tantamount to the Council of Europe itself).[8] These next steps may include referring the case to the European Human Rights Court. Alternatively (but this would be rarely done), the Ministers may instruct a government found in violation of the European Convention to adopt policies to bring it into compliance, and the named government is obligated to act in accordance with these instructions. The Committee of Ministers can act on these matters with a two-thirds vote.

The European Court of Human Rights   Composed of distinguished jurists from each of the member countries of the Council of Europe and sitting for nine-year, renewable terms, the Court of Human Rights has jurisdiction over all cases referred to it by either the Commission or one of the states party to the Convention. Individuals or nongovernmental groups can obtain a hearing from the Court if they can get the Commission or a friendly government to take their case into the Court. The Court has the authority to find a member government to be in conflict with its obligations under the Convention and, in such cases, to "afford just satisfaction to the injured party."[9] Moreover, "The judgment of the Court shall be final."[10] The Court, has in fact ordered in over 40 cases governments to give at least token financial compensation to injured parties, in amounts worth, in some instances, up to $160,000.[11]

An authoritative study of the European human rights regime published in 1989 found that "the European regime has been genuinely receptive to processing human rights grievances." But the study also concluded that even in this comparatively progressive system "statist imperatives [still] tend to outweigh the values of human dignity."[12]

The Inter-American System

In many respects the international regime in the Americas for promoting human rights and dealing with their violation is similar to the European regime. Resting on two overlapping, basic agreements—the Charter of the Organization of American States (as amended in 1970) and the American Human Rights Convention (negotiated in 1969 and entered

---

8. Ibid., Article 46.
9. Ibid., Article 50.
10. Ibid., Article 52.
11. See the account of the functioning of the European Human Rights Court by Mark W. Janis in his *An Introduction to International Law* (Boston: Little, Brown, 1993), pp. 257–265.
12. Burns H. Weston, Robin Ann Lukes, and Kelley M. Hnatt, "Regional Human Rights Regimes: A Comparison and Appraisal," in Claude Weston, ed., Human Rights in the World Community: Issues and Action (Philadelphia: University of Pennsylvania Press, 1989), pp. 209–211.

into force in 1978)—the Inter-American regime also functions through a human rights commission and court. The procedures of the Inter-American Commission on Human Rights and the Inter-American Court of Human Rights, and their relationship toward each other, might appear to be closely modeled on the European human rights commission and court. But as put by Jack Donnelly, a close student of these institutions, "In the Inter-American system there simply are not any enforcement powers," and, decidedly more so than in Europe, "sovereignty remains the overriding norm in the Inter-American human rights regime."[13] The United States has not yet helped to override this norm; it still has refused to ratify the American Human Rights Convention.

Like its European counterpart, the Convention provides that "Any person or group of persons, or any nongovernmental entity legally recognized in one or more member states of the Organization, may lodge petitions with the Commission containing denunciations or complaints of violations of this Convention by a State Party."[14] And it contains almost the identical set of criteria for judging the admissibility of such petitions. The Commission is authorized to investigate such cases and to try to reach a friendly settlement. But, in contrast to the traditions that are being established in the European system, the governments in the Western Hemisphere that are the most appropriate targets of complaints (and there have been many deserving targets) have been for the most part uncooperative with Commission investigations. The Commission can bring contentious cases to the Inter-American Court of Human Rights but has rarely availed itself of this option.

In some of the egregious cases of gross violations (in the 1980s, among those thus singled out were Chile, Cuba, El Salvador, Guatemala, Haiti, Nicaragua, and Paraguay), the Commission has issued condemnatory resolutions, which have often been echoed by similar resolutions in the Organization of American States. Typically, the offending governments try to brush off such reprimands as motivated by the political concerns of their regional and ideological rivals. But the fact that the governments brought up for review expend a great deal of effort in their attempts to avoid such negative reports indicates that they do worry about the impact of the negative publicity on their domestic constituents and, of no small moment, their relations with those countries who take human rights seriously (especially countries with policies restricting economic aid, loans, and arms sales to governments with poor human rights records). Moreover, Jack Donnelly reminds us

> that "the bottom line" includes individuals who are helped, even
> if the overall situation in the country remains repressive. States

---

13. Jack Donnelly, *International Human Rights* (Boulder, CO: Westview, 1993), pp. 88–89.
14. American Convention on Human Rights, Article 48.

often respond to adverse international human rights publicity by releasing or improving the treatment of prominent victims. These may be small victories for international action, but they are victories nonetheless of immense significance to the individuals involved.[15]

Donnelly's observation points to the reality that where international institutions are unable themselves to apply legal sanctions on human rights violators (which is still the case everywhere except in the Council of Europe regime), the hope of victims for redress lies almost entirely in the negative publicity that can be generated to embarrass the offending governments. It is not evident, however, that the resolutions of international institutions are the most effective means for creating the negative publicity; to be sure, an official international condemnation can give legitimacy to popular outrage, but unless that outrage is stirred and channeled against the offending governments by nongovernmental groups and the media, the official condemnatory resolutions will simply gather dust on the archival shelves of the international institutions.

THE GENERATION OF POPULAR OUTRAGE

Given the determination of most governments to retain as much sovereignty as possible within their jurisdictions and given the fact that it is the national governments of the world that must approve any supranational means (even monitoring and nonintrusive investigations) of implementing international human rights law, it is no wonder that many countries with notoriously poor human rights records remain largely immune from sanctions at the hands of international agencies. Negative sanctions, if they are to be applied at all, usually must come either directly from other governments or from a national government's own constituents at home. But such lateral sanctions or domestic "punishment from below" will not be forthcoming in the absence of widespread popular outrage at the human rights infractions.

Transnational citizen groups, like Amnesty International and Human Rights Watch, have come to realize that in order to have a significant impact on governments engaged in systematic and persistent human rights violations, they, as nongovernmental organizations, cannot confine themselves to quiet inquiries to governments about the condition and whereabouts of victims (the procedure most relied upon by Amnesty in its early years) or lawyerly maneuverings to activate the established international commissions and courts. Increasingly, their work involves the dissemination of information on human rights viola-

---

15. Donnelly, *International Human Rights*, p. 89.

tions to the news media and directly to the general public through books, videos, the Internet, and the organization of public forums.

TRANSNATIONAL LOBBYING TO AFFECT NATIONAL FOREIGN POLICIES

A government with aroused constituents, outraged at the way their fellow human beings are being treated in another country, does not have to wait on cumbersome international-agency procedures to bring pressure on the government of that country to rectify the situation. Unilateral diplomacy may be the preferred option, especially where the offending government is also represented in the cognizant official international body and where any attempts to seriously activate human rights procedures of international institutions are doomed to diversion and failure.

Indeed, the more gross and systematic the violation of human rights, the more likely it is that other governments and nongovernmental organizations will find themselves blocked by the offending government if they try to have the case taken up by the relevant international commissions. In such situations, human rights advocates have begun to rely increasingly on transnational nongovernmental political networks and

CONTROVERSY BOX
6

Religious Discrimination in Russia

Despite objections voiced by President Clinton and threats by the U.S. Senate to cut off aid to Russia, President Boris Yeltsin signed a law in September 1997 privileging the Russian Orthodox Church and permitting the government to restrict the rights of "nontraditional" religious groups to tax relief, the use of property, public assembly, and the use of print and electronic media to proselytize.[†]

Russian defenders of the new law (expressing anger at the United States for meddling) claim that it is needed to protect citizens against cults and totalitarian sects such as the Japanese religious group that launched a gas attack in the Tokyo subway in 1995. But some of Russia's mainline religious minorities charge that the legislation is so loosely worded that it could be used against them as well.

What can, and should, concerned people outside of Russia do about this issue?

[†]For details, see Michael R. Gordon, "Irking U.S., Yeltsin Signs Law Protecting Orthodox Church," *New York Times* (September 27, 1997).

organizations to lobby national parliaments and political parties around the world to compel their governments to apply sanctions on their own without waiting for international-agency blessing.

Such domestic political lobbying of national legislatures and executive agencies has become one of the major activities of such transnational organizations as Amnesty and Human Rights Watch and also of transnational ethnic and religious communities (see Controversy Box 6 on page 105) on behalf of their members around the world.[16] This mode of pressing for the injection of human rights considerations into foreign policy is, of course, nothing new; during the Cold War, with the UN human rights agencies often paralyzed when it came to dealing with repression within countries in the Soviet sphere, exiles from the USSR and Eastern Europe kept the political spotlight turned on the "captive" peoples of the region mainly through efforts to influence legislators and political parties in the Western democracies. The women's rights movement is becoming particularly active using this mode of advancing its concerns.[17] Tibetan exiles, blocked by China in their efforts to bring the Tibetan situation before UN human rights agencies, run a very active transnational lobbying operation.[18] The Inuit and other aboriginal people not only from the Canadian north but also from Alaska, northern Japan, northeastern Russia, and Greenland are mutually supportive of one another's lobbying efforts in all of the Arctic countries.[19]

The ability of constituency groups on human rights with members in countries around the world to concert their lobbying activities has been given an enormous boost by the widespread use of fax technology and the global accessibility of the Internet and other electronic sources of information. The global "civil society" that is evolving can perhaps manipulate the existing nation-state system on behalf of human rights concerns better than it can manipulate the still-embryonic organs of supranational regional and global governance.

But again, there is no guarantee that the transnational mobilization of human rights concerns will indeed result in changes of foreign policy, where other considerations—especially commercial considerations—mitigate any significant disruption in an ongoing, mutually advantageous, bilateral relationship. Exhibit A on behalf of the "realist" proposition that materialistic national self-interests will always win out over

---

16. See the annual reports of Amnesty International and Human Rights Watch.
17. Kathryn Sikkink, "The Power of Principled Ideas: Human Rights Policies in the United States and Western Europe," in Judith Goldstein and Robert O. Keohane, eds., *Ideas and Foreign Policy: Beliefs, Institutions, and Political Change* (Ithaca, NY: Cornell University Press, 1993).
18. Dong Dong Tian, "The Tibet Issue in U.S.-China Relations," (Ph.D. dissertation, Brandeis University, 1955).
19. Menno Boldt and J. Anthony Long, eds., *The Quest for Justice: Aboriginal Peoples and Aboriginal Rights* (Toronto: University of Toronto Press, 1985).

human rights and other moral considerations is the retention by the United States of most-favored-nation trading status for China even after the Tiananmen Square massacre raised the consciousness of the American people about the brutal character of the regime in Beijing.[20]

DIRECT ACTION—NONVIOLENT AND VIOLENT

When normal political processes, either international or domestic, fail to rectify conditions felt to be grossly unjust, the victims and their supporters in other countries can attempt to influence the perpetrators directly by interfering with *their* well-being and/or disrupting *their* lives.

Devotees of nonviolent direct action (of the kind organized by Gandhi or Martin Luther King) sometimes attempt to work on the *psychological* well-being of the perpetrators by actions designed to force them to confront, and to expose before the world, the immorality of their policies: These actions have included civil-disobedience campaigns against unjust laws, requiring governments to fill up its jails with gentle, otherwise law-abiding people, and voluntary fasting by victims' leaders in order to make the responsible powers conscious that they are causing unjustifiable suffering and have the ability to stop it. Again, as with the case of the South African apartheid regime, nonviolent direct action can also work on the physical or material well-being of the abusers of human rights. This action can be through transnationally organized boycotts of the goods produced by countries or corporations responsible for the violations (or sometimes directed against the goods of corporations with subsidiaries or major investments in the offending country) and, at the extreme, through countrywide general strikes designed to bring the economies to a halt and stop all normal civic life until the governments capitulate to the demands of the antigovernment forces (a device used in various capitals in Eastern Europe in the 1990–1991 period to bring down the Communist regimes). As direct-action demonstrations begin to disrupt the normal business of a country, the outside world also becomes involved, since the economies and even the military security of other countries can be negatively affected; in such cases (as in the People Power Revolt in the Philippines in 1986 against the Marcos government), foreign governments sometimes weigh in on the side of the human rights protesters and try to persuade governments to satisfy some of the demands in order to avoid a total collapse of law and order.

---

20. On President Clinton's reneging on his election campaign promise to take a tough stand against China's human rights violations, see Seyom Brown, *The Faces of Power: Constancy and Change in United States Foreign Policy From Truman to Clinton* (New York: Columbia University Press, 1994), pp. 602–604.

Human rights movements do not always restrict themselves to non-violent methods. Not infrequently, militants, who believe that brutal means are necessary to achieve their just ends, become the leaders; and terrorism, kidnappings, rape, and even genocidal "ethnic cleansing" become "legitimate" as long as they are used against the supporters of the government.

SELF-DETERMINATION AND SECESSION

In the name of exercising their right of self-determination, ethno-national or religious communities, convinced that they cannot obtain justice by remaining a subordinate part of the larger nation-state which has heretofore claimed sovereignty over them, may attempt to secede from that larger state (see Chapter 3). In some cases, the government in control will allow such secession to be effectuated peacefully (as Britain did with many of its colonies between 1945 and 1965 and as the Soviet Union did with most of its member republics in the 1989–1991 period). But where the existing government refuses to allow any such thing (as in Russia's reaction to Chechnya's attempted secession, Indonesia's on-going repression of the East Timorese, or Serbia's forcible expulsion of the Albanian population from Kosovo, the impasse may well degenerate into full-blown civil war.

Typically in such conflicts the revolutionary side justifies its resort to violence as retaliation for more horrible acts of violence perpetrated by the government. In such circumstances (as those in the former Yugoslavia in the 1991–1999 period), outside powers may feel compelled to intervene politically and even militarily—usually under the auspices of the United Nations or a regional security organization such as NATO—to stop or at least quarantine the carnage.

6

Some Illustrative
Human Rights
Struggles

Each of the five cases recounted in this chapter—the successful over-throw of the racist regime in South Africa; the resistance of China to international human rights pressures; the attempt to turn a human rights spotlight on the practice of female genital cutting; the international intervention against ethnic cleansing in the former Yugoslavia; and the effort to create effective international tribunals for dealing with violators of the most heinous human rights violations—illustrates a particular facet of the expanding role of human rights issues in world politics. More generally, they are all expressions both of the potential power of the human rights idea to shake the foundations of, and eventually transform, the nation-state system and the great resistance that still resides in the system against such a transformation. Chapter 8 offers speculations on the implications of these lessons for the future of the world polity.

The ultimately successful campaign against racial apartheid (segregation) in South Africa shows, on the one hand, that certain basic convictions about what are unalienable human rights have become world-community norms that now rival the foundational state-sovereignty, noninterventionist norms of the international system. But the South African case, when looked at along side of the still largely ineffective campaign by human rights advocates to mobilize comparable international pressures against China for its notorious human rights abuses, also reveals how difficult it is to translate the human rights norms, even when codified in international covenants, into operative international public policy. The question of how to deal internationally with the ritualistic cutting of the genitalia of females, as is widely practiced in many countries in Africa and the Middle East, raises in stark form the persistent issue of universalism versus cultural relativism. Lastly, the international responses to the genocidal acts committed in the former Yugoslavia and in Rwanda and the controversy over the establishment of a permanent international criminal court pose what is perhaps the most crucial question in world politics looking toward the twenty-first century: Are the nations of this planet finally ready to institutionalize— at least with respect to genocide and other universally condemned crimes against humanity—the accountability of persons, peoples, and governments to world law?

SOUTH AFRICA: THE ERADICATION OF APARTHEID

A dramatic success story in the field of human rights has occurred in South Africa. Although the largely peaceful overturning of that country's regime of racial discrimination is a unique development unlikely to be repeated elsewhere, it does reveal, perhaps more than any other case, the extent to which human rights struggles have the capacity to transform world politics. It stands as an exemplar of how the justice demands of people within a particular country can compel the statespersons of the world to override the traditional state-sovereignty norms of the international system.

Apartheid versus the Universal Affirmation of Human Rights

The promulgation of racial segregation as official policy by the Union of South Africa in 1948 ironically coincided with the nearly worldwide popular affirmation of human rights ideas, as reflected in the adoption that year of the Universal Declaration of Human Rights by UN General Assembly.

The ruling National Party in South Africa dismissed the Universal Declaration of Human Rights as merely a resolution by the UN General Assembly and as certainly not binding on a national government that refused to vote for it. Defiantly, Pretoria proceeded to deepen and rigidify its apartheid regime over the next few years: The Prohibition of Mixed Marriages Act (1949) outlawed any marriage between a European and non-European. The Immorality Act of 1950 criminalized sexual acts between blacks and whites. The Population Registration Act of 1950 established three classifications—white, colored, and native. The Suppression of Communism Act of 1950 allowed for suppression of any criticism of white supremacy. The Group Areas Act of 1950 established residential segregation in the cities.

The Cold War was also intensifying at this time. Communists and democratic capitalists were hardly of the same mind in their definition of human rights; but the United States and its allies on the one side and the Soviet Union and its allies on the other side, in their competition for the hearts and minds of the anticolonial self-determination movements in the Third World, agreed on at least one thing: national policies of racial discrimination were illegitimate.

The nonwhite communities in South Africa were able to tap into the international groundswell of support for self-determination and human rights. Denied domestic electoral or legislative power and frustrated in their attempts to assert their rights through the courts, the leaders of the anti-apartheid movement opted for direct action. In June 1952 the African National Congress of South Africa (ANC) and the South African Indian Congress initiated a nonviolent Campaign of Defiance against Unjust Laws. In emulation of the earlier campaigns of Mohandas Gandhi (in both South Africa and India), the protesters, making sure that the international media were alerted to the confrontations that might take place, courted arrest for refusing to obey discriminatory laws. As recounted by Nelson Mandela, then President of the Transvaal branch of the ANC,

> Africans, Coloureds, Indians and Europeans, old and young, all rallied to the national call and defied the pass laws and the curfew and the railway apartheid regulations. By the end of the year, more than 8,500 people of all races had defied. The Campaign called for immediate and heavy sacrifices. Workers lost their jobs, chiefs and teachers were expelled from the service, doctors, lawyers and businessmen gave up their practices and businesses and elected to go to jail. . . . It was one of the best ways of exerting pressure on the Government and extremely dangerous to the stability and security of the State.[1]

The government struck back. It arrested leaders of the Campaign of Defiance and promulgated a set of new laws restricting assembly and speech. Meetings of more than ten blacks were prohibited, and even *advocacy* of defiance of laws was made a criminal offense. Those convicted of defiance offenses were subject to harsh penalties, including whipping.

The news of Pretoria's 1952 crackdown galvanized Third World delegations at the United Nations to call for an investigation. In an historic breakthrough, on December 5, 1992, the General Assembly—over the objections from South Africa that this constituted a violation of Article 2, paragraph 7, of the UN Charter (the domestic-jurisdiction provision)—established a three-member United Nations Commission on the Racial Situation in the Union of South Africa.

---

1. Nelson Mandela, *The Struggle is My Life* (New York: Pathfinder Press, 1986), p. 34.

The UN Commission's 1953 report to the General Assembly found that South Africa's apartheid laws

> affect . . . nearly all aspects of the domestic, familial, social, political and economic life of the non-White population, who make up 79 per cent of the whole population of the country. They affect its most fundamental rights and freedoms: political rights, freedom of movement and residence, property rights, freedom to work and practice occupations, freedom of marriage and other family rights. They establish obvious inequality before the law in relation to the rights, freedoms and opportunities enjoyed by the 20 per cent of the population consisting of "Whites" or "Europeans." . . .
>
> . . .
>
> Four fifths of the population are thereby reduced to a humiliating level of inferiority which is injurious to human dignity and makes the full development of personality impossible or very difficult. . . .

Bypassing the issue of whether national governments were legally bound by the Universal Declaration of Human Rights, the Commission invoked the UN Charter itself, finding that

> All the . . . discriminatory legislative and administrative measures . . . laid down in pursuance of the apartheid policy . . . conflict with the solemn declaration in the Preamble of the United Nations Charter in which the signatories state that they are determined to "reaffirm faith in fundamental human rights, in the dignity and worth of the human person, in the equal rights of men and women and of nations large and small."
>
> . . .
>
> Those measures are also contrary to the purposes of international economic and social cooperation laid down in Article 55 of the Charter, which states that the United Nations should, "with a view to the creation of the conditions of stability and well-being which are necessary for peaceful and friendly relations among nations," promote "universal respect for, and observance of, human rights and fundamental freedoms for all without distinction as to race, sex, language, or religion."[2]

The Deepening Crisis in South Africa

Despite the embarrassing findings of the UN Commission, the regime in Pretoria showed no inclination to moderate its racist policies to please either its international or domestic critics. The repressive legislation

---

2. *Report of the United Nations Commission on the Racial Situation in the Union of South Africa*, A/2505 and Add.1. (1953); text in *The United Nations and Apartheid 1948–1944* (United Nations: Department of Public Information, 1994), pp. 228–231.

stayed on the books, and officials more assiduously than ever prosecuted leaders of activist organizations for violating the laws.

In the face of government intransigence, the leading umbrella organization of the anti-apartheid movement, the African National Congress, began to fractionate over alternative strategies of resistance. The centrists wanted to continue along the lines of the nonviolent Campaign of Defiance. By bearing witness and courting arrest on behalf of their commitment to a democratic multiracial society and with their struggle now endorsed by an attentive international community, they hoped to persuade enough white South Africans of goodwill that fundamental reforms were both morally and politically necessary. The Africanists (black nationalists), believing the time had come for the blacks to play the race card to their own benefit by asserting their own birthright to rule the area, disparaged cooperation with liberal or marxist whites and Indians in the ANC and the country at large. The communists in the movement, many of them white, wanted to mobilize a broad class-based alliance of labor organizations in all the racial communities. Straddling these various factions was the youthful and charismatic Nelson Mandela, a militant who did not rule out the use of violence, subversion, and sabotage but who, at this stage, was still a champion of broad-based, multiracial nonviolent demonstrations for democracy.[3]

Publicly, the ANC was able to maintain a united front, under the banner of a new Freedom Charter adopted in June 1955 by three thousand delegates from all over the country.

An amalgamation of Western liberal and socialist tenets and provisions in the Universal Declaration of Human Rights, the Freedom Charter outlined a transformed South Africa in which

> Every man and woman shall have the right to vote for and stand as a candidate for all bodies which make laws.
>
> . . .
>
> The preaching and practice of national, race or colour discrimination and contempt shall be a punishable crime;
> All apartheid laws and practices shall be set aside.
>
> . . .
>
> The national wealth of our country, the heritage of all South Africans, shall be restored to the people;
> The mineral wealth beneath the soil, the banks and monopoly industry shall be transferred to the ownership of the people as a whole;
> All other industries and trade shall be controlled to assist the well-being of the people.
>
> . . .

---

3. Stephen M. Davis, *Apartheid's Rebels: Inside South Africa's Hidden War* (New Haven, CT: Yale University Press, 1987), pp. 1–12.

> Restriction of land ownership on a racial basis shall be ended, and all the land re-divided amongst those who work it, to banish famine and land hunger.
>
> . . .
>
> No one shall be imprisoned, deported or restricted without a fair trial;
>
> . . .
>
> The law shall guarantee to all their right to speak, to organize, to meet together, to publish, to preach, to worship and to educate their children;
> The privacy of the house from police raids shall be protected by law;
> All shall be free to travel without restriction from countryside to town, from province to province, and from South Africa abroad;
> Pass laws, permits and all other laws restricting these freedoms shall be abolished.
>
> . . .
>
> Men and women of all races shall receive equal pay for equal work.
>
> . . .
>
> Free medical care and hospitalization shall be provided for all. . . .[4]

Nelson Mandela made it clear that he and his ANC colleagues considered the Charter "more than a mere list" of reforms. "It is a revolutionary document precisely because the changes it envisages cannot be won without breaking up the economic and political setup of present South Africa."[5] The government authorities agreed with this assessment, and in December 1956 they arrested Mandela and 155 other leaders of the anti-apartheid movement, accusing them of participating in a treasonable conspiracy inspired by international communism to overthrow the South African state by violent means. The treason trial dragged on five years until 1961 when the defendants were acquitted.

Meanwhile, the incarceration and treason trial of Mandela and his colleagues, rather than breaking the back of the movement, simply opened the way for the movement to be taken over by more radical black nationalists of the Pan Africanist Congress (PAC). It was a PAC-led, nationwide antipass demonstration, in which tens of thousands of blacks discarded their identifying passes and took to the streets to court arrest, that led to the so-called Sharpville Massacre of March 21, 1960.

Seventy-one blacks were killed and at least 200 were wounded when government police fired on the demonstrators at Sharpville, Vanderbijlpark, and Langa. In the days following, townships all around the country exploded in riots. With 30,000 angry blacks marching on

---

4. Text of the 1955 Freedom Charter in Mandela, *The Struggle Is My Life*, pp. 50–53.
5. Mandela, p. 55.

Cape Town, the government declared a state of emergency. In panic, under the authority of a hastily passed Unlawful Organizations Act, Prime Minister Hendrik Verwoerd banned both the ANC and PAC and dispatched government forces to break up their meetings and arrest their leaders. The government may have temporarily averted a breakdown of public order, but in its handling of the situation, Pretoria assured that the international human rights spotlight would be trained on its transgressions from then on.

International Condemnation and Sanctions

Ten days after Sharpville, the UN Security Council chastised the government of South Africa for bringing about the crisis and for disregarding resolutions of the General Assembly that had asked Pretoria to bring its policies into conformity with the UN Charter. In its resolution of April 1, 1960, the Security Council called upon the South African government "to initiate measures aimed at bringing about racial harmony based on equality in order to ensure that the present situation does not continue or recur, and to abandon its policies of apartheid and racial discrimination."[6]

The Security Council's admonitions to Pretoria were welcomed by the disenfranchised majority in South Africa, but words alone were not enough to induce the ruling minority to reverse its policies of increasing repression. Frustrated, the radical elements of the anti-apartheid movement now expanded their campaign of sabotage, insurgency, and escalating violence—actions which confirmed the suspicions of the most paranoid elements of the government that the ANC had been a front all along for violent revolutionaries and their international communist backers. A spiraling cycle of violent resistance and violent repression ending in full-scale civil war and foreign intervention now seemed almost unavoidable.

What started as a human rights issue had become a threat to international peace and security. On this ground and laying the blame squarely on the government of South Africa for "its determined aggravation of racial issues by enforcing measures of increasing ruthlessness involving violence and bloodshed," the UN General Assembly voted on November 6, 1962, to request all UN members to

- break off diplomatic relations with the Republic of South Africa

- close their ports to all vessels flying the South African flag

- prohibit their ships from entering South African ports

---

6. Resolution 134 of the UN Security Council, April 1, 1960; text in *The United Nations and Apartheid*, pp. 244–245.

- boycott all South African goods and refrain from exporting goods to South Africa

- refuse landing and passage facilities to all aircraft belonging to the government of South Africa and all companies registered under the laws of South Africa[7]

The Assembly also established a Special Committee on the Policies of Apartheid of the Republic of South Africa to "keep the racial policies of the Government of South Africa under review" and to report on compliance with the relevant UN resolutions.

Over the next few years many countries, in accordance with the General Assembly request, did substantially reduce their official political and economic relations with the Republic of South Africa, though few went so far as to totally break off relations. The United States joined the other members of the UN Security Council in calling for, and itself instituting, a ban on the sale and shipment of arms to South Africa. But most of the advanced industrialized countries refrained from preventing their private corporations from continuing to do nonmilitary business in South Africa.

Additionally, various UN bodies denied participation and services to the South African government. The International Labor Organization excluded the country's officials from its meetings. And, the Economic and Social Council voted to prevent the Republic of South Africa from taking part in the work of the Economic Commission for Africa until "conditions for constructive cooperation have been restored by a change in its racial policy."

For the remainder of the decade this combination of condemnatory resolutions and selective sanctions continued but to no avail; indeed, the regime in Pretoria seemed to be developing a siege mentality in reaction to its international isolation and to the success of anticolonial self-determination movements throughout the continent. For the time being, it was protected by a security belt in southern Africa of the Portuguese colonies of Angola and Mozambique and the white minority government in Rhodesia, and it did everything it could to help these regimes perpetuate themselves in power.

Domestically, the South African government pursued its opponents with new determination. In 1964 Nelson Mandela was one of those convicted and sentenced to life imprisonment for alleged acts of sabotage. A shocking blow to the morale and confidence of the anti-apartheid movement, the conviction of Mandela and his associates was followed by more factional splits within the ANC and a long period of regrouping,

---

7. Resolution 1761 of the UN General Assembly, November 6, 1962; text in ibid., p. 251.

much of it among secret underground societies preparing for the full-blown civil war that they now saw as their only hope.

The coming to power of the Nixon administration in the United States in 1969 ushered in an era of diminished pressure by the great powers on Pretoria that was consistent with the Nixon-Kissinger strategy of "selective relaxation" toward the remaining Portuguese and white regimes in Africa. But condemnations and sanctions from other international sources continued to grow. In 1970 the International Olympic Committee expelled South Africa for practicing racial discrimination in sports. In 1973 the UN General Assembly opened for signature the International Convention on the Suppression and Punishment of the Crime of Apartheid (the Convention received sufficient ratifications to come into force in 1976), branding apartheid as a crime against humanity; declaring as "criminal those organizations, institutions and individuals committing the crime of apartheid;" and authorizing state parties to the convention to try, in their own courts or by international tribunals, persons charged with the crime. In 1974, the General Assembly decided not to accept the credentials of the representatives of South Africa. The Security Council considered a resolution to expel South Africa from the United Nations, but the resolution was rejected as a result of the negative votes of the United States, the United Kingdom, and France.

The hopes of the United States and some of its allies that South Africa could be more effectively induced to reform its racist policies through increased international trade and contacts went up in smoke in June of 1976 in the fires of Soweto and during their aftermath. What began as a peaceful march of black schoolchildren demonstrating against the compulsory introduction of Afrikaans (the Dutch-derivative language of the dominant white supremacist group) turned into a spiral of violence and arson as government police charged into the ranks of the children and ripped up their placards. News of the violence in Soweto sparked rioting and counterviolence by police in at least 160 black communities in the ensuing weeks and months. By the time the Soweto-instigated eruptions played themselves out, as many as 1,000 blacks had been killed by government security forces. The post-Soweto cycle claimed the life of the internationally famous black nationalist leader Steve Biko, who was beaten and tortured to death during his interrogation by the police.[8]

Pretoria's political strategy for averting civil war and containing international condemnation now emphasized the creation of ostensibly autonomous black "Bantustans" within the larger white-run union. But the majority in the United Nations rejected this as a ruse and over the

---

8. Davis, *Apartheid's Rebels,* pp. 26–27.

next few years passed a series of resolutions branding such instances of "self-determination" as invalid.

The Final International Squeeze

The ruthlessness of the South African campaign against the anti-apartheid movement drove many of the ANC activists into foreign exile—especially to London, where new resources and recruits could be mobilized and plans could be devised for resuming the struggle in Africa. The latter 1970s seemed propitious for laying the groundwork for a full-blown war of national liberation since, given the collapse of the last redoubts of Portuguese colonialism in Angola and Mozambique and the installation of a black majority regime in Zimbabwe, attacks could now be launched from the territory of the states surrounding South Africa.

Much of the military infrastructure for the anticipated war of liberation was already in place in the bases and supply lines constructed by the Cuban troops who had been airlifted into southern Africa by the Soviets to help the anti-Portuguese forces during the last phase of their successful struggle. Thousands of Cuban troops stayed on to help the new black governments fend off counterrevolutionary remnants supported by Pretoria and, not incidentally, to provide logistics support and protection for the buildup of ANC forces preparing to liberate South Africa and for raids by the Southwest African Peoples Organization (SWAPO) into Namibia.

The Reagan administration, presiding over U.S. foreign policy for most of the 1980s, was less hostile to the South African government (which it regarded as a valuable Cold War ally) and more suspicious of the communist connections of the ANC than had been the human rights–championing Carter administration. But fearful of becoming trapped in an embarrassing, and potentially dangerous, special alliance with the white supremacist regime, particularly as South Africa's military confrontations with neighboring black-ruled states threatened to escalate into a hot war, the Reagan administration announced a policy of "constructive engagement"; that is, a policy where Washington too would work to persuade Pretoria to reform its apartheid policies but where Reagan (soon to be seconded by Britain's new prime minister, Margaret Thatcher) would rely more on the carrots of increased commerce and restored international legitimacy than the sticks of economic embargoes and political ostracism.

The Reaganites were inclined to credit South Africa's constitutional reform of 1983—establishing a tricameral parliament, with one house each for whites, coloreds, and Indians (but providing no representation for blacks)—as a gradual but significant step toward multiracial democracy. The UN majority, however, regarded the 1983 reforms as a transparent hoax and responded with the harshest yet of all the General Assembly resolutions against Pretoria.

Once again, calling apartheid "a grave menace to international peace and security" and "a crime against humanity," the December 1983 General Assembly resolution charged:

> The racist regime of South Africa, in its efforts to consolidate and perpetuate racist domination and exploitation, has forcibly moved and deported over 3 million people from their homes. It has imprisoned many millions of Africans under humiliating "pass laws". . . .
>
> In an effort to suppress resistance against its inhuman policies, it has banned many organizations and imprisoned . . . thousands of persons. Scores of persons have died of torture in detention. . . .
>
> The apartheid regime has not hesitated to resort to massacres, even of schoolchildren. . . .
>
> . . .
>
> It has, moreover, committed numerous acts of aggression, destabilization and terrorism against neighboring independent African States. . . .
>
> . . .
>
> It has amassed military equipment and acquired nuclear weapon capability, with the support of certain Western countries and Israel, thereby posing an enormous threat to Africa and the world.[9]

The time had come, said the General Assembly majority, for "outraged world opinion" to "translate these [UN] declarations and resolutions into universal action" against not only the government of South Africa but against all governments and corporations that continue to collaborate or engage in commerce with the regime in Pretoria. In addition to expanding the economic embargoes and sanctions to be applied and tightened by member governments and international organizations, the December 1983 resolution urged nongovernmental groups and organizations (corporations, labor unions, churches, educational institutions, artists, writers, and musicians) around the world to cease all positive interaction with the regime in Pretoria and with any businesses and private groups in South Africa that were associated with the regime and its policies. Endorsing pressure tactics devised by some church groups in the West, the resolution urged stockholders in corporations with investments in South Africa that were directly or indirectly perpetuating the apartheid regime to demand that these corporations divest any such funds and that institutions holding stocks in any corporations which continued to support the regime should immediately sell off their holdings in these corporations.[10]

---

9.   Resolution 38/39 B of the UN General Assembly , December 5, 1983; text in *United Nations and Apartheid*, pp. 379–380.

10. Ibid., pp. 385–389.

If the South African power elite were to be substantially hurt by the economic sanctions, those in the private sector—especially the huge U.S.-based transnational corporations and banks—would have to cooperate. And in the last half of the 1980s, this kind of decisive pressure did indeed materialize.

An ominous sign for the defenders of apartheid was Citibank's 1985 decision to refrain from making any more loans to the South African government. The next year Barclays Bank of the United Kingdom followed suit by cutting off all new lending to the government in Pretoria. Meanwhile key national governments were tightening the financial squeeze: France announced a ban on all new investments in South Africa, and in 1986 the Democratic-controlled U.S. Congress overrode President Reagan's veto of the Comprehensive Anti-Apartheid Act. In accordance with the Comprehensive Anti-Apartheid Act's disincentives for private investments, many large U.S. corporations with subsidiaries in South Africa, now a high-risk area for capital, began to shut down their operations.

The refusal of the major international banks to extend loans and the drying up of investments from abroad turned influential members of the South African business community into advocates of political reform. Starting in about 1987, the restoration of the country's international legitimacy became the highest imperative of many of the country's largest industrialists and political pragmatists within the government.[11]

Pretoria's Turn Toward Human Rights and Democracy

The ascendancy of the pragmatists in the government was signalled by the resignation of President P. W. Botha in the summer of 1989 and his replacement as National Party leader by F. W. de Klerk. In February 1990, President de Klerk, who for months had been engaged in secret negotiations with Nelson Mandela, surprised the world with his historic pronouncements rescinding the 30-year ban on the ANC and other anti-apartheid organizations and freeing long-imprisoned political prisoners, including Nelson Mandela.

The next few years featured a fitful dismantling of the segregationist regime and gradual progress toward the one-person–one-vote multiparty democracy that would bring South Africa into compliance with UN covenants and resolutions. The difficult negotiations between the government, led by de Klerk, and the ANC, once again led by Mandela,

---

11. Heribert Adam and Kogila Moodley, *The Opening of the Apartheid Mind: Options for the New South Africa* (Berkeley, CA: University of California Press, 1993), pp. 52–58.

were occasionally derailed by outbursts of violence provoked by extremists on both sides; but the direction was set, and the end of apartheid was finally in sight. As early as July 1991, President George Bush announced that South Africa had met the conditions for lifting the U.S. trade and economic sanctions prescribed by the Comprehensive Anti-Apartheid Act of 1986.

In December 1991, delegations representative of all major groups in the country convened in Johannesburg as the Convention for a Democratic South Africa (CODESA) with the objective of drafting, pending the adoption of a permanent constitution in 1999, an interim constitution for the country. Nearly two years later, CODESA issued the interim constitution and scheduled universal-suffrage elections for April 1994 to select the first post-apartheid government. Crediting this breakthrough, Nelson Mandela asked the United Nations in the fall of 1993 to begin lifting its economic sanctions but to maintain various special sanctions relating to arms, nuclear matters, and oil until the new democratically elected government was installed.

The April 1994 elections were, as expected, an overwhelming victory for the ANC. The interim constitution went into force, and a democratic, nonracial government was installed with Nelson Mandela as president and F. W. de Klerk as a deputy president. In his first state-of-the-nation address, President Mandela announced that South Africa henceforth would accede to all the human rights conventions of the United Nations; faithfully implementing their provisions, however, would pose new challenges, particularly with respect to guaranteeing the civil and property rights of the white minority and dealing with the self-determination demands of various tribal groups.

The Constitution now in force in South Africa, while containing one of the most extensive bill of rights in the world, has not disposed of some of these challenges. Adopted overwhelmingly by the multiracial but ANC-dominated parliament on May 8, 1996, the new Constitution was pronounced flawed by Deputy President de Klerk on the very next day as he resigned and pulled his nearly all-white National Party out of the coalition government headed by Mandela. De Klerk was dissatisfied with the Constitution's lack of provision for joint decision making between the parties, which the National Party had demanded as protection against the possibility of the one-person–one-vote electoral system producing a tyrannical black majority government. And de Klerk, along with Inkatha Freedom Party Chief Mangosuthu Buthelezi, the separatist Zulu provincial leader, was also displeased with the degree of autonomy to be permitted provincial governments and other ethnic enclaves within the federal union.

A controversial move of the new government was its establishment of a Truth and Reconciliation Commission for interrogating and granting amnesty to confessed perpetrators of human rights abuses during the apartheid era. Its remarkably even-handed proceedings have found brutal human rights violations on both sides of the anti-apartheid struggle, but many families of the victims resent the amnesty approach and are demanding prosecutions and punishments.

A symptom of post-apartheid ethnic rights problems to come was the still-unresolved question of the language of instruction in the schools in white Afrikaans-speaking localities. Another contentious issue pitted claims of property rights against the socialist orientation of the ANC. These problems, however, are issues that the international community tends to leave to national societies to work out on their own.

CHINA'S DEFLECTION OF WESTERN PRESSURE

The ability of the People's Republic of China to squelch its domestic critics, while fending off external critics of its human rights performance, provides the principal contemporary example of the persisting primacy in international diplomacy of traditional security and economic considerations. It also provides an exasperating case study of how an autocratic regime that other national governments are afraid to alienate can do and, for the most part, still does what it wants to the people in its jurisdiction. These confirmations of the dominance of materialistic power considerations are not very surprising. What is potentially of greater significance for the evolving world polity is the fact of the Chinese government's sensitivity to international criticisms of its human rights record and the intensity of its diplomacy to deflect such criticism. The Chinese leaders know that dictatorships in modern societies cannot survive a collapse in legitimacy in the minds of their own constituents—a fact their counterparts in the former Soviet sphere (the USSR and the communist regimes of Eastern and Central Europe) found out too late to save themselves—and that therefore, given today's global mobility of information and people, what the external world thinks of China can be internally explosive.

The Primacy of Geopolitics

Although in the high Cold War decades of the 1950s and 1960s the totalitarian character of Communist China figured prominently in the rhetoric of the West, especially that of the U.S. government, policy makers and publics had no expectation that the regime in Beijing was likely to change its repressive ways. Then, ironically, Mao Zedong's surprise opening to the West in the late 1960s and early 1970s, which led to the Washington-Beijing rapprochement of 1972, took virtually all the external pressure off the regime to liberalize its internal dictatorship. During most of the 1970s and 1980s—under the geopolitical imperative of balancing Soviet power in Eurasia—successive U.S. administrations and their international allies tended to hear no evil, see no evil, and speak no evil concerning even the most brutal policies of the "People's Republic."

Bush's "Realism"

With the waning of Soviet expansionism in the late 1980s, however, the champions of human rights had reason to hope that Washington's geopolitically motivated protectiveness toward Beijing would be lifted. The moment seemed to have arrived for a policy turnaround in June 1989 with the Chinese army's repression of student prodemocracy demonstrators in Tiananmen Square, which was broadcast into American homes by CNN and other international media. But the Bush administration's "realistic" approach to international relations for the emerging post–Cold War era was premised on mutually respectful relationships among the governments of the major military and economic powers, and this approach had little room for reactions to Tiananmen that could interfere with the carefully nurtured U.S.-China relationship.

To assuage the outrage in the United States at the brutal action of the Chinese soldiers (outrage heightened as some media reported as many as one thousand student demonstrators were killed), President Bush did issue a brief public rebuke, deploring "the use of force against citizens who were making a public statement in favor of democracy," to the authorities in Beijing. Coming under immediate criticism for not taking a stronger stand, Bush followed up with tangible sanctions: suspension of weapons sales to China, suspension of visits by high-level U.S. and Chinese officials, and suspension of technical exchanges with the Chinese military. Yet when asked by the press why he wasn't also imposing economic sanctions, the President explained that

> I don't want to hurt the Chinese people. I happen to believe that the commercial contacts have led. . . to this quest for more freedom. . . . I would argue with those who want to do something more flamboyant, because I feel that this relationship is vital to the United States of America.[12]

Behind the scenes, administration officials attempted to reassure their Chinese counterparts that business could go on as usual. Barely a month after Tiananmen, Bush sent National Security Adviser Brent Snowcroft and Deputy Secretary of State Lawrence Eagleberger on a secret mission to Beijing to work out the modalities of putting Sino-U.S. relations back on track. For the Chinese, the big test of the Bush administration's professions of continued friendship was its ability to fend off Congressional efforts to deny China normal trading privileges—accorded

---

12. George Bush's statements of June 3 and June 5, 1989, *Weekly Compilation of Presidential Documents*, Vol. 25, no. 23 (Washington, DC: GPO, 1989), pp. 838–843.

under most-favored-nation (MFN) status—in the U.S. market. Beijing was not to be disappointed as Bush repeatedly threatened to veto the punitive legislation. The administration's argument, made time and time again, was that not only would the denial of MFN status for China produce a general worsening of U.S.-Chinese relations but that it would also hurt important U.S. economic groups, including aircraft manufacturers, wheat farmers, and fertilizer companies.

Bush's success in reassuring the Chinese was purchased at some domestic political cost to him, however. Congressional Democrats charged that the administration's China policy was a throwback to the Nixon-Kissinger amoral realpolitik. And in the presidential-candidate debates in the 1992 election, Bill Clinton recalled how "all those kids went out there carrying the Statue of Liberty in Tiananmen Square, and Mr. Bush sent two people in secret to toast the Chinese leaders and basically tell them not to worry about it." Bush's rebuttal was that Congress and Clinton wanted to isolate China and by "putting conditions on MFN and kind of humiliating them . . . you . . . turn them inward, and then we've made a terrible mistake. I'm not going to do it."[13]

Clinton's Retreat

Consistent with his election campaign pledges to deny China MFN status unless there was clear evidence of substantial betterment of the human rights situation in the country, President Clinton, a few weeks after his inauguration, sent a stern letter to the government in Beijing that stipulated various reforms it had to institute if it were to continue receiving normal trading privileges. The bill of particulars included the release of political prisoners, a cessation of inhumane treatment of prisoners, the permission of international radio and television broadcasts to China, and substantial cultural autonomy for Tibet. But by the late spring deadline for his recommendation to Congress on the trade issue, Clinton began to have second thoughts about making human rights the linchpin of the U.S.-China relationship. He asked for another year's extension of MFN for China, ostensibly to give Beijing time to accommodate to the new seriousness about human rights in the White House but in reality to allow the new administration to undertake a full-dress review of its overall China policy.[14]

The comprehensive reassessment focused on China's growing impact on both the world's economy and global political-military relationships.

---

13. From presidential debate in St. Louis, October 11, 1992, ibid., Vol. 28, no. 42, pp. 1914–1915.
14. This early shift in the Clinton administration's thinking about China is analyzed in Seyom Brown, *The Faces of Power: Constancy and Change in United States Foreign Policy from Truman to Clinton* (New York: Columbia University Press, 1994).

China wanted access to the U.S. market, but U.S. exporters also wanted access to China's 1.2 billion consumers. Some economist were speculating that before the middle of the next century, China's gross domestic product, international trade, and market share could make it the number-one economy in the world.

With a larger army than any other nation and as the only Third World country with a major nuclear-weapons capability, China was now more than ever a crucial component of both the Asian and global balances of military power. Additionally, China had become a big player in the global arms market, and her cooperation was crucial to the Clinton administration's policy of discouraging the sale of advanced weapons, particularly long-range missiles that could be outfitted with nuclear or chemical warheads, to Third World clients. An alienated China would also be less likely to help hold the line against the further spread of nuclear weapons—a concern that became acute for the Clinton administration just a few months after it assumed office when North Korea announced its intention to withdraw from the Nuclear Non-Proliferation Treaty.

The result of the China-policy review was a shift in grand strategy—though not publicly presented as such—away from reprimanding Beijing for its human rights violations and toward drawing China more fully into a web of international and transnational relationships. In accordance with the new strategy, Clinton agreed to meet in November 1993 with China's president, Jiang Zemin, at the November Asia-Pacific Economic Conference in order to open a new high-level dialogue on improving Sino-U.S. relations.

The administration's position was not that it was downgrading the significance of human rights but that for China the better route to a more open and democratic society was through the modernization that would come with increasing integration into the world capitalist system. "Engagement" rather than "containment" became the new byword in Washington.

When the annual ritual of considering MFN status for China came around again in the spring of 1994, Clinton recommended the extension, with virtually no conditions attached for future extensions, despite the fact that the State Department's report to Congress on China's human rights record showed little, if any, improvements over the year. Clinton's announcement made it clear that his administration would no longer use the MFN privilege as a lever to compel Beijing to make progress on human rights.

Again, administration officials stressed that they had not abandoned the cause of human rights in China. They were merely switching to the presumably more productive path of stabilizing the basic relationship with Beijing and of providing incentives for the Chinese to further transform their socialist system into a capitalist economy while relying mostly on quiet diplomacy and private channels to persuade the regime to enlarging the scope of political freedom.

Almost two years after MFN was "delinked" from human rights, however, the U.S. Department of State was unable to tell the White House and the Congress that the policy of official Sino-U.S. respectfulness was working as hoped. The Department's annual country report on human rights practice in China, submitted to the Congress in March 1996, concluded that the Chinese government was continuing to commit "widespread and well-documented human rights abuses in violation of internationally accepted norms, stemming both from the authorities' intolerance of dissent and the inadequacy of legal safeguards for basic freedoms."

A sampling from the detailed report of abuses gives some specific examples:

> The [Chinese] Government still has not provided a comprehensive, credible public accounting of all those missing or detained in connection with the suppression of the 1989 demonstrations. . . .
>
> . . .
>
> Former detainees have credibly reported that officials [in order to obtain confessions] used cattle prods, electrodes, prolonged periods of solitary confinement and incommunicado detention, beating, shackles and other forms of abuse. . . .
>
> . . .
>
> In theory [China's] Administrative Procedure Law permits a detainee to challenge the legality of his or her detention. In practice, however, lack of access to legal counsel inhibits the effective use of this law. . . .
>
> . . .
>
> Although the Constitution states that freedom of speech and freedom of the press are fundamental rights enjoyed by all citizens, the Government interprets the Communist Party's "leading role" as circumscribing these rights. It does not permit citizens to publish or broadcast criticism of senior leaders or opinions that contradict basic Communist Party doctrine. . . .
>
> . . .
>
> While the Constitution has provisions for freedom of peaceful assembly and association, the Government severely restricts these rights in practice. The Constitution provides, for example, that activities may not infringe upon the "interests of the State." Protests against the political system or its leaders are prohibited.
>
> . . .
>
> The Government continued to implement comprehensive and highly intrusive family planning policies . . . [which rely] on education, propaganda, and economic incentives as well as more coercive methods. . . .Disciplinary measures . . . include fines, withholding social services, demotion, and . . . loss of employment.
>
> . . .

> There are no independent Chinese organizations that publicly monitor or comment on human rights conditions in China. The Government has made it clear that it will not tolerate the existence of such groups.
>
> . . .
>
> The Government permitted increased international correspondence and information access when commercial accounts became available in May [1995]. . . . [New] regulations appear to be designed to impose the same restrictions on internet as now limit public discourse in China.[15]

Human rights groups and the press took every opportunity to wave such violations in front of the Clinton administration as evidence of the naïveté (or cynicism) of its arguments for democratizing China through increased commercial intercourse. Embarrassed, and prodded by congressional riders to various bills, pro–human rights officers in the administration tried to ensure that U.S. diplomats and delegates to international forums would seek out opportunities to implement the engagement part of the constructive-engagement strategy. But it was not clear that the president really wanted to do anything that might interfere with the burgeoning U.S.-China commerce; and without firm presidential backing, conveyed to other heads of state as well as to U.S. negotiators, U.S. protestations that greater access by the Chinese to global trading and capital markets must be accompanied by progress on human rights lacked credibility. Instead, the world was treated to a sequence of China-U.S. meetings at the cabinet, vice-presidential, and presidential levels in which, according to the U.S. participants, human rights issues were discussed but which produced no reform commitments the Chinese would publicly accept.

Nor were U.S. partners in the Group of Seven advanced industrial countries inclined to alienate the managers of the world's fastest growing economy. In 1995 meetings of a European Union/China Joint Committee were planned for long-term enlargement of Sino-European economic relationships, and the Western European heads of state competed with one another for invitations to President Jiang Zemin to visit their countries.

Evidently emboldened by the competitive kowtowing among the rival capitalist powers, Beijing became in the last half of 1995 considerably more confrontational with Washington—not only on human rights issues but also on other matters, such as fair trade practices and

---

15. U.S. Department of State, *Country Reports on Human Rights Practices for 1995*; submitted to the Committee on International Relations, U.S. House of Representatives, and the Committee on Foreign Relations, U.S. Senate (Washington, DC: GPO, 1996), pp. 574–594.

international armaments transfers, about which the United States had been pushing China.

The Chinese government's rearrest of and denial of due process to prominent dissidents in November 1995 garnered official U.S. reprimands that, even though they were perfunctory, provoked new angry allegations from Beijing that Washington was trying to interfere in the domestic affairs of other countries. Popular outrage in the United States was reflected in a *New York Times* editorial stating that "it is now clear that the White House's muted concern about Chinese human rights abuses has only encouraged Beijing to pursue a Stalinist policy of repression."[16]

Meanwhile, the electronics software industry was pressing U.S. trade officials to sanction or retaliate against the Chinese for pirating copyrighted material. At the same time, U.S. arms control specialists were prodding the administration to implement congressional legislation that would deny financial credits to China for her foreign sales of advanced missile and nuclear technologies in violation of international arms control accords.

All this was taking place in the midst of escalating Sino-U.S. tensions over the posturing of high Taiwanese officials, in advance of Taiwan's spring 1996 general elections, in the direction of greater autonomy (possibly even eventual independence) for the island nation. China's threats to use military force to keep its "province of Taiwan" in line—made all too real by her live missile exercises in the Taiwan Straits in the week before the Taiwanese election—were countered by a redeployment of major U.S. aircraft carriers toward the Straits.

By the middle of April 1996, with the Taiwanese elections over, relations between Taiwan and the mainland had simmered down. But popular passions in the United States had been rekindled to a level not seen since the Tiananmen Square massacre. Although official Washington and Beijing must have hoped for a rapid return to normalcy (meaning an emphasis on commercial negotiations), the human rights constituency was now highly exercised. Responsive to the national mood, the Clinton administration revealed that it would be taking a strong line on the human rights situation in China at the forthcoming annual meeting of the United Nations Human Rights Commission. Predictably, Beijing bristled and blasted the United States in numerous international forums, particularly those in the Third World, as an arrogant, imperialist, ignorant, and disrespectful of other cultures.

In the April 1966 session of the Human Rights Commission, the Chinese were able to marshal sufficient support to prevent a vote on the U.S.-sponsored resolution taking note of complaints that China had

---

16. "The Misrule of Law in China," *New York Times*, November 23, 1995.

instituted "severe restrictions on the rights of citizens to freedom of assembly, association, expression, religion as well as to due legal processes and fair trial" and had subjected dissidents to long-term imprisonment for nonviolent acts. The resolution would have mandated that the Commission keep a watch on China and issue a public report on its findings at the Commission's 1997 session. Appealing to other Third World countries, the Chinese delegate, Wu Jianmin, warned, "What is happening to China today will happen to any other developing country tomorrow." Disappointed at the outcome, the U.S. delegate, Assistant Secretary of State John Shattuck, vilified the Chinese maneuver of preventing serious consideration of its record as "an assault on the basic integrity of the Commission." The United States delegation was particularly chagrined at the fact that not only traditional autocratic regimes but also leading Third World democracies, such as India, supported China's position.[17]

Nor did the Group of Seven industrial countries give the United States the solid and visible backing it wanted in its efforts in 1996 and 1997 to call Beijing to account before the Human Rights Commission. This timidity reflected the not-incidental fact that their own commercial negotiations with China had been intensifying while Sino-U.S. relations were deteriorating.[18]

Expressions of displeasure with China's human rights violations were voiced in the 1996 U.S. elections by candidates of both political parties. But as he got back to business at the start of his second term, President Clinton continued to hold his ground against the critics. With a letter of support in hand from three former presidents—George Bush, Gerald Ford, and, yes, human rights champion Jimmy Carter—the president once again successfully urged the Congress not to revoke China's MFN trading status. As explained to the Senate Finance Committee by Secretary of State Madeleine Albright,

> If the United States, the world's largest and most open economy, were to deny China's normal trading relationship, China's stake in the international system would shrink. The consequences would be grave indeed.
>
> First, . . . we could lose China's critical cooperation on dismantling North Korea's nuclear program. . . .
>
> Second, . . . It would disrupt our initiatives to curtail China's transfers of advanced weaponry to unstable regions.
>
> Third, we would risk losing Chinese support for U.S. initiatives at the UN—including . . . peacekeeping and sanctions on Iraq. And

17. Barbara Crosette, "China Outflanks U.S. to Avoid Scrutiny of Its Human Rights," *New York Times* (April 24, 1996).
18. On China's economic courtship of the Europeans, see William J. Dobson, "China's Europe Card," *New York Times* (April 13, 1996).

China, destined to displace the United States as the largest producer of greenhouse gases, could withhold its participation in a global agreement on preventing climate change. . . .

Fourth, the withdrawal of MFN would devastate our economic relationship. It would invite Chinese retaliation against our exports . . . [and] would also damage future opportunities for American investment, as China would steer contracts to our many economic competitors. . . .

Fifth, the damage to our commercial ties would well spill over into our efforts to improve human rights in China. Because non-state firms account for half of China's exports, the revocation of MFN would weaken the most progressive elements of Chinese society. It would also create a tense atmosphere in which Chinese leaders might be even less likely to take the actions we have been encouraging to release political dissidents, to allow international visits to prisoners and to open talks with the Dalai Lama on increasing Tibetan autonomy. . . .

. . .

In sum, revoking a normal trade relationship could seriously undermine our ability to influence China's development and instead turn China further in the direction of isolation, suspicion and hostility.[19]

But the policy of constructive engagement, the Clinton administration hastened to assure Congressional critics from both parties, did not mean approval of Beijing's human rights performance. Rather, the policy was portrayed as the preferable *means* for opening up China's political system, by drawing it further into communication and dialogue with governments and nongovernmental groups committed to proposition that capitalism and democracy need one another to function effectively. Meanwhile, if the leaders in both countries could be relieved of the fear that Sino-U.S. economic and strategic cooperation would be held hostage to the human rights issue, their differences over human rights might be able to be explored even more openly.

Indeed, as if to confirm the premise that constructive engagement could allow for a more candid U.S.-Chinese dialogue on human rights, an unprecedented public argument ensued between President Clinton and President Jiang during their fall 1997 summit meeting in Washington in response to a reporter's question on the legacy of the Tiananmen Square episode.

PRESIDENT JIANG: The political disturbances that occurred . . . in 1989 seriously disrupted social stability and state security. Therefore, the Chinese Government had to take necessary mea-

---

19. Statement of Secretary of State Madeleine K. Albright before the Senate Finance Committee, June 10, 1997 (Department of State Press Release).

sures, according to law, to quickly resolve the matter to ensure that our country enjoys stability and that our reforms and opening up proceeds smoothly.

The Communist Party of China and the Chinese Government have long drawn the correct conclusion on this political disturbance, and facts have also proved that if a country with an over 2.2 billion population does not enjoy social and political stability, it cannot possibly have the situation of reform and opening up that we are having today.

Thank you.

PRESIDENT CLINTON: . . . I think it should be obvious to everyone that we have a very different view of the meaning of the events and Tiananmen Square. I believe that what happened and the aftermath and the continuing reluctance to tolerate political dissent has kept China from politically developing the level of support in the rest of the world that otherwise would have been developed.[20]

Following the Jiang-Clinton verbal confrontation, however, both governments took new initiatives toward removing the human rights issue as an irritant in their thickening relationship. In response to Beijing's release from prison of a number of prominent political dissidents on medical grounds, its limited cooperation with the International Red Cross's efforts to gain access to China's jails, and its promise to sign the Covenant on Political and Civil Rights, the Clinton administration in March 1998 abandoned its annual campaign to get the UN Commission on Human Rights to censure China for human rights violations.

Human rights advocacy groups charged that the 1998 backing off by the Clinton administration in the UN Commission was a return to Bush's approach toward human rights abuses in China of "hear no evil, see no evil, and speak no evil." But U.S. officials insisted they were continuing in bilateral negotiations, where real bargaining can take place, to press China for reforms.

In the 1999 meeting of the UN Human Rights Commission, however—a meeting that followed a new State Department report scathingly condemning China's lack of significant progress on human rights—the United States shifted ground and joined in a resolution condemning China for its violations of human rights. Although only a symbolic move, itself carrying no attached sanctions, this shift in U.S. policy reflected changes occurring in the domestic support base for Clinton's constructive-engagement policy. Sectors of the broad coalition of commercial interests that had backed the delinking of trade and human rights issues were becoming increasingly dissatisfied with Beijing's foot-dragging on measures to open up the Chinese market to U.S. goods and

---

20. News conference of President Clinton and President Jiang, October 29, 1997, *Weekly Compilation of Presidential Documents,* Vol. 33., no. 44, p. 1677.

investments, even as the huge U. S. trade deficit with China continued to widen. In a concession to this increasing discontent, coupled with complaints from firms and labor unions in textile-producing states that the flood of Chinese textiles into the U.S. market was causing an alarming rate of bankruptcies, President Clinton in April 1999 announced he was still not ready to support China's long-standing bid to enter the World Trade Organization (WTO). This announcement surprised and embarrassed Chinese Prime Minister Zhu Rongji whose visit to the United States was premised on the expectation of a joint communiqué featuring WTO membership for China. The growing sourness on Sino-U.S. relations in the commercial sectors coincided with new concerns among defense and arms-control experts about Chinese military intentions and programs. These concerns were heightened in early 1999 by charges that China was engaged in a larger than suspected espionage operation and had stolen nuclear weapons secrets from the Los Alamos National Laboratory in New Mexico. There were also worries that the Chinese were converting technologies presumably purchased for commercial space satellites to military use and, in particular, to improving the accuracy of their strategic missiles. (In addition, there were allegations that agents for some of the participating firms had made illegitimate contributions to the Clinton-Gore election campaign.)[21]

Did the emergent economic and security tensions with China free President Clinton to take a more confrontational stance on human rights issues—in accordance with his own values? Or was such an interpretation wishful thinking on the part of human rights activists? A more realistic interpretation is that the tougher U.S. stance on human rights in 1999 was only a bargaining ploy for leveraging Chinese accommodation of U.S. economic and strategic interests.

THE CAMPAIGN AGAINST FEMALE GENITAL MUTILATION

The international campaigns against apartheid and genocide have been able to command nearly universal support—support among those in the North, South, East and West; among secularists and theocrats; and among devotees of virtually every religious and ethical worldview. And they have given rise to significant permutations of the norms and structures of the state-sovereignty system. Notably, the acts targeted by these

---

21. Jeff Gerth and David E. Sanger, "Citing Security, U.S. Spurns China on Satellite Deal," *New York Times* (February 23, 1999); David E. Sanger, "U.S. to Back the Censure of Beijing Over Rights," *New York Times* (March 27, 1999); James Risen, "White House Said to Ignore Evidence of China Spying," *New York Times* (April 13, 1999).

campaigns have been brutalities and violations of human dignity inflicted by one community or ethno-national group against another.

By contrast, the acts opposed in the campaign against female genital mutilation (FGM) are primarily acts inflicted by members of particular cultural communities against other members of their own communities. The physical procedures and rituals in question tend to be defended by cultural authorities in these communities as essential and valuable parts of their traditions. As such, they have generated controversy that, as much as any issue before the international community, involves a collision of universalist and relativist approaches to human rights. Moreover, the controversy centers on practices in the private sphere (as distinct from the public sphere) for which, even if they are held to be in violation of various international covenants, it is difficult to prescribe remedies that can be internationally monitored or enforced.

The Offending Acts

Throughout much of Africa and in many countries in the Middle East and Southeast Asia, there are many communities in which girls and young women are compelled by their families and community traditions to endure the cutting away and alteration of parts of their genitalia so as to make them eligible wives.[22] The operations, usually performed by older women of the community specializing in these rituals, may involve any or some combination of the following procedures: partial or total removal of the clitoris and removal or excision of outer and inner lips of the vulva and a stitching together of its two sides—a procedure called infibulation—that leaves only a small opening for the passage of urine or menstrual blood (the opening is enlarged just prior to the woman's marriage).

In rural areas these clitoridectomies and infibulations are often performed with rudimentary tools such as knives, razor blades, or even splinters of glass and without anesthesia. In some urban areas the procedures may be performed by medical professionals with the use of anaesthetics.[23]

Defenders of the genital alterations typically claim that they guarantee the woman's virginity—the infibulation making premarital coitus impossible and the clitoridectomy reducing her sexual desire—up until her wedding night. The removal or reduction of the clitoris is also supposed to reduce the woman's sexual appetite after marriage and thus lessen the likelihood of promiscuity. Another presumed benefit is the

---

22. Credible estimates by researchers range as high as 2 million of such operations each year and add up to a total of nearly 115 million girls and women who have been genitally mutilated. Nahid Toubia, "Female Genital Mutilation," *Women's Rights, Human Rights: International Feminist Perspectives* (New York: Routledge, 1995), p. 224.

23. Efua Dorkenoo, *Cutting the Rose* (London: Minority Rights Group, 1994).

enhancement of the husband's pleasure (the result of the wife's loss of interest in clitoral stimulation, allowing her to focus on vaginal intercourse). Some traditional justifications also claim—contrary to all medical evidence—that clitoridectomy improves fertility and prevents maternal and infant mortality.[24]

What has been established by medical evidence is the substantial risks to the woman's physical health emanating from these surgical procedures and their after-effects. These include hemorrhage leading to anemia and death, acute infections, chronic infections causing infertility, dangerous blockages of menstruation and urination, major obstetric complications including the inability to dilate during childbirth, and increased susceptibility to HIV infection and AIDS.[25] As yet there has been little research on the psychological consequences to the affected women, most of whom are poor and are not likely to avail themselves of psychiatric counselling, but most medical professionals who have begun to study and treat women who have had their genitalia mutilated are convinced there are severe implications for psychological health from the trauma and shock of the procedure itself, let alone from the physiological and sexual after-effects.[26]

A Politically Charged Controversy

Physicians and medical researchers who brought the health consequences of FGM to the attention of the World Health Organization (WHO) in the 1970s were dismayed at the strength of the opposition even to the discussion of the problem. But at a WHO seminar held in Khartoum in 1979, Western feminists, armed with information supplied by the Women's International Network (WIN), were able to pass a reso-

---

24. Toubia, "Female Genital Mutilation," p. 231.
25. From medical reports that were gathered by Kristin Foellmer in "Female Genital Mutilation" (Senior Honors Thesis, Brandeis University, 1996) and include K. P. Bimal, "Maternal Mortality in Africa: 1980–1987," *Social Science and Medicine* 37 (1993); J. A. Black and G. D. Debelle, "Female Genital Mutilation in Britain," *British Medical Journal* 310 (1995); Colette Gallard, "Female Genital Mutilation in France," ibid.; Mary McCaffey, "Female Genital Mutilation: Consequences for Reproductive and Sexual Health," *Sexual and Marital Therapy* 10, 2 (United Kingdom, 1995); and Nadia Toubia, "Female Genital Mutilation and the Responsibility of Reproductive Health Professionals," *International Journal of Gynecology and Obstetrics* 46, 2 (1944); D. B. Hardy, "Cultural Practices Contributing to the Transmission of Human Immunodeficiency Virus in Africa, " *Review of Infectious Diseases* 9 (1987); and Fran P. Hoskin, "Medical Facts and Summary," in *The Hoskin Report: Genital and Sexual Mutilation of Females* (Lexington, MA: Routlege, 1990).
26. Toubia, "Female Genital Mutilation," pp. 229–230.

lution calling for the rapid abolition of FGM. Many participants from African nations, however, were appalled at the aggressiveness of WIN militants and accused them of insensitivity toward their African sisters that was reminiscent of the arrogance of the colonial imperialists who tried to impose Western cultural norms on the peoples they subjugated. Similar confrontations occurred at the 1980 UN Conference on Women, held in Copenhagen, and in various UN bodies. The Western delegates were increasingly able to get the topic on the agenda (for example, the Working Group on Slavery of the UN Commission on Human Rights considered FGM for the first time in 1981) but often at the cost of alienating even some of the Western-educated women from the Third World countries who wanted to eradicate the practice in their countries.[27]

These politically sophisticated women counseled their Western counterparts that progress in reducing FGM would come less from official admonitions by world forums and more from educational efforts conducted by women leaders and health care professionals from within the Third World countries. This more culturally respectful approach was symbolized by the appointment in 1983 of Mrs. Halima Embarek Warzazi of Morocco by the UN Subcommission on the Prevention of Discrimination and the Protection of Minorities to study FGM. Meanwhile, WIN and other transnational, nongovernmental organizations promoting women's reproductive and sexual rights began to direct their efforts both toward helping their counterparts around the world to gain and disseminate information on the health consequences of FGM (including psychological ones) and toward lobbying UN commissions to pass condemnatory resolutions.

Relying on the female political activists, health care specialists, and educators from the countries in which FGM is widespread to erode the myths surrounding it has the virtue of bypassing the issue's potential for exacerbating the polarization of the North versus the South and the West versus the non-West on human rights (which occurs when FGM is treated as a violation of international human rights law).[28] But meanwhile, particularly where there is most need of reform, this culturally

27. On the confrontations between feminists and African women over the FGM issue in UN forums, see Claude E. Welch, Jr., *Protecting Human Rights in Africa: Roles and Strategies of Non-Governmental Organizations* (Philadelphia, PA: University of Pennsylvania Press, 1995), pp. 92–94.

28. For an African perspective on the causes of and remedies for the unproductive polarization between Western and non-Western women's movements, see Oloka-Onyango and Syllvia Tamale, "'The Personal is Political,' or Why Women's Rights are Indeed Human Rights: An African Perspective on International Feminism," *Human Rights Quarterly* 17, 4 (November 1995), pp. 691–731.

deferential approach often leaves political and legal control over sexual and reproductive norms under the authority of officials who are hostile to any efforts to enhance the status of women in their societies.

Refugees from FGM—A New Human Rights Issue

However, enlightenment about FGM *is* spreading in the countries where the practice is prevalent, particularly among women in cities and other areas accessible to the health professionals and educators. And as these ideas filter into even the most traditionally controlled areas, increasing numbers of women are fleeing communities and countries where, if they remained, they would be forced to suffer the fearsome operations.

Fleeing is hard enough. Finding a place of refuge is often even harder. International human rights law is quite clear about the right to leave a county for whatever reason—to escape poverty, brutality, cultural oppression, and so on. But it is ambiguous, weak, and often of no help at all to refugees when it comes to establishing obligations on countries to receive and provide domicile, let alone citizenship, for international refugees. Thus, the new category of refugees—refugees from FGM—may compel some countries to reassess their own immigration laws, and in turn this, for reasons of sharing the anticipated burden of an influx of young, poor women, could stimulate fresh multilateral efforts to humanize and strengthen international obligations to provide asylum.

Currently, a major test of U.S. immigration law as it affects FGM refugees is entering the U.S. judicial process. The case is that of a 19-year-old woman who fled her country of Togo to avoid being mutilated and who was imprisoned in the United States for more than a year on grounds of illegally entering the country. Under existing U.S. immigration law, asylum is generally to be granted to refugees from persecution that they have suffered in their home countries because of their race, religion, nationality, political opinions, or membership in a particular minority group. But no provision exists for refugees from practices like FGM in which the intent is not to punish or deny basic civil rights to people belonging to minorities or dissident groups but rather to require community members to adhere to a long-established custom.

Attorneys on behalf of the Togolese refugee from FGM are arguing that not only the degree of brutality in the procedure itself but also the community-sanctioned coercion and ostracism of those who refuse to submit to it constitute a type of societal persecution and punishment comparable to, if not worse than, the standard grounds for granting asylum. U.S. immigration attorneys opposed to granting asylum to the Togo woman argue that to so loosen the category of acceptable asylum claims would open the country to a flood of refugees from all sorts of societal practices and conditions found objectionable. This landmark case has already received considerable media attention in the United States, since its outcome could have enormous implications not only for women's rights but for the rights of refugees all around the world.[29]

Paradoxically, legal and political strategies for dealing with the FGM issue have been made even more difficult because some countries in which the practice is prevalent have officially outlawed it. Togo is one of the African countries that, responding to the growing international pressures, has banned FGM; in doing so, it has joined Burkina Faso, Central African Republic, Djibouti, Ghana, Guinea, and Senegal. Where official prohibitions coexist with the widespread continuation of the practice, it is virtually impossible to get foreign immigration authorities to grant asylum to women from these countries or to obtain official international censure. This is a 'game"—in the name of cultural diversity—that sensitive nationalists can play to prevent individuals from obtaining international redress that their own societies deny them.

HUMANITARIAN INTERVENTION AGAINST ETHNIC CLEANSING

The last decade of the twentieth century marked the entry of a new concept into the lexicon of human rights violations: ethnic cleansing, the term originally applied by Serbian nationalists in the early 1990s to their efforts to drive non-Serb, particularly Muslim, populations out of areas of Bosnia-Herzegovina. The purpose was to make these areas homogeneously Serbian and Orthodox Christian and thus validate the Serbian claim, in the name of self-determination, that at least these areas should be part of the state of Serbia. The Muslims and Roman Catholic Croats in areas they dominated similarly attempted to change the ethnic/religious composition of the parts of the former Yugoslavia they hoped to control. By the end of 1995, when the international community, led by the United States, imposed a cease-fire under the Dayton Accord, over 1 million inhabitants of Bosnia-Herzegovina (nearly one of every two persons) had been displaced. Most had fled the country and had swelled the ranks of international refugees seeking residence in Western Europe.

The most brutal campaigns of ethnic cleansing in the Bosnian conflict were undertaken by the Serbs in areas they controlled. Typically, local Serbian paramilitary forces, sometimes aided by troops from Serbia proper, incarcerated Muslims in detention camps; destroyed their homes; selectively executed political leaders, teachers, intellectuals, and other professionals; and systematically raped Muslim women. This

---

29. Celia W. Dugger, "U.S. Hearing to Decide Rights of Women Who Flee Genital Mutilation," *New York Times* (May 2, 1996).

pattern was replicated, sometimes in a spiral of mutual revenge, by all three communities against populations of the others. But in the words of a highly authoritative account, "In the last analysis, given the number of Muslims expelled from the Serb-controlled territory and the brutality that accompanied their expulsions, the sum total of atrocities committed by the Serbs was in a category by itself."[30]

The ethnic cleansing campaigns, along with the potential effects of the mass migrations on the stability of the entire Balkan region, were invoked in the UN Security Council and in the political debates within member countries as sufficient grounds—humanitarian *plus* those of international peace and security—for international military intervention in the Bosnian civil war. The first UN interventons had been more traditional, namely, peacekeeping missions to police the 1991 cease-fire between Serbia and Croatia after Croatia's secession from Yugoslavia in 1991 had prompted a Yugoslav/Serb invasion to retain Serb-populated areas as part of the Yugoslav federation. But Bosnia-Herzegovina's subsequent secession rapidly turned into a three-sided, interethnic civil war that the European powers, the United States, and the United Nations—although initially reluctant to become involved—felt compelled to pacify when the carnage escalated to include the massacre and forced relocation of civilians. When a succession of negotiated cease-fires monitored by the lightly armed UN Protection Force (UNPROFOR) broke down, the Security Council authorized NATO airstrikes in retaliation against the culprits, unusually the Serbs. Even so, taking advantage of their inheritance of the major portion of the Yugoslav armed forces, the Serbs were able to exploit the failure of international diplomacy to achieve a political settlement by consolidating and expanding their ethnic cleansing effort. But, a regrouped and refurbished Croatian military, in cooperation with Bosnian Muslims, was able to inflect major losses on the Serbian forces in the Krajina region in the summer of 1995. Vicious counterattacks by the Serbs in cities throughout Bosnia provided the occasion for NATO to launch major airstrikes against Serb miliary concentrations in August and September of 1995, and it was the threat of additional NATO strikes which would produce even higher levels of destruction that finally permitted the U.S. government and its allies, with Richard Holbrook as their chief negotiator, to force the warring Bosnian communities to swallow the Bosnia partition/federation agreement known as the Dayton Accord.

Paradoxically, the Dayton Accord, largely a reaction to the genocidal dimension the conflict in Bosnia was assuming, made it difficult to hold the perpetrators internationally accountable or to prevent an even more horrendous phase of ethnic cleansing to be reinstituted by the Serbs four

---

30. Steven L. Burg and Paul S. Shoup, *The War in Bosnia-Herzegovina: Ethnic Conflict and International Intervention* (London. M. E. Sharpe, 1999), pp. 172–173.

years later in Kosovo. As is recounted later in this chapter in the discussion on the establishment of the International Tribunal for the Former Yugoslavia, the leading statespersons of the major powers perceived that to bring the high officials responsible for ethnic cleansing to trial, quite plausibly for acts of genocide, would have meant that those who were depended upon to implement the Dayton Accord—officials like Yugoslav President Slobodan Milosevic—would lose their authority.

Four years after the Dayton Accord, as relative calm prevailed in Bosnia under the watchful presence of UN peacekeeping forces—despite the forebodings of a collapse of the federal arrangement there—the most notorious sponsor of ethnic cleansing, Slobodan Milosevic, was at it again in Kosovo.

A part of the Federal Republic of Yugoslavia, but having a population that was 90 percent Albania, the province of Kosovo had been granted substantial autonomy by the Yugoslav communist dictator, Tito, in 1968 in response to increasingly violent demands by Albanians for self-determination. But in reaction to renewed rebelliousness by the Kosovar Albanians in the 1980s, President Milosevic abolished the province's autonomy and instituted direct rule from Belgrade along with measures to give a Serbian character to all public functions and harsh controls against any further nationalistic agitation by the Albanians.[31] Instead, the Kosovar Albanians intensified their activities, forming a province-wide dissident society.

Initially espousing nonviolent means of achieving independence, the independence movement, in reaction to Milosovic's harsh countermeasures, soon came under the sway of the militant Kosovo Liberation Army (KLA). The KLA's violent insurgency was used by Milosovic to justify an increasingly brutal policy of ethnic cleansing in the province, including forced deportation, incarceration, and summary execution of Kosovars involved in or suspected of participation in the independence movement—the so-called ethnic cleansing of Kosovo.

Stimulated by media reports of the intensifying ethnic-cleansing campaign, the United States and its NATO allies, while unwilling to support full independence for Kosovo, demanded—and made a threat of military action if Milosovic refused—Belgrade grant the Kosovars an even greater degree of autonomy within the Federal Republic of Yugoslavia than they had perviously achieved under Tito. The systematic air assault by NATO in the spring of 1999, in response to Milosovic's rejection of these terms, was accompanied by an escalation of the Serbian atrocities against the Albanian Kosovars.

As documented in the May 27, 1999, indictment of Milosovic and four of his aides by the International Criminal Tribunal for the Former

---

31. For background on the crisis in Kosovo, see William W. Hagen, "The Balkans' Lethal Nationalisms," *Foreign Affairs*, July/August 1999, pp. 52–64.

Yugoslavia, the ethnic-cleansing campaign conducted by the forces of the Federal Republic of Yugoslavia and Servia included

- the forced deportation of some 740,000 Albanian civilians from Kosovo
- murder, rape, and other physical atrocities against men, women, and children throughout Kosovo in numbers yet to be verified
- the systematic destruction of property belonging to Kosovar Albanians.

NATO only agreed to stop its bombing of Yugoslavia when Milosovic agreed to withdraw all of his forces from Kosovo, to allow an international force controlled by NATO to escort the Kosovar deportees back into the province and to protect them during at least the early phases of reconstruction of civil life, and to grant essential political autonomy (though not yet full independence) for Kosovo.

The international community's handling of the crisis in Kosovo, even more than its intervention in Bosnia, has opened up a huge question for statespersons, political philosophers, and the citizens of countries around the world: Is there in fact a world polity of enforceable law and order emerging, grounded in fundamental human rights principles, that is beginning to override the norms and structures of the state-sovereignty system? And, who will support and who will oppose this development?

BRINGING GENOCIDAL AND WAR CRIMINALS TO TRIAL

Nearly a half century after evidence in the international courtroom of Hitler's genocidal policies moved world leaders to incorporate basic human rights protections into international law, new eruptions of genocidal violence in the Balkans and central Africa have pushed the world toward an even deeper institutionalization of the proposition that there are some human rights so fundamental that their violation anywhere on Earth must be made a punishable crime. But as was revealed in the debate over the creation of a Permanent International Criminal Court and as reflected in the statute adopted by 120 countries in Rome during the summer of 1998, the establishment of effective supranational mechanisms for apprehending, prosecuting, and punishing the guilty are as controversial as ever among international lawyers and statespersons.

The Legacy of the Nuremberg and Tokyo Tribunals

The atrocities and killings inflicted by the Nazis on many millions of Jews and other communities Hitler wanted eliminated and the brutal treatment of prisoners by the Japanese military during World War II were central counts in the indictments and convictions of German and Japanese leaders in the international tribunals of Nuremberg and Tokyo following the war. These were victors' trials of the vanquished, not only for crimes against humanity perpetrated during the war, but also for starting the war in the first place. There were no comparable trials of those in the victor governments who ordered the total incineration bombing of cities and the use of the atomic bomb and no willingness on the part of the Western governments and the Soviets to admit, even in theory, that they too might have been partly to blame for the war.

This lack of symmetry—some would say double standard—in the immediate postwar effort to define and prosecute international crimes bothered many international jurists and legal philosophers. The result was a divergent, two-branched legacy of the Nuremberg and Tokyo trials among international lawyers and scholars. On one side, the war-crimes trials reinforced the arguments of the traditionalists that international law must not (indeed, cannot) be supranationally enforced on the sovereign countries of the nation-state system; Nuremberg and Tokyo were anomalies, not precedents to be emulated. On the other side, the war crimes trials energized the commitment of reformers to deepen and make truly universal the obligations and potential liabilities of all states with respect to genocide and war crimes. This branch of the legacy produced the 1948 Convention on the Prevention and Punishment of the Crime of Genocide, the 1949 Geneva Convention Relative to the Protection of Civilians in Time of War, and the 1949 Geneva Convention Relative to the Treatment of Prisoners of War; it also led to proposals for a permanent international criminal tribunal.

During the Cold War members of each ideological bloc and nonaligned countries frequently charged that their adversaries had violated one or another of these "humanitarian" international conventions. But interbloc politics and the persisting influence of the conservative wing of the international legal fraternity prevented anything comparable to the post–World War II tribunals from materializing—that is, until the post–Cold War paroxysm of violence in the former Yugoslavia galvanized a concerted international determination to put a stop to such excesses.

The International Tribunal for the Former Yugoslavia

Reacting to the deteriorating situation in the former Yugoslavia and reports that the rival communal groups were engaging in internationally prohibited acts—acts that included mass forcible expulsions and deportation of civilians (called ethnic cleansing); imprisonment and abuse of civilians in detention centers; deliberate attacks on noncombatants, hospitals and ambulances; impediments to the delivery of food and medical supplies to civilian populations; and wanton devastation and destruction of property—the United Nations Security Council passed a series of resolutions in the summer and fall of 1992

- reminding the parties to the conflict that they were bound to comply with their "obligations under international humanitarian law," especially the 1949 Geneva Conventions, and warning that persons who commit or order grave breaches of these obligations would be held individually responsible[32]

- demanding that all parties to the conflict "cease and desist" from their breaches of international humanitarian law, and threatening that their failure to do so would compel the Security Council to take further action under Chapter VII (the peace and security provisions) of the UN Charter[33]

- establishing an "impartial Commission of Experts" to determine the extent of the violations of humanitarian law and to consider what legal remedies were available through the United Nations[34]

Finally, in its historic Resolution 808 of February 22, 1993, the Security Council, taking the advice of the Commission of Experts, decided

> that an international tribunal shall be established for the prosecution of persons responsible for serious violations of international humanitarian law committed in the territory of the former Yugoslavia since 1991.[35]

A detailed Statute for International Tribunal for the Prosecution of Persons Responsible for Serious Violations of International Humanitarian Law Committed in the Territory of the Former Yugoslavia Since 1991 was prepared by Secretary General Boutros-Boutros Ghali and adopted by the Security Council in May 1993 under Resolution 827.[36]

The Tribunal is comprised 11 independent judges elected by the General Assembly from a list provided by the Security Council. Indictments and presentations to the Tribunal of the charges against the accused are prepared by the prosecutor, an independent officer appointed by the Security Council on nomination by the secretary-general.

With respect to events transpiring in the former Yugoslavia, beginning with the outbreak of violence among its Serbian, Croatian, and

---

32. Resolution 764 of the UN Security Council, July 13, 1992.
33. Resolution 771 of the UN Security Council, August 13, 1992.
34. Resolution 780 of the UN Security Council, October 6, 1992.
35. Resolution 808 of the UN Security Council, February 22, 1993.
36. The text of the statute for international tribunal for the former Yugoslavia is included in the report of the secretary-general pursuant to Resolution 808 of the UN Security Council (United Nations Document No. S/25704 & Add.1, 1993).

Muslim communities in 1991, the Tribunal has had authority to investigate, indict, order the arrest of, prosecute, convict, and sentence to imprisonment "persons committing or ordering to be committed" acts of *genocide* (defined as acts with the "intent to destroy, in whole or in part, a national, ethnical, racial, or religious group"); *crimes against humanity* (defined as violent or inhumane wartime acts against civilians, such as murder, enslavement, deportation, imprisonment, torture, and rape); and other *violations of the laws of war* (including inhumane treatment of prisoners; the destruction of cities, towns, or villages not justified by military necessity; and the plunder of private property).[37]

The debate over the role of the Tribunal has not abated during the early phases of its operation, and expectations are that the fulfillment of its mandate will take many years—perhaps more than a decade. Opponents and skeptics argue that there has been a contradiction all along between (a) the basic mandate of the Tribunal and (b) efforts to construct and internationally guarantee a tripartite peace in the former Yugoslavia among the warring Croats, Serbs, and Muslims; for among the governing authorities in each of these communities (authorities who are now expected to accord each other legitimacy and respect and to be so treated by the international community) are quite a number of individuals who fall within the category of indictable international criminals under the Tribunal statute. Either the Tribunal does its job and orders the arrest of many of those who are supposed to be responsible upholders of the peace, or in the interests of securing the peace, it exempts some of the most notorious perpetrators of genocidal acts and thus drastically undercuts its own authority and invites the charge of hypocrisy. Many human rights scholars agree with the pessimistic forecast of Professor David Forsythe that "The leaders of the various fighting parties—those who ordered or allowed the systematic rapes, the torture and summary execution of prisoners, the policy of intentionally targeting civilians and nonfortified cities and towns and objects essential to the survival of the civilian population—are unlikely ever to be convicted."[38]

The United States and its allies attempted to overcome this dilemma by making the obligation to cooperate with the Tribunal an integral part of the Dayton Peace Agreement of 1995 for ending hostilities in Bosnia. The Agreement includes a provision prohibiting individuals indicted by the Tribunal from holding public office, and the implementing accords authorize the Implementation Force (IFOR), deployed into Bosnia under the command and control of the North Atlantic Treaty Organization(NATO), to arrest any indicted person "it comes across" in the areas of its patrols. But the IFOR commanders and NATO

---

37. Ibid.
38. David P. Forsythe, "Politics and the International Tribunal for the Former Yugoslavia," *Criminal Law Forum* 5, 2–3 (1994), pp. 401–422; quote from p. 417.

political authorities have interpreted their mission as not involving proactive search-and-arrest operations. Nor does the Dayton Agreement *require* public authorities in Bosnia or in its Serb and Muslim/Croatian subregions to arrest and turn over to the Tribunal all indicted war criminals in their jurisdictions; such persons, however, are formally subject to arrest on behalf of the international community at any time, not only in their home regions, but also in neighboring or foreign jurisdictions in which they might appear (which would be more likely).

Critics impatient for retributive justice against the war criminals contend it is naïve to expect that the Dayton peace provisions and implementing instruments will ever produce the "big fish" (such as, Radovan Karadzic, the Bosnian Serb political leader, and General Ratko Mladic, allegedly directly responsible for some of the most horrible atrocities) as defendants before the Tribunal.[39] But supporters of the UN/Dayton approach see the top criminals suffering substantial punishment even if they are never taken into custody. International pariahs, fearful of apprehension if they travel abroad, they are imprisoned, as it were, in their own lands; even at home, they can no longer hold or legally seek public office. Such a political delegitimation is "particularly devastating [to] . . . leaders such as Karadzic and Mladic," argues Payam Akhavan, legal adviser in the office of the prosecutor. The insolent pride of those who thought they could commit genocide with impunity has been followed by their downfall and humiliation. . . .

> It might be said . . . that absent their arrest and surrender to the Tribunal, the indictment of political and military leaders, and their consequent stigmatization, deprivation of liberty, and removal from office, has had the effect of an "interim justice."[40]

The case for such limited interim justice, even if the most prominent persons indicted for war crimes and crimes against humanity are never apprehended and brought into court, is that it nevertheless provides a basis for breaking the chain reaction of escalating retributive violence. This reasoning has it that it is crucial to provide the aggrieved victim communities with designated *individuals* to hold responsible for the atrocities that have been committed; for if such internationally (and legitimately) named culprits are not made targets for justifiable retribu-

---

39. Tribunal Judge Fouad Raid, in issuing the indictments for Karadic and Mladic, said that the evidence gathered by the prosecutors showed "scenes of unimaginable savagery: thousands of men executed and buried in mass graves, hundreds of men buried alive, men and women mutilated and slaughtered, children killed before their mother's eyes, a grandfather forced to eat the liver of his own grandson." See Anthony Lewis, "No Peace Without Justice, *New York Times* (November 20, 1995).

40. Payaam Akhavan, "The Yugoslav Tribunal at a Crossroads: The Dayton Peace Agreement and Beyond," *Human Rights Quarterly* 18, 2 (May 1966), pp. 259–285; quote from p. 273.

tive anger, the prospects are high that the aggrieved communities will attempt to take retributive justice into their own hands by violently punishing the entire enemy community they believe to be the source of their suffering, and this in turn is likely to provoke righteous counterretaliation for the innocents who have been attacked. "If individuals are not brought to book," argues the Tribunal's chief prosecutor, Judge Richard Goldstone, "then there is collective guilt. The victims and their survivors cry out for justice against a group. That's why there are these cycles of violence in the former Yugoslavia."[41]

Prosecuting the Perpetrators of the Rwanda Genocide

In November 1994, this time with the objective of stopping an epidemic of interethnic violence in the center of Africa, the UN Security Council created another ad hoc tribunal—one mandated to bring to justice those responsible for the massacre of hundreds of thousands of Rwandan Tutsi civilians by Rwandan Hutu militia earlier that year. (Some estimates ran as high as 1 million slaughtered.) Formally named the International Criminal Tribunal for the Prosecution of Persons Responsible for Genocide and Other Serious Violations of International Humanitarian Law Committed in the Territory of Rwanda and Rwandan Citizens Responsible for Genocide and Other Such Violations Committed in the Territory of Neighboring States, Between 1 January 1994 and 31 December 1994,[42] the Tribunal has in some respects a more simple task for Rwanda, and in other respects a more formidable one, than its counterpart Tribunal for the former Yugoslavia.

In this case, the leaders of *one* of the country's ethnic groups (the Hutus, which comprise 85 percent of the population) were clearly to be held responsible. Moreover, the group they had victimized, the Tutsis, were now in control of the government of Rwanda and were presumably able and willing to arrest individuals indicted by the Tribunal. But the slowness of the international Tribunal on the one hand (no indictments were issued by the end of 1995)—resulting from its meagre staff and funds and the fact that its chief prosecutor, Richard Goldstone, was preoccupied with his other assignment as chief prosecutor for the Yugoslav Tribunal—and the desire of the Tutsis, back in power in Kigale, for swift justice, on the other hand, do not bode well for the prospectus of due process. In the view of many Tutsi leaders, thousands of Hutus were complicit perpetrators of the genocidal massacres of 1994, and the

---

41. Judge Richard Goldstone, quoted by Anthony Lews, "No Peace Without Justice," *New York Times* (November 20, 1995); see also Randolph Ryan, "Prosecutor: Leaders Not Immune" Boston Globe (November 19, 1995).
42. Resolution 955 of the UN Security Council, November 8, 1994.

government in Kigale, which is not waiting for indictments from the Hague, therefore feels justified in making arrests on its own. Many of the presumed-guilty Hutus, however, have fled into the neighboring countries of Burundi and Zaire and are hiding out among millions of Hutus reluctant to return to Rwanda out of fear of reprisal from the Tutsi community. The potential for renewed outbreaks of intertribal warfare are high, and the violence could easily escalate into the neighboring countries. The ability of the Rwandan Tribunal to function in the midst of regionwide relapse into genocide would be problematical, to say the least.

A Permanent International Criminal Court

Seizing upon the readiness of the international community to create special tribunals to prosecute those responsible for the atrocities in the former Yugoslavia and Rwanda, the United States and other major governments instructed their representatives in the United Nations to give fresh attention and support to the long-standing effort to create a permanent tribunal to deal with such cases.[43] The effort culminated in a UN-mandated Conference in Rome in the summer of 1998 that was attended by governmental delegates from 160 countries, by representatives of pertinent international agencies, and by nongovernmental organizations that had been accredited observers in the preparatory conferences. After five weeks of intense deliberation, the Conference adopted the Rome Statute of the International Criminal Court by a vote of 120 in favor to 7 against (including the United States), with 21 abstentions.

The jurisdiction of the International Criminal Court (ICC), in the words of the Statute, "shall be limited to the most serious crimes of concern to the international community as a whole," namely, genocide, "crimes against humanity," war crimes, and "the crime of aggression." But, given the Statute's definition and the listing of these crimes in it, an activist ICC could establish for itself quite a sweeping mandate.

In the Statute *genocide* is defined in accordance with the now-standard definition of killing or attempting to destroy, in whole or in part, a national, ethnic, racial, or religious group.

Crimes against humanity are considerably broadened from the original Nuremberg formulation, being extended in the ICC Statute to encompass also deportation or forcible transfers of population; "imprisonment or other severe deprivation of physical liberty in violation of fundamental rules of international law;" "rape, sexual slavery, enforced prostitution, forced pregnancy, enforced sterilization, or any other form of sexual violence of comparable gravity; enforced disappearance of per-

---

43. See David J. Scheffer, "International Judicial Intervention," *Foreign Policy* 102 (Spring 1996), pp. 51.

sons;" and other "inhumane acts of a similar character intentionally causing great suffering, or serious injury to body or to mental or physical health."

War crimes are enumerated in a long list that is essentially in accordance with the standing Geneva Conventions and their protocols.

The *crime of aggression* is undefined in the Statute, which explicitly stipulates that the ICC's jurisdiction over the acts to be covered is left for future deliberation and amendments.

The debate in the Rome Conference reflected such fundamental differences among various influential delegations that it looked for a time as if the whole effort would break down. The most intense controversies revolved around the issue of the autonomy to be granted the ICC to initiate proceedings in particular cases. Another contentious issue involved the ICC's jurisdiction over crimes alleged to have been committed by, or in, countries not party to the Statute authorizing the Court.

The United States and the other permanent members of the UN Security Council made it clear during the drafting process that they were opposed to allowing the ICC's prosecutors and judges to initiate trials on their own. The United States wanted to restrict the Court's jurisdiction to cases brought to it either by the Security Council or by a national government. France proposed that the Security Council should have the power to veto the ICC's consideration of any particular case, which would mean that complaints about Russian actions in Chechnya or Chinese actions in Tibet, for example, would rarely, if ever, come before its judges. The outcome of this debate is reflected in those provisions— strongly opposed by the U.S. delegation—that allow the ICC to take jurisdiction in a particular case on the basis of an investigation authorized by a state party, by the UN Security Council, or by the ICC Prosecutor. The Security Council, however, can vote at any time to stop, for a period of 12 months, an investigation that has already commenced.

The other highly controversial issue had to do with the reach of the ICC into the affairs of countries that have not become parties to the Statute. Here those in favor of a restrictive mandate won out, but not completely. International crimes committed by nationals of a state that has not ratified the Statute are beyond the jurisdiction of the ICC. But international crimes that are committed by nationals of a party to the Statute, independent of where they have been committed, will come under the Court's jurisdiction, and the culprits shall be subject to arrest *as long as they (the crimes or the alleged criminals) are in the jurisdiction of a state that is a party to the Statute or has otherwise accepted the Court's jurisdiction for the crime in question.*

Consistent with the covenants establishing other international and regional courts and commissions with adjudicatory power, the Statute has a complementarity provision that restricts the ICC from taking up a case unless the state in which the alleged crime has been committed is unable or unwilling to take up the case. Even so, the United States and a few other countries, most prominently India and Israel, claimed that the ICC could too intrusively violate their national sovereignty.

In explaining the refusal of the United States to approve the Statute, the U.S. delegate raised the specter of states hostile to the United States bringing indictments against American military and other personnel, who are characteristically deployed around the world, in order embarrass and harass the country. But in seeking absolute security against such harassment by not joining this innovative institution instead of finding other ways to assure that cases are responsibly handled by the prosecutor and judges of the ICC, the United States seriously undermined the prospect of holding members of the international community account-able to standards of behavior Americans claim to believe in.

Champions of a stronger global human rights regime are disap-pointed at the way that political expediency appears to have prevailed in the United States and in other governments over what appears to be the obvious case for a supranational judicial body to prevent states from shielding acts universally regarded as horrible and unjustifiable. But if half a loaf is all the oven of outrage over today's genocidal conflicts can bake, the human rights constituency will, for the time being, settle for the constricted permanent tribunal, even absent the world's superpower, rather than none.

Chapter 7

Persisting Issues
and New Dilemmas in
U.S. Foreign Policy

This chapter focuses on the way the United States in particular has been grappling with the problem of incorporating human rights objectives into its foreign policy. There are two reasons for singling out the United States for such analysis. First, having participated in some of the relevant policy debates, I have direct knowledge about how human rights have been handled in U.S. foreign policy. Second, what the United States decides to push or oppose in the human rights field will unavoidably have profound influence on the ways the international community deals with this dimension of world politics.

This is not to say that the United States can dictate the rules and determine the outcome of struggles in the international human rights arena. Indeed, when it comes to human rights issues, all countries—big and small—tend to claim legal and moral equality not only in the exercise of sovereignty over what happens within their borders but also in the formulation of the principles and covenants of the emerging global human rights regime. Yet, realistically, the fact that the United States has a uniquely large bag of carrots and sticks that it can select from to induce other countries to respect its preferences ensures, even in the sovereignty-sensitive sphere of human rights, that these preferences will impact heavily on international deliberations and frequently also on the domestic policies of many countries.

HUMAN RIGHTS VERSUS
OTHER INTERESTS

A persisting debate in the U.S. policy community since World War II has centered on the question of what role and what weight should be given to human rights considerations in this country's foreign relations.

Influential answers—that is, positions that have been reflected in actual policy—have ranged across a wide spectrum including the following:

- Henry Kissinger's realpolitik proposition that the external behavior of states, not the internal character of their regimes, should be the focus of international diplomacy.

- The early Cold War policies of the Truman and Eisenhower administrations that tolerated autocratic characteristics of countries which would join U.S. alliances against the communists.

- John F. Kennedy's view that a credible U.S. posture against repressive governments of both the left and the right was a powerful instrument in waging the Cold War.

- The Clinton administration's insistence that human rights objectives, while part of the American purpose abroad, should not be emphasized to the extent that other more important interests (such as arms control and economic globalization) are held hostage to them.

- Jimmy Carter's effort to elevate human rights to a cardinal value that the United States should actively promote around the world.

WHICH RIGHTS HAVE PRIORITY?

Another set of questions, which intersects the basic question of how much to emphasize human rights, deals with the *kinds* of rights that should be most strongly supported abroad by the United States. There has been close to unanimity in the U.S. policy community for the proposition that the United States in its human rights policy should be uncompromising and loud, at least in its rhetoric, in opposing genocide, ethnic cleansing, forced disappearances, and the systematic employment by governments of torture and other severe brutalities against opposition groups. When it comes to decisive *action* on behalf of these positions, however, the consensus often falls apart, especially when the implementation strategies would risk war and/or substantial expenditure of national resources on which there are competing claims.

Beyond the right not to suffer acts of extreme brutality, many of the human rights appearing in the principal international covenants have not obtained unequivocal, official U.S. support. The extent to which the United States should pressure other countries to respect these rights and the priority to be accorded various categories of rights have been matters of considerable debate.

Thus, the question of how much preference should be given in U.S. foreign policy to the rights featured in the Covenant on Civil and Political Rights as compared with the social-justice rights in the Covenant on Economic, Social and Cultural Rights has often pitted human rights officers in the Department of State against officials in the Department of Commerce, with the latter typically pushing for policies of constructive economic engagement even with autocratic regimes. And within the political parties as well, there also has been division over the priority to give the adoption of an economic free-market system over political democracy. These debates have been reflected in major variations in the thrust of the human rights policies of successive U.S. administrations. Some examples are

- the insistence by the Kennedy administration that governments that expected economic development aid from the United States *must* make determined and credible efforts to institute constitutional democracy

- Nixon's turning a blind eye to gross violations of human rights in the Soviet Union and China in order to further detente with the former and rapprochement with the latter

- Carter's effort to champion both liberty and economic-amenity rights, particularly among Third World peoples, insisting that each was a co-requisite of the other

- Reagan's emphasis on property rights and free enterprise as necessary conditions for political freedom and his willingness to return to the Truman-Eisenhower policies of embracing politically authoritarian regimes as long as they cooperated in the good fight against communism and socialism

- Bush's desire to purge ideological means tests from U.S. post–Cold War relationships, particularly in his constructive-engagement policies toward China (see the discussion of U.S. China policy in Chapter 6) following Beijing's brutal suppression of the student democracy movement in Tiananmen Square in 1989

- Clinton's continuation of the Bush administration's constructive-engagement policies toward China, Turkey, Algeria, Peru, and other countries with politically repressive regimes, in effect giving primacy—at least in countries whose cooperation the administration has deemed vital to U.S. strategic and/or economic interests—(as did Reagan) to property rights and economic freedoms over civil and political rights

POLICY INSTRUMENTS

A third set of issues deals with the means the United States should use to induce other countries to improve their human rights practices. Although the public debate over these issues is often framed between the opposed poles of sanctions and constructive engagement, the policy instruments actually considered, and chosen, in particular cases usually involve a melding of these two approaches. On occasion, the debate will be over military intervention to secure human rights.

In the U.S. policy community, sanctions are thought of as coercive pressures short of the use of force. They range from acts to register displeasure against a government with a poor human rights record (such as the canceling of ceremonial diplomatic visits or denial of aircraft landing rights) to withdrawal of normal trading privileges in the U.S. market, to votes in the International Monetary Fund and the World Bank against loans to the country, and to efforts to inflict extreme economic hardship on the offending government by cutting off virtually all of its international commerce.

A middle ground in sanctions policy—and the approach most often invoked—is the cessation of special assistance (military and/or economic) to a heretofore friendly government. The legislative mandate for this type of sanction, found in both the Foreign Assistance Act (1974) and the Arms Export Control Act (1976) states,

> No assistance [of this kind] may be provided . . . to the government of any country which engages in a consistent pattern of gross violations of internationally recognized human rights, including torture or cruel, inhuman punishment, prolonged detention without charges, causes the disappearance of persons, or other flagrant denial of the right to life, liberty and the security of person . . . [including]] internment or imprisonment . . . for political purposes.[1]

As with all such legislatively imposed restrictions of this kind, the Congress permits the appropriate executive agencies to exempt a country that would otherwise qualify for the sanctions if the president makes an explicit finding that the exemption is important for the national interest. During the Cold War, presidents were often inclined to make such a determination when the country with a bad human rights record was a weighty ally in the effort to maintain a balance of power against the Soviets. Since the end of the Cold War this exemption option has provided a means of maintaining loan and military assistance packages for

---

1. United States Congress, Foreign Assistance Act of 1974 and Arms Export Control Act of 1976.

countries that are important to the U.S. economy or whose cooperation is deemed important for de-escalating regional conflicts or controlling the spread of weapons of mass destruction.

GOOD INTENTIONS COMPROMISED

The presidential campaigns of Jimmy Carter (in 1976) and Bill Clinton (in 1992) both featured harsh criticisms of the realpolitik policies of their predecessors and promised to make the promotion of human rights a centerpiece of U.S. foreign policy. Upon election, Carter and then Clinton appointed human rights advocates, many of them former congressional staffers active in drafting and politicking the human rights amendments that were regularly attached to trade and foreign assistance bills in the early 1970s, to subcabinet and working-level posts in their administrations. Expectations in the human rights constituency were particularly heightened by Carter's appointment of civil rights leader Andrew Young to be ambassador to the United Nations. Sixteen years later, after the Reagan and Bush years, hopes were again raised by Clinton's appointment of Anthony Lake, who had been a strong advocate of human rights from within the Carter administration, to be his national security adviser. However, the human rights constituency was to be disappointed by both of the human rights–professing presidents.

Carter's Commitments and Frustrations

Some of the foreign policy officials in the incoming Carter administration in 1977 were worried about the president's commitments to human rights. Those for whom improving relations with the Soviet Union were the overriding concern tried to convince the president early in his first term that serious negotiations with the Kremlin on arms control, an even higher priority for Carter, could be derailed by the new moralism in the White House. Concerned, the president asked secretary of state, Cyrus Vance, to sort things out and to fashion a workable human rights policy.[2]

The result of Secretary Vance's efforts was the appointment of a high-level, interagency committee, chaired by Deputy Secretary of State Warren Christopher, mandated to review and apply human rights considerations to virtually all the administration's international programs on a case-by-case basis. The human rights considerations were outlined in a

---

2. The various factions in the Carter administration are detailed in Seyom Brown, *The Faces of Power: Constancy and Change in United States Foreign Policy From Truman to Clinton* (New York: Columbia University Press, 1994), pp. 311–388.

basic policy paper developed by Vance and other high-level administration officials that was approved by the president and on which Vance based a major public address articulating the new policy.

Delivered at the University of George Law School on April 30, 1977, the Vance speech put forward a sweeping definition of "what we mean by 'human rights'" that encompassed the rights against government oppression, usually championed by Western liberals, and also the social-justice rights that developing countries and countries in the Soviet camp were insisting should be given priority.

> *First, there is the right to be free from government violation of the integrity of the person.* Such violations include torture; cruel, inhuman or degrading punishment; and arbitrary arrest or imprisonment. And they include denial of fair public trial, and invasion of the home.
>
> *Second, there is the right to the fulfillment of such vital needs as food, shelter, health care, and education.* We recognize that the fulfillment of this right will depend, in part, upon the stage of a nation's economic development. But we also know that this right can be violated by a Government's action or inaction—for example, through corrupt official processes which divert resources to an elite at the expense of the needy, or through indifference to the plight of the poor.
>
> *Third, there is the right to enjoy civil and political liberties—* freedom of thought, of religion, of assembly; freedom of speech; freedom of the press; freedom of movement both within and outside one's own country; freedom to take part in the government.
>
> Our policy is to promote all these rights. . . . There may be disagreement on the priorities these rights deserve, but I believe that, with work, all of these rights can become complementary and mutually reinforcing.[3]

Vance's remarks were designed to convey to the world that the U.S. government, under the leadership of President Jimmy Carter, was now more seriously than ever committed to this policy. He quoted the poet Archibald MacLeish, "The cause of human liberty is now the one great revolutionary cause. . . ," and the president's own statement to the UN General Assembly that "no member of the United Nations can claim that mistreatment of its citizens in solely its own business."

Having laid out the new human rights–oriented foreign policy in grand terms, the U.S. secretary of state then proceeded to outline a highly restrained, pragmatic approach for implementing it, one that was mindful of "the limits of our power and wisdom." He cautioned that "A sure formula for defeat of our goals would be a rigid, hubristic attempt to

---

3. Cyrus Vance, "Human Rights and Foreign Policy," address at University of George Law School, April 30, 1977, in *Department of State Bulletin* (May 23, 1977), pp. 505–508.

impose our values on others. A doctrinaire plan of action would be a damaging as indifference."

We must be realistic, he said. "Our country can only achieve our objectives if we shape what we do to the case at hand." Vance said that this would require applying the following three sets of questions to each situation in determining whether and how to act:

> First, what is the nature of the situation in the country of concern?
>
> > What kinds of violations or deprivations are there?
> >
> > Is there a pattern to the violations? If so, is the trend toward concern for human rights or away from it?
> >
> > What is the degree of control and responsibility of the government involved?
> >
> > And finally, is the government willing to permit outside investigation?
>
> A second set of questions concerned the prospects for effective action.
>
> > Will our action be useful in promoting overall cause of human rights?
> >
> > Will it actually improve the specific conditions at hand? Or will it be likely to make things worse instead?
> >
> > Will the country involved be receptive to our interests and efforts?
> >
> > Will others work with us, including official and private international organizations dedicated to furthering human rights?
> >
> > Finally, does our sense of values and decency demand that we speak out or take action anyway, even though there is only a remote chance of making our influence felt?
>
> A third set of questions focused on the difficult policy dilemmas and tradeoffs:
>
> > Have we been sensitive to genuine security interests, realizing that the outbreak of armed conflict or terrorism could itself pose a serious threat to human rights?
> >
> > Have we considered all the rights at stake? If, for instance, we reduce aid to a government which violated the political rights of its citizens, do we not risk penalizing the hungry and the poor, who bear no responsibility for the abuses of their government?

Thus, the pressures to be brought against human rights offenders would also have to be assessed on a case-by-case basis. The means available ranged "from quiet diplomacy in its many forms, through public pronouncements, to withholding assistance. . . . In the end, a decision whether and how to act in the cause of human rights in a matter for informed and careful judgment."[4]

Human rights idealists were not at all pleased with this articulation of Carter's human rights policy and pointed out that with all the qualifications and tradeoffs outlined by the secretary of state, the administration could not claim to be offering anything new. The administration's political opponents took delight in contrasting the circumspect and seemingly inconsistent implementation of the policy with the standards of Carter's earlier idealistic rhetoric, which they now vilified as hypocrisy. Many in the human rights constituency sadly agreed with the charge of hypocrisy, as they witnessed Carter showering praise on the Shah of Iran (albeit for Cold War balance-of-power reasons), continuing high levels of military support to the repressive military autocracy running South Korea, and publicly ignoring to the continuing brutality toward dissidents by the government of the People's Republic of China.

Despite its unpopularity, the president and Vance believed they had formulated the only workable way of making human rights a central consideration in U.S. foreign policy. And they indicated to their subordinate officials that they expected the bureaucracy to be resourceful in applying the legislation already on the books. Responding to this mandate, the interagency group headed by Warren Christopher saw to it that foreign assistance and international loans were reduced, on grounds of poor human rights performance, to Afghanistan, Guinea, Central African Empire, Chile, Nicaragua, Paraguay, and El Salvador. Meanwhile, findings of positive human rights developments brought about increased assistance to India, Sri Lanka, Botswana, Gambia, the Dominican Republic, and Costa Rica.

The officially unspoken, but internally admitted, premise of the Carter human rights policy when it came to applying sanctions against offenders was that the United States would get tough with the little fish but had neither the wherewithal, nor the political will, to prevent the big fish (like China, the USSR, Iran, Turkey, Brazil) from getting away.

Clinton's Bold Rhetoric and Ambivalent Action

Bill Clinton too has found it difficult to translate his impulses to do good in the world into concrete policy. Whereas in theory it might be expected that the end of the Cold War imperative of supporting friendly tyrants against the geopolitical rivals of the United States should have enlarged the opportunities for more forthright promotion human rights, in practice being denied the national security rationale for diverting human and

---

4.   Ibid.

material resources to external purposes, President Clinton has faced a tougher burden of justification than did his predecessors when it comes tangible commitments to affect the human rights situation in another country. Moreover, as commercial considerations began to rival, if not supplant, geopolitical considerations in defining the priority national interests of the United States, it became even more difficult for policy makers to sort out the "good guys" from the "bad guys."

As detailed in the previous chapter, the biggest embarrassment for President Clinton in the human rights field was his reversal of the promise he made on the way to the White House to link Beijing's violations of human rights to the issue of extending normal trade privileges to China. Perhaps he was sincerely converted to the constructive-engagement proposition that the expansion of the middle and entrepreneurial classes which would result from China's opportunities for increased commercial interaction with the outside world would lead to a more open, pluralistic, and free society. Yet it was no secret in Washington (and surely no secret also in Beijing) that Clinton was ready to maximize trade with China whether or not it produced near-term improvements in the human rights of the Chinese and Tibetan peoples and even if future improvements remained highly uncertain.

The issue of Haitian refugees was another human rights embarrassment, but one that Clinton was able to obscure somewhat through the dramatic moves by which he forced the Haitian military dictator Raoul Cedras to relinquish power. During his 1992 campaign for president, Clinton had excoriated as inhumane President Bush's policy of refusing asylum to the more than twenty thousand Haitians who were trying to escape in small boats from crushing poverty and political repression in their country. But when as president he faced the prospect of a flood of refugees on Florida's shores, Clinton conceded that he might have been too harsh in condemning Bush's policy and announced that the policy of interception would continue for the time being, while his administration developed a plan for improving conditions in Haiti itself.

The fact that in 1991 General Cedras had grabbed power from Haiti's elected president, Jean-Bertrand Aristide, in a military coup provided the Clinton administration with the grounds for changing the human rights issue from that of the condition of the refugees to the brutality of the regime in Haiti. This emphasis was consistent with a new foreign policy doctrine the Clinton White House was formulating to define its post–Cold War foreign policy. As explained by National Security Adviser Anthony Lake, "The successor to a doctrine of containment must be a strategy of enlargement, enlargement of the world's free community of market democracies."[5]

---

5. Anthony Lake, address at the Johns Hopkins School of Advanced International Studies, Washington, DC, September 23, 1993, *Department of State Dispatch*, Vol. 4. no. 39.

With diplomatic pressures and economic sanctions failing to move General Cedras to reinstall Aristide or to hold new, internationally monitored elections, the Clinton administration got the United Nations Security Council in July 1994 to authorize member states to form a multinational force and "to use all necessary means to facilitate the departure from Haiti of the military leadership, . . . the prompt return of the legitimately elected President and the restoration of the legitimate authorities of the Government of Haiti."[6] Under the authority of this and related Security Council resolutions, President Clinton ordered the U.S. military to prepare to invade Haiti in September to forcibly remove General Cedras and then, backed by a UN peacekeeping force, to establish the conditions for the restoration of democratic processes. In preparing a skeptical public for the forthcoming military action, Clinton charged that "Haiti's dictators . . . control the most violent regime in our hemisphere. Cedras and his armed thugs have conducted a reign of terror, executing children, raping women, killing priests."[7]

In the days preceding the planned invasion, due to commence on September 18, 1994, Secretary of State Warren Christopher and other high officials of the administration reiterated the case for military intervention: (1) It was intolerable that democratic governments in the Americas be overthrown by military coups; (2) terrible human rights violations had been committed by the Haitian military regime; and (3) continuing waves of immigrants from Haiti would destabilize the hemisphere.

With U.S. planes carrying paratroopers already in the air, three Clinton emissaries—former President Jimmy Carter; former chairman of the joint chiefs of staff, Colin Powell; and Senator Sam Nunn, chair of the Senate Armed Services Committee—persuaded General Cedras and other members of his junta to step down and to give way to a UN-supervised election to restore civilian rule. As part of the last-minute deal for calling off the invasion, the Cedras group were to be granted amnesty by the Haitian parliament and the United States would provide them with financial assistance for leaving the country and settling elsewhere.

The feature of the U.S.-imposed arrangements in Haiti that was most criticized by human rights groups was the "golden parachute" provided to General Cedras for leaving the country. Why not a trial to prosecute him for his brutal human rights crimes? But former Jimmy Carter and Colin Powell defended the deal they negotiated on the grounds that if sacrificing full justice bought the avoidance of the bloodshed of a military invasion and also a restoration of democracy in Haiti, it was worth it.

Ambivalence in the U.S. policy community concerning how the international community should handle individuals, especially high government officials, who have been responsible for gross human rights

---

6. Resolution 940 of the UN Security Council, July 31, 1994.
7. President Clinton, address to the nation, September 1. 1994. Text in the *New York Times,* September 2, 1994.

abuses has also been reflected in the Clinton administration's coolness toward the establishment of a permanent international criminal court (see Chapter 6) and toward efforts by other governments to put former Chilean dictator Augusto Pinochet on trial for crimes committed under his regime in the 1970s.

Some U.S. officials fear that because of Washington's Cold War activism (both military and covert) and its post–Cold War superpower assertiveness, governments around the world may be tempted to seek applause from their constituents by demanding that U.S. leaders, past and present, be put on trial in international tribunals for war crimes and human rights violations. Could George Bush be indicated for the suffering and deaths of Iraqi civilians from disease and malnutrition produced by the economic sanctions and bombings Bush ordered during the Gulf War? Could President Truman be tried posthumously for the atomic bombing of Hiroshima and Nagasaki? What about the complicity of Richard Nixon and Henry Kissinger with the violent coup in Chile in 1973 that resulted in the murder of elected President Salvador Allende and the assumption of power by Pinochet? To fend off criticisms that U.S. government was being unduly self-protective with regard to its own possible human rights criminality, the Clinton administration decided in December 1998 to declassify some secret documents on the killings and torture policies of the Pinochet regime.[8]

The Clinton administration's unsteady and vacillating human rights posture was also evident in its policies toward political crises in various of the Asian countries suffering from the collapse of financial markets in 1998. Although initially announcing support for market *democracies,* the administration had been quite tolerant of autocracy in countries such as South Korea, Indonesia, Malaysia, and Singapore, given their openness to economic globalization and their success with capitalism. But when economic collapse translated into severe unemployment, a dramatic constriction of needed health and other social services, and repressive responses by the governments in power to demands by dissidents for greater democratic accountability, second thoughts surfaced in the the the minds of U.S. policy makers.

Still, the U.S. government offered only belated support to the prodemocracy forces in Indonesia that forced the resignation of dictatorial President Suharto in 1998. Subsequently the Clinton administration stood by ambivalently as Suharto's successor, B. J. Habibie, began his own crackdown on opposition groups who were mobilizing support for the spring 1999 elections. Indonesia, clearly, was one of those countries too big and too much of a factor in the global economy, as Asia's largest oil producer, to be pushed around.

---

8.   Tim Weiner, " U.S. Will Release Files on Crimes Under Pinochet," *New York Times,* (December 2, 1998).

By contrast, at the November 1998 meeting in Kuala Lumpur of the Asia Pacific Economic Cooperation forum, Vice President Al Gore, substituting for President Clinton, lambasted his Malaysian hosts for suppressing democracy and human rights (Prime Minister Mahathir Mohamad was at the time the object of intense protests by prodemocracy forces for imprisoning his reformist deputy, Anwar Ibrahim, on charges of corruption and sexual offenses and allowing him to be beaten by prison officials). The U.S. vice president, in his prepared speech, praised "the brave people of Malaysia" who were calling for democracy along with economic reform. "Democracies have done better in coping with economic crises than nations where freedom is repressed," he said. "Democracy confers a stamp of legitimacy that reforms must have in order to be effective." Prime Minister Mahathir was reported to be deeply offended by Gore's remarks, and the Malaysian trade minister told representatives of the world's press that "It was the most disgusting speech I've heard in my life." The foreign minister, Abdullah Badawi, went even further, denouncing "incitement by the U.S. government to lawlessness by certain undemocratic elements," and threatening that Malaysia will "hold the U.S. responsible" for any violence. Even countries normally allied with the United States were not particularly pleased. Australian Prime Minister John Howard complained that "You don't necessarily achieve a desirable outcome by . . . hectoring other nations."[9]

Reactions by the attentive public in the United States were mixed. Some leading newspapers editorialized against the Gore démarche in Kuala Lumpur, calling it rude, sanctimonious, and likely to galvanize nationalistic support for Mahathir's dictatorial methods. Others, like the *New York Times*, opined that the vice president was "right to be rude. America's interest in Asia is to encourage human rights and democratic change, not to flatter embattled autocrats."[10]

Human rights critics continued to ask (rhetorically, since they, of course, knew the answer) Why just Malaysia? Why not Indonesia? Or China? Not surprisingly, as this review of U.S. policy shows, human rights, having become a prominent part of world politics and no longer the preserve of reformist lawyers and activists, are subject to the same kinds of instrumental manipulation by powerful and small countries alike in the service of their perceived national interests.

---

9. Mark Landler, "Gore, in Malaysia, Says Its Leaders Suppress Freedom," *New York Times* (November 17, 1998); and Indira A. R. Lakshmanan, "Asian Nations Angered by Gore Comments," *Boston Globe* (November 18, 1998).

10. "Championing Democarcy in Malaysia," *New York Times* (editorial, November 18, 1998).

8

Human Rights and the Future of World Politics

Even before the convulsions of the post–Cold War era began, R. J. Vincent, a sage British scholar of international relations, speculated that the global system was on the verge of experiencing "a transformation from international relations to world politics as significant as that which established the society of states, and for which the idea of human rights is a kind of midwife." Dr. Vincent was reacting to what he perceived to be an emerging transnational world in which "Individuals and groups other than states have forced themselves on the attention of world society."[1]

The events and debates recounted in this book support Dr. Vincent's diagnosis. The increasing mobility of persons and ideas, along with the mobility of economic goods and services, has been creating a world society (if not yet a world community) that requires strengthened international legal and political structures. In the process, traditional state-sovereignty norms and institutions are coming under increasing assault, both from intellectuals and from the international facts of life.

There is no going back to the older system in which how national governments treat the people within their jurisdictions is no one else's business. A system of international and transnational accountability is evolving, by fits and starts. Driven by competing ideas about justice as well as by material forces, the state-sovereignty system is in the process of transformation. Its basic shape—still up for grabs—will be substantially determined by the outcome of the human rights debates and struggles analyzed in these pages.

---

1. R. J. Vincent, *Human Rights and International Relations* (New York: Cambridge University Press, 1986), pp. 151–152.

THE FUNDAMENTAL "CONSTITUTIONAL" ISSUE

To be, or not to be, a world polity—that is *not* the question. Inescapably, like it not, we are. The question, rather, is what kind of a polity do we want to be, and that raises the fundamental, constitutional issue of what rights are to be guaranteed to human beings throughout world society and what rights are to be left to the world's particular communities, especially to its nation-states, to determine for themselves.

Political philosopher Michael Walzer joins the debate with his 1994 essay, *Thick and Thin*.[2] Walzer's thesis is that the dense, many-layered, complex, and often subtle norms of human relations—the *thick* aspects of culture and morality—vary from community to community and it would be imprudent to attempt to homogenize them into a unitary world polity. The product of historical experience, the thick fabric of formal rules and informal mores present in each community comprises its uniquely evolved determination of what arrangements are just and practicable for its people. Outsiders, despite their preferences, should accord presumptive validity to such community ways of life; each community should be given the benefit of the doubt for knowing what it is doing in its allocation of rights and duties among its people.

Walzer's communitarian philosophy has room for only a *thin* worldwide fabric of universal rules for how people should treat one another. This would appear to be consistent with how the so-called international system in fact works: Nation-states are unwilling to accord international regimes authority over anything but the most necessary arrangements for coordinating their interactions, and despite all the legal-sounding rhetoric in international human rights documents, countries have yet to grant international agencies anything but the most rudimentary scrutiny over their internal affairs.

Walzer's realism, however, should not be confused with the so-called realist school of international relations, which maintains that attempts to hold nation-states internationally accountable to any universal moral principles (such as those set forth in the core human rights covenants) are incompatible with the anarchic structure of the international system. As Walzer argues in his *Just and Unjust Wars*, states should and can be morally constrained by some elemental and universalistic principles of justice and human decency in how they treat one another and the citizens within their jurisdictions—even in wartime.[3] Some policies, such as those regarding genocide or a degree of systematic and massive oppres-

---

2. Michael Walzer, *Thick and Thin: Moral Argument at Home and Abroad* (Notre Dame: University of Notre Dame Press, 1994).
3. Michael Walzer, *Just and Unjust Wars: A Moral Argument with Historical Illustrations* (New York: Basic Books, 1977).

sion by one group of another that approximates slavery (Walzer puts apartheid in this category), clearly provide justifiable grounds for international intervention to stop them, if not by world agencies then by other national governments acting alone or in coalition.[4] Short of such extremes, however, Walzer would move cautiously when it comes to internationally institutionalizing his or any community's moral preferences. Outsiders, and the international community (to the extent that it can put together a consensus), may have serious reservations about aspects of a particular country's internal political arrangements and domestic policies, but these reservations should at least initially be explored through international dialogue and reasoned discourse rather than through UN censure and diplomatic isolation, economic sanctions, or military intervention.

Other contributors to this global, constitutional debate come out quite differently. Organizations like Amnesty International and Human Rights Watch regard the basic human rights covenants, now ratified by the vast majority of countries, as an international bill of rights (analogous to the function of the Bill of Rights vis-à-vis the U.S. Constitution) that gives specific elaboration to the general human rights objectives in the UN Charter. The provisions of the covenants—prescribing the kinds of thick societal arrangements that Walzer said should be the province of particular communities—are *already* international law, and people around the world, especially in countries that have ratified the covenants, are fully justified in demanding that their governments adhere to these provisions. From this perspective, Walzer and other communitarians are either behind the times or engaged in a reactionary campaign to undermine the basic world community consensus that has already been forged.

In fact, however, international law is still essentially a set of treaties and covenants among states that retain the power to renege on their obligations. The world polity is not yet a *supra*national system. What a nation-state has conceded to be its obligations by signing various international human rights covenants it may yet take back if it comes to believe that these covenants are being used against it by those disrespectful of its culture.

The observations of Dr. Vincent, quoted at the outset of this chapter, provide what I believe to be the right perspective on this fundamental constitutional issue, namely, that we are in a highly dynamic phase of the evolution of the world polity and that the human rights debate is at the center of this process. The international bill of rights is as yet hardly an analog of the U.S. Bill of Rights, which is centrally enforceable by U.S. citizens against the states. In the world system, the potential for

---

4. Ibid., pp. 89–90.

such supranational enforcement exists, and certain developments—the ability of individuals to sue for their human rights in the Council of Europe system, the ad hoc war crimes tribunals for Bosnia and Rwanda, and the move to establish a permanent tribunal—may indeed be prefiguarations of the birth of a new world polity for which, as Vincent put it, the midwife would be the human rights idea. Perhaps. But other developments—the growth of religious fundamentalism, antidemocracy backlashes in the states of the former Soviet Union and in the Third World, the revival of xenophobic anti-immigration policies in affluent industrial countries—may be indicators of deeper systemic resistance to change than some of us were forecasting at the start of the post–Cold War era.

In other words, the constitution of the world polity is not yet set, either in its structure or its norms. Indeed, the most fundamental features of its structure and norms are still evolving, and we are all its founding fathers and mothers—especially when it comes to the issue of which rights of persons and peoples should be universally guaranteed and which rights should be contingent upon their compatibility with the traditions and current values of particular communities.

MOVING INTO THE "FOURTH GENERATION"

This contemporary constitutional debate over human rights can be viewed simply as the latest expression of the perennial philosophical debate between universal moral absolutism and cultural relativism. As shown in Chapter 4, Aristotle and Cicero, Locke and Burke, Kant and Rousseau, Hegel and Mill, and their more recent counterparts have had illuminating things to say on the issue, which statespersons and politicians sometimes explicitly invoke on behalf of their preferences. Unfortunately, at the level of the competing philosophical logics themselves, the central issues are probably unresolvable.

But we should not be stymied by the philosophical impasse, for the political struggles are continuing anyway, and new patterns of relationships between persons, communities, and governments are evolving around globe. Respectful attention to what people around the world have been claiming as their rights can provide a starting point for informed analysis of (and, for those who want to, intelligent participation in) the evolution of the new world polity. What does such analysis show?

First, and most important, virtually all people resent (and many will try to subvert) norms and structures they feel are imposed on them by people who are not members of their own community. Empires are inherently unstable, and

community self-determination is ultimately the most powerful political force.

*Second, a basic long-term, global trend is the growing
moral legitimacy and practical force of claims of minorities against oppressive national governments.* This is an
irreversible result of the expanding mobility of people and
information, which provides such minorities with increasing opportunities to establish transnational connections
with their ethnic, religious, professional, and ideological
brothers and sisters in other countries. The implication is
that countries (and their national governments) are losing
moral standing, relatively speaking, in comparison with
other communities and nongovernmental organizations.

*Third, another long-term, global trend is the increasing
moral legitimacy of the claim of individual rights vis-à-vis
communities and the empowerment of individuals to
assert their rights against community efforts to induce conformity.* This too is an irreversible result of the expanding
mobility of people and information.

These trends are part and parcel of the increasing prominence of
human rights issues in world society. They reflect the ways that the proliferation of human rights claims and groups advancing them are changing the face of both domestic and international politics. They also indicate how the changing world polity is affecting the discourse on human
rights.

It is commonplace in the literature on human rights to characterize
the political discourse as having moved from one generation to another:

- An emphasis on the civil and political rights of individuals against
  repressive governments (the first generation)

- An emphasis on the basic needs of the economically disadvantaged in domestic and world society (the second generation)

- An emphasis on the empowerment of minorities or other communities that have been historically neglected or repressed by the
  dominant cultural groups in the larger society. This empowerment is sometimes called "collective rights" or "solidarity rights"
  (the third generation)

I see a fourth generation of discourse emerging, namely, the on-going
confrontations among all of these previous generations and their champi-

ons in the international forums that are fashioning the norms and institutions of the evolving world polity. The largest question for this fourth generation is whether the on-going confrontations will confirm political scientist Samuel P. Huntington's ominous forecast of a clash of civilizations between the West and the rest[5] or whether they will engender an intense but mutually respectful "cross-cultural dialogue and internal cultural discourse" (a phrase from human rights legal theorist Abdullah Ahmed An-Nàim.).[6] This book has been written to promote the latter.

---

5. Samuel P. Huntington, "The Clash of Civilizations?" *Foreign Affairs* 72, 3 (Summer 1993), pp. 22–49.
6. Abdullah Ahmed An-Nàim, ed., *Human Rights in Cross-Cultural Perspective* (Philadelphia, PA: University of Pennsylvania Press, 1992). See especially An-Nàim's own chapter, "Toward a Cross-Cultural Approach to Defining International Standards of Human Rights," pp. 19–43.

Obtaining Information on Human Rights

by Leslie Stebbins*

This is an introduction to the literature on human rights. Most of the sources are available in the United States through university and public libraries. Increasingly, this information is accessible from organizations and individuals with established sites on the Internet.

Comprehensive Guides to the Literature on Human Rights

Comprehensive guides are listed here. Guides to specific topics are listed in subsequent sections as well as in many of the comprehensive guides listed here.

Andrews, John A., and William D. Hines. *Keyguide to Information Sources on the International Protection of Human Rights.* New York: Facts on File Publications, 1987. Useful background information on pertinent international instruments and institutions and a general review of the literature. Includes large bibliography of resources and annotated list of official and nongovernmental organizations active in the human rights field.

Tobin, John J. *Guide to Human Rights Research.* Cambridge, MA: Harvard Law School Human Rights Program, 1994. Comprehensive bibliography on resources for human rights research. Special emphasis on legal materials useful to both professionals and laypersons. Details on location of human rights information in reports and records of the United Nations and other intergovernmental organizations as well as nongovernmental organizations. Full text available online at www.law.harvard.edu/groups/hrp2/.

Walters, Gregory J. *Human Rights in Theory and Practice: A Selected and Annotated Bibliography.* Metuchen, NJ: Scarecrow

---

* Leslie Stebbins is Coordinator of Library Instruction, Goldfarb Library, Brandeis University.

Press, 1995. An annotated bibliography, particularly strong on the philosophical, ethical, and religious foundations of human rights. Also covers works on international law, intergovernmental organizations, and nongovernmental organizations.

Hall, Katherine C. *International Human Rights Law: A Resource Guide.* Queenstown, MD: Aspen Institute, 1993. A guide to primary and secondary sources for international human rights law. Includes capsule history of the international human rights system. Provides citations with brief annotations to treaties, agreements, court opinions, resolutions of intergovernmental and international organizations, and reports of nongovernmental organizations. Symonides, Janusz and Vladimir Volodin. *Access to Human Rights Documentation: Documentation, Bibliographies and Databases on Human Rights.* Paris: UNESCO, 1994. Identifies major works on human rights from 1949 to 1993, documents of intergovernmental and nongovernmental organizations, and some useful databases. Also contains an extensive list of bibliographies on specific issues within the field.

Indexes and Overviews of the Work of International Organizations

General

The Yearbook of International Organizations. Brussels: Union of International Associations, 1948–. Provides background information on intergovernmental organizations, including historical information, major activities, structure, publications issued, and lists of affiliated nongovernmental organizations.

Journal of Government Information, Volume 6, every year. Tarrytown, NY: Pergamon Press, 1994–. (Previous title was *Government Publications Review.*) Annual index of reports and studies by intergovernmental organizations.

United Nations (all agencies)

United Nations Action in the Field of Human Rights, issued every five years. Describes all the UN human rights bodies, provides detailed summaries of current human rights activities within the UN, and includes references to recent UN documents on human rights.

United Nations Sub-Commission on the Prevention of Discrimination and Protection of Minorities. *List of Studies and Reports,* published as E/CN.4/Sub.2/[year]/2. Annual list of human rights–related studies prepared for the General Assembly, the Economic and Social Council, the Commission on Human Rights, and the Sub-Commission on the Prevention of Discrimination and Protection of Minorities and reports under preparation by special rapporteurs of the Sub-Commission. (Includes references to UN sales publication numbers when available for sale.)

Index to United Nations Documents and Publications. (Available on CD-ROM and on the Web at www.readex.com) Lists documents of the six main bodies of the UN; masthead documents; official records; sales publications; limited and restricted documents; documents emanating from sessional and standing committees, functional commissions, conferences and regional bodies; articles appearing in UN periodicals; and bilateral and multilateral treaties in the UN Treaty Series. Also includes citations to reports from the Commission on Human Rights, the annual report of the Human Rights Committee, and country reports by special rapporteurs.

Human Rights on CD-ROM. Citations to over 12,000 UN documents and publications related to human rights issued since 1980. Updated annually. Some of the information is taken from the UN materials database of the UN Bibliographic Information System.

United Nations Web site at www.un.org. Contains general information about the UN; Press releases (including current press releases from the Human Rights Committee), a daily list of documents released by the UN; a list of sales publications. Includes some texts of selected documents from the Commission on Human Rights and the Economic and Social Council. Includes over 30,000 treaties and related subsequent actions.

Reports of United Nations and Specialized Agencies Dealing with Human Rights

United Nations Commission on Human Rights (UNCHR)—most important UN human rights agency and an organ of the Economic and Social Council.

The annual report of the Commission on Human Rights, including its decisions, resolutions, and record of deliberations is found in United Nations, Economic and Social Council, *Official Records.*

Theme reports and country reports, including those of special rapporteurs or special representatives of the Commission, are published as E/CN.4/[year] and indexed in the *Index to United Nations Documents and Publications.* Recent years are available at www.unhchr.ch.

For highlights of Commission sessions see *The Review* (International Commission of Jurists, 1969–) and *Human Rights Quarterly* (Johns Hopkins University Press, 1981–).

United Nations Sub-Commission on the Prevention of Discrimination and Protection of Minorities—body of experts elected by the Commission and subordinate to it.

Documents of the Sub-Commission are found in the same sources indicated for the Commission on Human Rights. Its country and theme reports are published as E/CN.4/Sub.2/[year].

Human Rights Committee—body of experts set up by the Covenant on Civil and Political Rights to oversee the implementation of its provisions.

Report of the Human Rights Committee, [session no.]. Issued annually. Contains summaries of Committee documents and decisions (the full text of reports is published in small numbers, subject to the Committee's rules of restricted distribution, and are difficult to obtain).

International Labour Organization (ILO)—independent agency, associated with the United Nations, specializing in labor union rights, worker health and safety standards, child labor, and so forth.

Official Bulletin of the ILO. Issued three times a year. Summarizes activities of the ILO. Includes texts adopted by the International Labour Conference (its plenary body).

International Labour Review. Issued six times a year. Articles on recent ILO activities and other research related to international labor issues.

LABORDOC. Available on CD-ROM, online, and in print as *International Labour Documentation.* Indexes all ILO publications and other resources collected by the ILO library. Portions of this index are available at www.ilo.org.

Reports of Regional Organizations

European Commission of Human Rights—intergovernmental body of first resort for cases brought under the Council of Europe's Convention for the Protection of Human Rights and Fundamental Freedoms.

European Human Rights Reports. Bimonthly selection of decisions of the Commission, plus extracts of cases before the European Court of Human Rights. Recent reports can be found at www.dhcommhr.coe.fr

Minutes of the Plenary Session held at [city]. Account of each session.

European Court of Human Rights—adjudicates cases on appeal from the European Commission of Human Rights or brought by member governments of the council of Europe.

Publications of the European Court of Human Rights. Series A, Judgments and Decisions. Text of recent judgements can be found at www.dhcour.coe.fr.

Council of Europe: Directorate of Human Rights

Documentation Sources in Human Rights. Booklets containing lists of human rights publications of the council, and judgments and reports of the European Human Rights Commission and Court.

Inter-American Commission on Human Rights—The Organization of American States' intergovernmental body of first resort for cases brought under the American Human Rights Convention.

Annual Report—Inter-American Commission on Human Rights [year]. These reports are available at www.oas.org.

Inter-American Court of Human Rights—hears cases on appeal from the Inter-American commission of Human Rights or brought by member governments of the Organization of American States.

Series A—Judgments and Opinions. Texts of the Court's advisory opinions.

Series B—Pleadings, Oral Arguments and Documents. Texts of pleadings, briefs, and other legal materials.

Series C—Decisions and Judgments. Opinions of cases decided by the Court.

Press Release. Recent judgments of the Court and agendas of future sessions.

African Commission on Human and Peoples' Rights—Human rights agency of the Organization of African Unity, established by the African Charter on Human and Peoples' Rights.

Review of the African Commission on Human and Peoples' Rights. Reports on Commission sessions. Includes scholarly articles on human rights in Africa.

Nongovernmental Organizations

Directories containing current information on nongovernmental organizations:

Human Rights Internet Reporter. Listed below under the Human Rights Internet, directory is a valuable source for locating many NGO publications.

Master List of Human Rights Organizations and Serial Publications. Cambridge, MA: Human Rights Internet, Harvard Law School, 1994 (5th ed.; supplement to <I>Human Rights Internet Reporter<I>)

The Yearbook of International Organizations. Munich: Saur, 1948–. (Biennial)

Encyclopedia of Associations: International Organizations. Detroit: Gale, 1961–. (Annual)

Amnesty International—The largest human rights organization in the world. Works to free prisoners of conscience, to ensure fair trials for all political prisoners, and to abolish torture and executions.

Amnesty International
U.S. office:
322 Eighth Avenue
New York, NY 10001
212/807-8400
www.amnesty.org

Amnesty International Report [year]. Country-by-country survey of human rights. Summaries available at www.amnesty.org.

Newsletter. Monthly publication containing articles on human rights violations around the world. Includes "urgent actions" for members.

Human Right Watch—Investigates human rights abuses in about 70 countries. Documents and denounces murders, disappearances, torture, arbitrary imprisonment, exile, censorship, and other abuses of internationally recognized human rights.

Human Rights Watch
U.S. Office:
485 5th Avenue, 3rd Floor
New York, NY 10017
(212) 972-8400
www.hrw.org

World Report. Surveys and analyzes the U.S. government's human rights policies in other countries and describes human rights developments in those countries.

Human Rights Watch Quarterly Newsletter. Contains information on specific topics and updates on activities in particular countries.

Critique of the Department of State's Country Reports on Human Rights Practices for [year]. Published jointly with the Lawyer's Committee for Human Rights and available on the Lawyer's Committee gopher listed below.

Human Rights Internet—International communications network and clearinghouse on human rights. Collects publications from other human rights organizations from around the world.

Human Rights Internet
8 York Street, Suite 202
Ottawa, Ontario K1N5S6
613/789-7407
www.hri.ca

Human Rights Tribune/Tribune des Droits Humains. Quarterly containing a calendar of human rights events, short reports on country conditions, activities of NGOs, and some information about international organizations.

Human Rights Internet Reporter. Citations and abstracts to publications produced by NGOs, with some coverage of IGO reports. Information from the *Reporter* is available on a database at HRI from 1985 to the present, and many documents have been reproduced on microfiche by the InterDocumentation Company and are available at some libraries.

International Commission of Jurists—Multinational organization of jurists representing legal systems around the world working to promote human rights through the rule of law.

International Commission of Jurists
U.S. office:
777 UN Plaza
New York, NY 10017
212/972-0883

The Review. Semiannual. Contains brief articles on human rights conditions in individual countries and articles on human rights topics, including reviews of sessions of UN human rights bodies.

ICJ Newsletter. Reports on current activities

Attacks on Justice: The Harassment and Persecution of Judges and Lawyers. Annual account of cases of summary execution, detention, physical attacks, threats of violence, and professional sanctions against judges and lawyers.

International Committee of the Red Cross—Provides protection and assistance to victims of war; ensures application of the Geneva Conventions, including visits to prisoners of war and internment camps, transport and distribution of relief, information to families, and searches for the missing; and promotes the development and dissemination of international humanitarian law.

International Committee of the Red Cross
19 av de la Paix
CH-1202 Geneve, Switzerland
41 22/734 60 01
www.icrc.org

International Review of the Red Cross. Record of activities and events

Annual Report . Includes operational activities by country.

ICRC's Internet site includes the above two publications and a catalog of ICRC's publications.

Committee to Protect Journalists—Monitors abuses against the press and promotes international press freedom.

The Committee to Protect Journalists
330 Seventh Avenue, 12th Floor
New York, NY, 10001
212/465-1004,
www.cpj.org

American Association for the Advancement of Science—Documents human rights violations affecting the scientific community worldwide. Promotes use of scientific methods in the documentation and prevention of human rights violations. Promotes support for human rights and academic freedom within the scientific community.

> American Association for the Advancement of Science
> Science and Human Rights Program
> 1200 New York Avenue NW
> Washington, DC 20005
> 202/326-6600
> shr.aas.org

International Women's Rights Action Watch—Monitors law and policy developments affecting women throughout the world under the Convention on the Elimination of all Forms of Discrimination Against Women.

> International Women's Rights Action Watch
> Humphrey Institute of Public Affairs
> University of Minnesota
> 301 19th Ave. South
> Minneapolis, MN 55455
> 612/625-5093

> *Women's Watch.* Reports on law and policy change in accordance with the principles of CEDAW.

> Lawyers Committee for Human Rights
> 330 Seventh Avenue, 10th Floor
> New York, NY 10001
> 212/629-6170
> www.lchr.org

Lawyers Committee for Human Rights—Protects fundamental human rights as established by the International Bill of Human Rights and other international instruments. Focuses on the legal side of human rights.

> *Bulletin of the Lawyers Committee for Human Rights.* Information on the activities of the Committee.

> *In Defense of Rights* . Documents the persecution of judges and lawyers around the world

> *Critique: Review of the Department of State's Country Reports on Human Rights Practices,* available through 1996 on LCHR's gopher site, organized by country.

PEN (Freedom-To-Write Committee)—Defends the right to freedom of expression and to resist censorship.

PEN (Freedom-To-Write Committee)
568 Broadway
New York, NY 10012
212/334-1660
www.pen.org

Freedom-to-Write Bulletin, reports on recent casework and encourages letter-writing campaigns for profiled cases.

Physicians for Human Rights—Investigates and tries to prevent violations of international human rights and humanitarian law using the medical and forensic skills of health professionals, scientists, and concerned citizens.

Physicians for Human Rights
100 Boylston Street, Suite 702
Boston, MA 02116.
617/695-0041
www.phrusa.org

General Texts and Treatises

Alston, Philip., ed. The United Nations and Human Rights: A Critical Appraisal. Oxford: Clarendon Press; New York: Oxford University Press, 1992.

Am-Na'im, A. *Human Rights in Cross-Cultural Perspectives: A Quest for Consensus.* Philadelphia: University of Pennsylvania Press, 1992.

Claude, Richard Pierre, Burns H. Weston, and others. *Human Rights in the World Community: Issues and Action.* Philadelphia: University of Pennsylvania Press, 1992.

Donnelly, Jack. *International Human Rights.* 2nd ed. Boulder, CO: Westview Press, 1998.

Forsythe, David P. *Human Rights and World Politics.* Lincoln, NB: University of Nebraska Press, 1989.

Ratner, Steven R. *Accountability for Human Rights Atrocities in International Law:* Beyond the Nuremberg Legacy. Oxford: Oxford University Press, 1997.

Shue, Henry. *Basic Rights: Subsistence, Affluence, and U.S. Foreign Policy.* Princeton, NJ: Princeton University Press, 1996.

Steiner, Henry J., and Philip Alston. *International Human Rights in Context: Law, Politics, Morals.* Oxford: Clarendon Press; New York: Oxford University Press, 1996.

Vincent, R. J. *Human Rights and International Relations.* Cambridge: Cambridge University Press, 1986.

Human Rights Legal Instruments

Blaustein, Albert, Roger Clark, and Jay Sigler, eds. *Human Rights Sourcebook.* New York: Paragon House Publishers, 1987.

UN Centre for Human Rights. *Human Rights: A Compilation of International Instruments.* New York: United Nations, 1994. (ST/HR/1/Rev. 5)

Lawson, Edward. *Encyclopedia of Human Rights.* 2nd ed. New York: Taylor & Frances, 1996.

Brownlie, Ian, ed. *Basic Documents on Human Rights.* 3rd ed. Oxford: Clarendon Press; New York: Oxford University Press, 1993.

International Labour Conventions and Recommendations. Geneva: International Labour Office, 1996.

Lillich, Richard, ed. *International Human Rights Instruments: A Compilation of Treaties, Agreements, and Declarations of Especial Interest to the United States.* Buffalo, NY: W. S. Hein Co., 1990.

Council of Europe. *European Convention on Human Rights: Collected Texts.* Strasbourg: Council of Europe Press, 1994.

Human Rights in International Law: Basic Texts. Strasbourg: Council of Europe Press, 1992.

Organization of American States. *Basic Documents Pertaining to Human Rights in the Inter-American System.* Washington, DC: General Secretariat, Organization of American States, 1996.

Hamalengwa, M., C. Flinterman and E. Dankwa, comps. *The International Law of Human Rights in Africa: Basic Documents and Annotated Bibliography.* Dordrecht, Netherlands, and Boston, MA: M. Nijhoff, 1988.

Electronic Compilations of Instruments on the Internet

University of Minnesota Human Rights Library
(www.umn.edu/humanrts)
Full text of hundreds of international and regional human rights treaties and other instruments, materials relating to the work of UN organs, committees, agencies and criminal tribunals, and collections of documents on human rights in specific regions.

Fourth World Documentation Project
(www.halcyon.com/FWDP/fwdp.html)
Sponsored by the Center for World Indigenous Studies, currently archives over 400 documents including essays, position papers, resolutions, treaties, UN documents, speeches and declarations relating to Fourth World nations in the Americas, Africa, Asia, Europe, Melanesia and the Pacific. The text of a number of human rights treaties and other instruments are included.

Multilaterals Project (www.tufts.edu/fletcher/multilaterals.html)
A project of the Fletcher School of Law and Diplomacy at Tufts University, this site is designed to make available the texts of international multilateral conventions and other instruments, including those on human rights. Provides the full text of current as well as historical texts including the 1648 Treaty of Westphalia and the Covenant of the League of Nations.

United Nations High Commissioner for Human Rights
(www.unhchr.ch)
Large collection of international human rights instruments and UN human rights documents.

Other Internet Sources on Human Rights

Diana Database (diana.law.yale.edu)
A project of the Urban Morgan Human Rights Institutes at the University of Cincinnati College of Law and the Schell Memorial Human Rights Institute of Yale Law School to make available over the Web a collection of full-text human rights materials including treaties, court decisions, legal briefs, and secondary sources.

Directory of Human Rights Resources on the Internet
(shr.aaas.org/dhr.htm)
A comprehensive database of human rights organizations on the Web compiled and indexed by the American Association for the Advancement of Science and Human Rights Program.

University-based Web Sites—Several university-based Web sites with useful collections of human rights materials:

Center for Human Rights and Humanitarian Law, Washington College of Law, The American University (www.wcl.american.edu/pub/humright/)

Lillian Goldman Library at Yale Law School (elsinore.cis.yale.edu/lawweb/hrpage.htm)

University of Michigan Documents Center

(www.lib.umich.edu/libhome/Documents.center/psintl.html#rights){/BIB}

Journals Specializing in Human Rights

Canadian Human Rights Yearbook. Toronto: Carswell, 1983–. Articles, essays on law, case notes, and a bibliography on the Canadian Charter of Rights and Freedoms.

Columbia Human Rights Law Review. New York: Columbia University School of Law, 1972–. Semiannual, articles on human rights and civil rights with a focus on the United States.

Harvard Human Rights Journal. Cambridge, MA: Harvard Law School, 1988–. Annual publication includes articles and book reviews on human rights issues.

Human Rights Quarterly. Baltimore, MD: Johns Hopkins University Press, 1979–. Key journal in the field. Sponsored by the Urban Morgan Institute for Human Rights at the College of Law, University of Cincinnati. Articles are from a range of disciplines in law, the social sciences, and the humanities. Includes book reviews.

Human Rights Law Journal. Arlington, VA: N.P. Engel, 1980–. Monthly journal includes scholarly articles focusing on European human rights issues and has extracts of European Court and Commission of Human Rights decisions and reports. Also provides annual list of the current ratification status of international human rights instruments.

Human Rights Monitor. Geneva: International Service for Human Rights, 1988–. Review of UN activities and summaries of the UN Commission on Human Rights and the Sub-Commission on Prevention of Discrimination and Protection of Minorities and other treaty-monitoring bodies.

The International Journal of Human Rights. London: Frank Cass & Co., 1997–. Quarterly journal covering broad spectrum of human rights issues.

International Journal of Refugee Law. Oxford: Oxford University Press, 1989–. Quarterly publication on refugee law and its development.

Israel Yearbook on Human Rights. Tel Aviv: Faculty of Law, Tel Aviv University, 1971–. Articles and book reviews focused on Israeli or other Middle East human rights issues.

Netherlands Quarterly of Human Rights. Utrecht :Studie-en Informatiecentrum Mensenrechten, 1983–. Covers the theory and practice of international and European human rights protection. Articles, news, and documents from around the world.

New York Law School Journal of Human Rights. New York: The School, 1987–. Semiannual student-edited journal of articles and book reviews on U.S. civil rights and international human rights issues.

Refugee Survey Quarterly. Geneva, Switzerland: UNHCR, Centre for Documentation on Refugees, 1994–. (Continues *Refugee Abstracts*) Includes a bibliography of books, articles, reports, book reviews, announcements of new publications, meetings and conferences, country reports, and refugee- or human rights–related legal documentation.

South African Journal on Human Rights. Braamfontein, South Africa: Revan Press, 1985–. Issued three times a year, contains articles, cases and book reviews.

Topical Surveys and Analyses

Studies and reports by scholars and nongovernmental organizations (NGOs) usually provide more candid information than do reports of United Nations agencies and of other official international organizations, since the reports of the inter-governmental agencies are often purged of statements that member governments find embarrassing. The reports by national governments, though less watered down, are characteristically selective in praising their international allies and condemning their adversaries. Reports by the major human rights NGOs and reputable independent scholars are not entirely free of their own biases in this controversial field, but this has more to do with their philosophies of human rights than with efforts to protect or subvert a particular government.

Note that using search terms designating violations rather than the rights themselves—for example, using *genocide* rather than *racial survival* or *torture* rather than *protection against brutal treatment*—will produce more useful results in searching online indexes and catalogs.

Genocide and War Crimes

Steiner, Henry J., and Philip Alston. "International Crimes and Criminal Tribunals." Chapter 15 in *International Human Rights in Context: Law, Politics, Morals.* Oxford: Clarendon Press; New York: Oxford University Press, 1996, 1021–1109.

Human Rights Watch. *Slaughter Among Neighbors: The Political Origins of Communal Violence.* New Haven: Yale University Press, 1995.

Kuper, Leo. *The Prevention of Genocide.* New Haven: Yale University Press, 1985

Tutorow, Norman ed. *War Crimes, War Criminals and War Crimes Trials: An Annotated Bibliography and Source Book.* New York: Greenwood Press, 1986.

"A Critical Study of the International Tribunal for the Former Yugoslavia." *Criminal Law Forum* 5, 2–3 (1994).

Payam, Akhavan. "The Yugoslav Tribunal at a Crossroads: The Dayton Peace Agreement and Beyond." *Human Rights Quarterly* 18, 2 (May 1996), 259–285.

Meron, Theodor. "The Case for War Crimes Trials in Yugoslavia." *Foreign Affairs* 72, 3 (summer 1993), 122–135.

Human Rights Watch. *Iraq's Crime of Genocide: The Anfal Campaign against the Kurds.* New Haven: Yale University Press, 1995.

Niarchos, Catherine N. "Women, War, and Rape: Challenges Facing the International Tribunal for the Former Yugoslavia." *Human Rights Quarterly* 17, 4 (November 1995), 649–690.

"Draft Statute for the International Criminal Court" can be found at www.un.org/law/n9810105.pdf

Torture and Other Cruel and Inhuman Punishment

Human Rights Watch/Middle East. *Torture and Ill-Treatment: Israel's Interrogation of Palestinians from the Occupied Territories.* New York: Human Rights Watch, 1994.

Human Rights Watch/Middle East. *Behind Closed Doors: Torture and Detention in Egypt.* New York: Human Rights Watch, 1992.

Women's Rights

United Nations Committee on the Elimination of Discrimination Against Women. *Report on the Implementation of the Convention on the Elimination of All Forms of Discrimination Against Women.* (Issued annually as a General Assembly document)

Human Rights Watch. *The Human Rights Watch Global Report on Women's Human Rights.* New York: Human Rights Watch, 1995.

The Women's Watch. Minneapolis, MN: International Women's Rights Action Watch, Humphrey Institute of Public Affairs, 1987–.

MacKinnon, Catherine A. "Crimes of War, Crimes of Peace." in Stephen Shute and Susan Hurley, eds. *On Human Rights.* New York: Basic Books, 1993, 83–109.

Dorkenoo, Efua. *Female Genital Mutilation: Proposals for Change.* London: Minority Rights Group, 1992.

Peters, Julie, and others. *Women's Rights, Human Rights: International Feminist Perspectives.* New York: Routledge, 1995.

Gay and Lesbian Rights

Sanders, Douglas. "Getting Lesbian and Gay Issues on the International Human Rights Agenda." *Human Rights Quarterly* 18, 1 (February 1996), 67–106.

Breaking the Silence: Human Rights Violations Based on Sexual Orientation. London: Amnesty International, 1997.

Thomas, Michael. "Teetering on the Brink of Equality: Sexual Orientation and International Constitutional Protection." *Boston College Third World Law Journal* 17 (spring 1997), 365–394.

Long, Scott. *Public Scandals: Sexual Orientation and Criminal Law in Romania.* New York: Human Rights Watch, 1998.

The Rights of Ethnic Communities and Indigenous Peoples

Gurr, Theodore R. *Minorities at Risk: A Global View of Ethnopolitical Conflicts.* Washington, DC: United States Institute of Peace Press, 1993.

Brownlie, L. *Treaties and Indigenous Peoples.* Oxford: Clarendon Press; New York: Oxford University Press, 1992.

Halperin, Morton H., and David J. Scheffer with Patricia L. Small. *Self-Determination in the New World Order.* Washington, DC: Carnegie Endowment for International Peace, 1992.

Kymlicka, Will. *Multicultural Citizenship: A Liberal Theory of Minority Rights.* Oxford: Clarendon Press; New York: Oxford University Press, 1995.

Horowitz, Donald L. *Ethnic Groups in Conflict.* Berkeley: University of California Press, 1985.

Buchanan, Allen. *Secession: The Morality of Political Divorce from Fort Sumter to Lithuania and Quebec.* Boulder, CO: Westview, 1991.

Hannum, Hurst. *Autonomy, Sovereignty, and Self-Determination: The Accommodation of Conflicting Rights.* Philadelphia: University of Pennsylvania Press, 1996.

Phillips, Allan, and Allan Rosas, eds. *Universal Minority Rights.* Turku/Abo, Finland: University Institute for Human Rights, 1995.

Crawford, James, ed. *The Rights of Peoples.* Oxford: Clarendon Press; New York: Oxford University Press, 1992.

Gilbert, Geoff. "The Council of Europe and Minority Rights." *Human Rights Quarterly* 18, 1 (February 1996), 160–189.

Wilmer, Franke. *The Indigenous Voice in World Politics.* Newbury Park, CA: Sage, 1993.

Wright, Jane. "The OSCE and the Protection of Minority Rights." *Human Rights Quarterly* 18, 1 (February 1996), 190–205.

The Rights of Refugees

Prohibited Persons: Abuse of Undocumented Migrants, Asylum-Seekers, and Refugees in South Africa. New York: Human Rights Watch, 1998.

Taylor, Clark. *Return of Guatemala's Refugees: Reweaving the Torn.* Philadelphia: Temple University Press, 1998.

Burma/Thailand: No Safety in Burma, No Sanctuary in Thailand. New York: Human Rights Watch, 1997.

In Search of Safety: The Forcibly Displaced and Human Rights in Africa. New York: Amnesty International, 1997.

Refugees: Human Rights Have No Borders. New York: Amnesty International, 1997.

Hannum, Hurst. *The Right to Leave and Return in International Law and Practice.* Dordrecht, Netherlands: M. Nijhoff, 1987.

Lillich, Richard B. *The Human Rights of Aliens in Contemporary International Law.* Manchester: Manchester University Press, 1984.

Plaut, W. Gunther. *Asylum: A Moral Dilemma.* Westport, CT: Praeger, 1995.

United Nations High Commissioner for Refugees. *The State of the World's Refugees 1993: The Challenge of Protection.* New York: Penguin Books, 1993.

Zolberg, Aristide. *Escape from Violence: Conflict and the Refugee Crisis in the Developing World.* Oxford: Clarendon Press, 1989.

Human Rights Problems in Particular Countries

Annual reports (in considerable detail) on the human rights situation of various countries can be found in the following:

Amnesty International Report [year]. New York: Amnesty International.

Human Rights Watch World Report [year]. New York: Human Rights Watch.

United Nations Human Rights Commission, publication E/CN.4 [year]. See also listing of Country Reports in *Index to United Nations Documents and Publications.*

United Nations Sub-Commission on Prevention of Discrimination and Protection of Minorities, publication E/CN.4/Sub.2/[year].

European Commission on Human Rights. *European Human Rights Reports [year].*

United States Department of State. *Country Reports on Human Rights Practices for [year].* Washington, DC: GPO. Prepared each year by the U.S. Department of State and submitted to the Committee on International Relations of the U.S. House of Representatives and the Committee on Foreign Relations of the U.S. Senate. Also accessible on the Department's Web site: www.state.gov

Organization of American States. *Country Reports [year].* Washington: General Secretariat, OAS.

Index